FROM THE GOLDFIELDS TO THE 'G
A One-Eyed Look at Aussie Rules

FROM THE GOLDFIELDS TO THE 'G

KEVIN REED

Introduced by Dr Paul Callery

Publisher's Apprentice (2014) an imprint of Connor Court Publishing Pty Ltd
Copyright © Kevin Reed 2014

ALL RIGHTS RESERVED. This book contains material protected under International and Federal Copyright Laws and Treaties. Any unauthorised reprint or use of this material is prohibited. No part of this book may be reproduced or transmitted in any form or by any means, electronic or mechanical, including photocopying, recording, or by any information storage and retrieval system without express written permission from the publisher.

PO Box 224W
Ballarat VIC 3350
sales@connorcourt.com
www.connorcourt.com

ISBN: 9781925138146 (pbk.)

Cover design by Ian James

Printed in Australia

CONTENTS

Introduction vii
Prologue ix

1850s-1918

1: The Guildford Goldfields and George Coulthard 1
2: The Jubilee Carnival and Jack Worrall 19
3: Footy at Costerfield and "Dick" Lee 28
4: World War I and Bruce Sloss 37

1919-1940s

5: Peace and Frank Maher 45
6: The Depression and Bob Pratt 58
7: World War II and John Coleman 73
8: A Fitzroy Flag and Fred Fanning 94

1940s-1959

9: School Footy and John Kennedy 105
10: The "Oaks" and "Chooka" Howell 120
11: Lalbert, Lake Boga and the Finn Brothers 134
12: Some Country Footy and Rose Brothers 150
13: The Demon Era and "Bluey" Shelton 165

1960s-1990s

14: De La "Old Colls" and "Black Jack" Coughlan 180
15: VFA Sundays and Frank Davis 196
16: The Vietnam War and Glen James 212
17: 'Bool Days and Wayne Schwass 230
18: The "Sharks" and Gary Ablett Snr 255

1990s-2010s

19: The "Krushers" and the Carrolls	271
20: Back to Lalbert and Tony Free	285
21: Back to the Costerfields and the MUGARS	300
Epilogue	318
References	322
Acknowledgements	327
Key Player Index	331

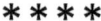

Dedication

This book is dedicated to the memory of my parents, Mick and Muriel Reed, who took the time to foster their children's interest in sport, particularly Aussie Rules Football.

Introduction

This wonderful book offers a unique account of the development of Australian Rules football in both rural and suburban Victoria. The context of the commentary ranges from the goldfields of Central Victoria to football's establishment in a proud suburban football centre.

The author, Kevin Reed, grew up about a dozen or so years ahead of me, in the same Melbourne suburb as I did. He is a proud descendant of George Reed, born in 1860, who lived and worked in the small mining town of Costerfield, about 15 kilometres from the larger Heathcote. George Reed was an avid Costerfield supporter and encouraged his sons to play football. Kevin, in his narration, relates how sport, in particular football, affected the development of his family lineage.

Authors of many Australian Rules football books, such as Martin Blake, Martin Flanagan and Russell Holmesby, have written about the VFL/AFL game but few, if any, have pursued football development as the author, Kevin Reed, has done.

As Kevin provides the story of the development of football around the mining fields, he also aligns the development of our great game and its famous names of the then-VFL to those great names of today. This dualism makes his book fascinatingly unique.

Kevin Reed has inadvertently set a challenge for potential writers and researchers to publish a myriad of similar unique accounts about their own country football and sport development. These histories will be lost unless someone as "obsessed" as Kevin is sufficiently brave and energetic to do so about their own community.

This book on football is much more than men and boys playing a match a week. The game of football can be seen to be the cement in the social fabric of a community for both genders, young and old.

The famous football identities Reed describes are fascinating to read about, especially when we consider that so many of these individuals came from small but proud Victorian regional districts. I was equally enthralled to read about some of the unknown locals of the Heathcote district. It could be said that people in the late 19th century and early 20th century were more passionate about their footy, than people are today. In this earlier era the community rivalries, amalgamations, abandonments, despairing accounts, accusations of fixing games were as rife as they are today. Football is about passion! Kevin Reed has encapsulated all these feelings.

From a personal perspective I could feel the emotions of the experiences brought on by football in and around the goldfields right to where I played junior football with Oakleigh YCW. I also remember the height of such emotions in the 1960s watching and even playing, as a youth, a couple of times with South Purrumbete, close to the Stony Rises near Colac. Reading this narrative helped me relive such experiences. How many football districts are there? Just read the Sunday papers for the community football results to see what football contributes to the whole of Victoria.

Kevin Reed, you are to be congratulated for your passionate endeavours in tracing and writing about the importance of the development of football; starting in our own lives, past and present.

Dr Paul Callery

Prologue

George Reed was born at the goldfield town of Guildford in Central Victoria in 1860, around the same time as Thomas Wills was penning his rules for our Australian game. George and his descendants have been involved in the Australian winter sport as players, coaches, administrators or supporters across five generations from the Goldfields to the 'G, the cathedral home of our game.

In their participation in our sport their journeys have crossed the paths of many well-known players and clubs.

George was attending the Guildford primary school in 1872 when an Act of Parliament made education free, secular and compulsory for all Victorian children up to the age of 14 years. Some time later descendants, a father and son, of an Italian migrant who came to Guildford in search of gold attended the same school. These two lads were bearers of one of the most famous names in Aussie Rules.

In 1919, just after the end of World War I, my father, Mick Reed, played alongside the local school teacher in a premiership team for Costerfield, another mining town in Central Victoria. The teacher's great-grandson later won a Brownlow Medal while playing with Essendon.

In the 1940s, my brother Ramon and I went to the same primary and secondary schools with a tall youngster who later became a multiple premiership player for the Demons. His father had played in a premiership team for Melbourne a generation earlier.

During the 1960s I played footy in a local church competition. Coming up through the under-age ranks in my club at that time was a defender, who later became a Melbourne premiership player and a captain of the Demons. Also with the club was a courageous rover who later became a well known rover for the Demons and the Saints.

In the 1980s, one of our sons played in a premiership team for South

Warrnambool under-18 side in the Hampden Football League. A future Club Best and Fairest winner at both North Melbourne and Sydney Swans was showing great potential with that team.

Another son broke his collar-bone while training with South Warrnambool in the 1990s. Running around the footy field at the same time was a tall, well-built, young forward who was to become a triple premiership player for Brisbane.

Twenty years later that same son lives two doors down in their street in Geelong from a lady whose maiden name is one of the most famous names in that football-mad town.

One of our daughters enjoyed a couple of seasons of Aussie Rules with the Melbourne University Girls Aussie Rules Squad (the MUGARS). Her bridesmaid, an outstanding premiership player for MUGARS, is a Life Member of that club.

And of course our paths have crossed those of many lesser known players and our journeys have taken us to many lesser known clubs.

By following the stories of some of George's progeny, it has been possible for one of his descendants to trace a history, albeit a little "one-eyed", of the game itself. Nevertheless, it can be said that to truly understand a sport that you love, it helps to know its history from different perspectives.

You might find similarities with your own family's Aussie Rules story in this book.

1
The Guildford Goldfields and George Coulthard

A Tense Grand Final, Guildford; Costerfield Football Club (FC), Heathcote FC, South Melbourne FC, Geelong FC, Carlton FC, the VFA, the VFL; William Gent, Richard Casey, Albert Franks, Tom Wills, Theophilus Marshall, Charles Brownlow and David Higgenbotham.

The Costerfield supporters, including my grandfather, George Reed, were furious about the result. Predictably, they were all a bit "one-eyed" but they knew when something wasn't right. And what Heathcote did to Costerfield, in order to win the 1906 Grand Final certainly wasn't fair.

Costerfield is a small mining township, about 15 kilometres north-east of the larger Heathcote which is a service town for nearby hamlets.

The rivalry between Costerfield and Heathcote was strong. Costerfield had won the flag in 1905 in the Heathcote District Football Association (HDFA). There was no Grand Final that year. The team on top at the end of the eight-game season (often called the minor premiers) was named as the "premiers". By the time of the last match in the two-team competition, Costerfield ("Coster") had won two more games than their rival so that match was just a formality. Nevertheless the game was to be keenly fought.

Dalton from Costerfield was the best man on ground, his cool and clever play winning admiration from all quarters. Other good players for Costerfield were G. and W. Bradley, as well as Tice, Woods, Brown and Young. Heathcote's best were Morey and Madden.

The *McIvor Times* noted that, at the conclusion of that game:

> a scene of wild enthusiasm followed. A Union Jack representing the Costerfield colours was nailed to a long pole which was carried and erected in the centre of the ground, while the local supporters gathered round it and cheered loudly.

The 1906 Grand Final

The next season, 1906, was different. There were five teams in the competition and it was decided to play a Grand Final, after the home-and-away matches, between the two top teams. This turned out to be a match between Costerfield and Heathcote again and was played on the Barrack Reserve at Heathcote.

George Reed and seven of his nine children managed to get there – the older boys on horseback with George taking the others in the family cart. One of George's sons, George Jnr, nicknamed "Kelly" after the bushranger, had to get there early because, although not a star player, he was in the team. Kelly was 20 years old at the time. Annie, my grandmother, stayed home with the two younger boys, my dad, Mick, then eight, and young Frank only three.

Heathcote was very keen to reverse the result of the previous year and the HDFA executive agreed that each club could have three players, imported from outside the district, playing in the Grand Final. It was thought that this would increase the standard of the game and also attract a larger crowd.

There was no stated agreement as to from where the players on permit could be recruited, but Coster signed three players from nearby Nagambie – a team that played in a different competition. This, Coster believed, was within the spirit of the agreement. There was also a proviso that the secretary of each club must see the opposing team's permits before the match started.

The great rivalry between the clubs plus the beautiful spring day brought a large crowd to the Heathcote oval and the spectators enjoyed a hard-fought and low scoring contest throughout the afternoon. Goals were at a premium. Into the final quarter Heathcote was seven points ahead when one of Coster's "imports" grabbed the ball at around centre half-forward and kicked it goalwards. There was a scrimmage about 15 metres out from goal and a Costerfield player kicked the ball off the ground towards the goal. As it bounced through for what the Coster players and supporters believed was a goal, a Heathcote player dived and touched the ball. To the consternation of the Coster boys the umpire ruled that the ball was touched before it crossed the line and a behind was awarded.

The teams battled it out for another five minutes with Coster attacking most of the time. However they were held up on every occasion, particularly by the Heathcote "imports", who had played outstanding and very aggressive football throughout the afternoon, often causing the Costerfield players to lose concentration and, in their efforts to retaliate, give away free kicks. With the supporters from both sides shouting encouragement to their boys and, on occasions, abuse to their counterparts from the opposition, the bell rang and Heathcote won by one goal – the score being 5.9.39 to 4.9.33. There was only a kick in it, but Heathcote really enjoyed their victory.

Amongst the Costerfield players and supporters there was great despondency as they felt that they were cheated of a goal when there was still time for them to score again and win the match. They were also anxious to find out more about the Heathcote "imports" who had played such tough and talented football. Many rushed to the Costerfield secretary to get some information about these players, only to find that he claimed not to have seen their permits before the game.

It didn't take long for the Costerfield committee to lodge a protest on two grounds. Firstly, that a score which was registered to them as a behind should have been a goal as it was touched after it had gone through the goals. And secondly, that the Costerfield Club Secretary didn't see the permits for the three Heathcote "imports" before the match.

A review panel, comprising the HDFA Chairman and a representative from each of the three clubs who didn't play in the Grand Final, was set up.

With regard to the non-awarded goal the appeal was dismissed on the grounds that the umpire's decision is final.

The appeal about the permit forms drew the same fate. The Heathcote secretary produced the signed documents and said that he had attempted to show the forms to the Costerfield secretary before the game but "he didn't want to see them". Costerfield argued that the Heathcote secretary didn't try hard enough to show the forms to his Costerfield counterpart as he wanted to keep quiet about the backgrounds of the imported footballers. Again the review panel voted to dismiss the appeal and the Chairman declared that Heathcote had won the premiership.

Then the Chairman dropped a "bombshell". After declaring Heathcote the premiers, the Chairman of the panel resigned saying that he was not pleased with the way that the panel members from three clubs banded themselves together against Costerfield. Clearly the Chairman felt that there was some skullduggery afoot, as did most of the Costerfield supporters, particularly George Reed who never forgot how Heathcote had "cheated" to win the Grand Final in 1906.

Heathcote's role in winning the flag must have come under even more suspicion when the backgrounds and football experience of their "imports" was considered. It is apparent that Heathcote was so desperate to beat the Costerfield upstarts that they broke from the spirit of the "import player" agreement even if it couldn't be proven. It was never intended that imported players would come from VFL clubs.

The Imported Players

While Costerfield looked to Nagambie for their new recruits, Heathcote spread their net as far as South Melbourne who, at that time, was a strong VFL club being runners-up to Carlton in 1907 and winning the flag in

1909. The three imported players (Gent, Casey and Franks) were not just ordinary players. The *Encyclopedia of AFL Footballers* says of **William Gent** that:

> he was a gifted and brilliant rover who had a chequered VFL career. He was suspended late in 1904 for the rest of the season and the whole of season 1905 for unsportsmanlike conduct.

The above book says of **Richard Casey** that:

> he was a combative and aggressive footballer. His approach even raised the ire of the normally conservative reporters of the day. Once or twice (one reporter wrote that) he (Casey) stuck out his boot in an attempt to trip an opponent. "He will do well to nip that in the bud."

Casey was reported in June 1910 and suspended for the rest of the year. He played 112 games and kicked 93 goals.

The Encyclopedia had the following to say about **Albert Franks**:

> A fine drop kick, he had good pace for a big man, he had endurance but there was a darker side to his game and one writer of the time said he frequently resorted to unsportsmanlike and unwarranted tactics ... In 1910, after Franks abused an umpire, the League stood him down indefinitely, however he was allowed to play again in 1912.

The three recruits between them played 273 games of VFL football and kicked 187 goals. All of them were at the height of their careers at the time and all of them had been suspended in the VFL for lengthy periods for rule infringements. Heathcote really wanted to win!

Footy at Costerfield

Like many towns, both small and large, Costerfield and Heathcote had men interested in playing football in the second half of the 19th century.

Eventually there was enough interest for clubs to be formed. Towns had played "friendly" matches, both within their respective clubs and against other clubs, for many years. In fact, as early as 1862, two hotels in Heathcote organised a team which played against another team made up of players from the rest of the town.

It took some time for competitions to be formed. This occurred at different times in different places. No competition had been formed in the Heathcote area before 1905 because it would have tied the players down to regular matches in the winter at a time when farmers worked most Saturdays, and travel between townships was not easy.

By 1905 travel conditions had improved and the growth of jobs such as mining, teaching and banking, which gave some free time to the workers at weekends, meant that there were enough young men available to play. Even some farmers could make themselves available for a short season.

Three clubs, Costerfield, Heathcote and Knowsley, had been represented at the initial meeting to form a competition early in 1905 although Knowsley couldn't field a team that year. The competition was named the Heathcote District Football Association (HDFA). In 1906, the competition expanded in that year to include Emu Flat, Tooborac and South Heathcote as well as Costerfield and Heathcote.

Disgusted by the way that they were treated in 1906, Costerfield didn't field a team in the HDFA in 1907, as a form of protest.

Background

George Reed, a son of William and Ann Reed, who had migrated from England in 1850, was born at Guildford, near Castlemaine in Victoria in 1860. Annie Reed, George's wife, was the daughter of John and Mary Dempsey who had migrated as single people from Ireland and were married in Geelong in 1858. Annie was born at River Street, Richmond Flat, in 1859.

Around the time of the births of George and Annie, an idea was conceived in the mind of **Tom Wills**, a member of the Melbourne Cricket Club and the son of a wealthy pastoralist, who had been educated in England. He wrote a letter to the sporting weekly paper *Bell's Life in Victoria* on 10 July 1858, calling for a winter sport, football, to be established. An outstanding cricketer himself, he argued that this would be beneficial to cricketers as it would keep them fit over the winter months. He proposed that a committee of three or more be formed to draw up a code of rules.

Earlier Matches

As it turned out a number of games took place before Wills had managed to get together his committee to agree on rules for the game. These matches involved large numbers and concluded when one of the teams scored a goal. Such games took place in parts of the colony other than in Victoria. The population was largely rural and, with the gold rushes, was growing rapidly. Both the rural workers and those seeking gold were itinerants who travelled to where employment or gold might be found. The idea of amusing themselves with games of football went with them.

Some Early Rules

Eventually **Tom Wills** did get his small committee together in May 1859. It produced ten rules from which, it could be said, the present Australian game evolved and continues to evolve.

A number of aspects of the rules are of interest and bear pointing out.

The width of the playing field was to be not more than 220 yards while its length and the distance between the goal posts were to be decided by the captains before the game started. A goal was scored if it was kicked between the posts.

The game was started with a "kick off" rather than from a centre bounce.

A catch was called a "mark" which gave the player a free kick. In no circumstances was the ball to be thrown. Tripping and pushing were allowed, but not hacking. Hacking is kicking an opponent's leg with the view to tripping him.

The ball could only be handled if it was caught from a kick or picked up after it had bounced. It could not be picked up directly from the ground. This rule resulted in "scrummages" where large numbers of players from both teams tussled with each other and tried to kick the ball in the direction of their goals. If the ball went out of bounds it was to be thrown back in at right angles to the boundary line.

The Committee's set of rules left open questions such as who would umpire the game, whether a player could run with the ball and, if so, how far? No mention was made of how long the match should last; whether there should be breaks in the game or whether scoring ends should be changed at any time during the match. Nor was there a specification of the number of players on each side.

Furthermore, the Wills' Committee did not specify the size and shape of the ball to be used. Should it be round like a soccer ball or more oval-shaped like the balls used in rugby?

Often decisions about the above issues were decided by the captains of the teams involved in the match before the game started.

Long and short games

The variability of the rules can be shown from a piece in the *In Black and White* section of the *Herald Sun* dated 5 July 2011. Under the heading *Long and Short* there is a report of aspects of the football career of **Theophilus Marshall**. It is apparent from his story that some football matches in 1859 lasted until two goals were scored, not one goal as in the match reported above. Theophilus' story follows:

Theophilus Marshall doesn't figure highly in footy record books. Probably he doesn't figure in them at all, but he might have a claim to fame. Researching for Kensington Primary School's 130th birthday, Mark Ryan found out Marshall – the first head master – played in the longest footy match yet, and also possibly the shortest.

He first played with Melbourne in 1859 against Richmond, back when games started about 2 pm and went on until a team kicked two goals. Mark says Marshall played in a match against Richmond that went for three weeks. Melbourne kicked a goal on the first Saturday and Richmond goaled on the next Saturday. On the third, Melbourne scored the winning goal. The shortest match Marshall remembered ended in 10 minutes when Melbourne scored two goals against University.

Over the next couple of decades many changes were seen in the Australian game. Clubs were formed, and both intra-club and inter-club games were arranged and played. They tended to be friendly, but rugged, winter events. Initially large numbers of players, far in excess of eighteen, were involved. Very few goals were scored, with behinds not being counted.

In those early years players had no designated positions and, because other games such as soccer and rugby used rectangular grounds, the early Australian Rules games were played on such shaped grounds. This made it very difficult for players to extricate the ball from the pockets.

The captains often acted as umpires and, when independent umpires were introduced in the 1880s, a captain had to appeal to the umpire if he thought his team deserved a free kick, just as a bowler appeals to the umpire if he/she thinks a batsman is out. The times of play also varied from place to place and time to time.

Eventually, with the formation of the Victorian Football Association (VFA) in May 1877, a number of the stronger clubs were linked under a set of common rules. At first the VFA did not arrange competition matches. These were arranged between the clubs themselves. Some teams played many more games than others. Initially, there were no finals with the newspapers determining which team may have been the best for the season, that is, the premiers.

The game, as codified by Wills and his committee with later variations, spread across the country, particularly in the southern colonies. When competitions were formed, these often involved only a few teams as was the case with the Heathcote District Football League (HDFL) which the HDFA was later re-named. And there was some inter-colonial rivalry at the time. The *South Australian Advertiser* (17 July 1886) reported on a visit by the Geelong team to Adelaide to play matches against four South Australian sides: Norwood, Port (Adelaide), South Adelaide and Adelaide. The Geelong team was victorious against the first three teams although the result of the match against Adelaide was not reported as it had not been played at the date of the article.

A "Grand Final"

In 1886 when undefeated teams, South Melbourne and Geelong, had not met each other during the season, the occasion of their scheduled match was seen as a "Grand Final". The winner would clearly be the premiers. There was huge interest in the game and a record crowd attended at the Emerald Hill (South Melbourne) ground.

According to an article, (written in *The Daily News*, Perth on 2 July 1937) reflecting on developments in the game in the late 19th century:

> Special trains and the old "Edina" and "Courier", bay steamers, must have carried some thousands of 'Geelongeese' to Melbourne that Saturday and the ground was packed tight with spectators. "South" had imported from Adelaide a huge fellow to play at centre. I think his name was Bushby. But stocky **Davie Higginbotham** ran rings around him.

David Higginbotham (NEWSPIX)

Geelong defeated South Melbourne rather easily with the score being 4.19.43 to 1.5.13. The 1886 victory was one of which Geelong long remained proud.

As well as discussing the rivalry between the two clubs, the above mentioned article pointed out that up until 1886, "football received but brief notice in the Press. However *The Argus* (newspaper) gave a two-column report of the game written by that brilliant and versatile journalist, Donald McDonald, an old footballer himself. From that day football reports have been featured in the Press".

Although there were no official finals played in the VFA days it was said that the "Pivitonians", as Geelong team was then known, was the best side in the first decade of VFA football.

From the VFA to the VFL

In the 1870s more than 60 clubs were started in the country with over 40 clubs beginning in Melbourne. The Melbourne clubs were initially inner suburban clubs such as Carlton, Melbourne, St Kilda, Collingwood, Hawthorn and South Melbourne. Geelong and Ballarat also had teams that competed against the Melbourne clubs.

With the founding of these clubs, football matches became regular Saturday events in Victoria with some key games in Melbourne attracting crowds of around 10,000 fans.

Interest in the game continued to grow throughout the 19th century until the depression of the 1890s when unemployment meant that people could not afford to go to the football. The less wealthy clubs found it difficult to field teams.

In 1897, in an attempt to revive the game, eight of the better-off clubs broke away from the VFA and formed the Victorian Football League (VFL).

The initial clubs were Collingwood, South Melbourne, Essendon, Melbourne, Fitzroy, Geelong, Carlton and St Kilda. The teams played two games against each other then the top four teams played each other once to determine the premiers. Thus there were six final matches in all with Essendon, winning all three of its final games, being the premiers in the first year of the competition.

From its first season in 1897 the VFL slowly, but surely, became the dominant football body in Victoria. The game was then beginning to look something like the game we see today with behinds being included in the scoring, umpires dressed in white, boundary umpires, 100 minutes of play, and the centre bounce being used to start a match. Over time, different systems of finals were tried to determine the premier team.

Miners and Footballers at Guildford.

Guildford, where George Reed's parents William and Ann Reed settled, is a gold mining town about 130 kilometres north-west of Melbourne between Castlemaine and Daylesford. Early settlers included Swiss, Italians and Chinese seeking gold, as well as miners from Great Britain.

Like other youngsters at the time, my grandfather, young George Reed, had some experience of football when he was growing up in Guildford. One of the earliest recorded football matches was played at nearby Castlemaine in 1859.

Playing football, particularly "kick to kick" in the senior grades, was one of George's pleasures at the Guildford State School, (photo at right) a fine building, evidence of the town's successful past. As he grew older

Guildford School (Private photo / Marj Reed)

and stronger George and his mates were involved in scratch matches around Guildford and Castlemaine. In doing this they experienced the changes in the game as it evolved.

Castlemaine Football Club was formed in 1877, when George was 17. It played intra-club and inter-club matches until 1889 when it joined the Castlemaine Football Association (CFA). In 1889 the CFA comprised only two clubs, Castlemaine and Foundry United. Castlemaine were premiers.

Snippet

In the 20th century, a father and son who were to make names for themselves in VFL football also spent time at the Guildford School. Both were named Ron Barassi. Their forebears were part of the Italian group of families who settled in the district about the same time as George Reed's parents.

Ron Barassi Snr was born in 1913. He was the grandson of Guiseppi Barassi who was the first Barassi to settle at Guildford. Ron Snr's father was Carlo Barassi. After initially playing football for Castlemaine, Ron Snr was recruited to Melbourne where, as a courageous rover, he played 58 games for 84 goals. Ron Snr played football for Castlemaine but he played cricket for Guildford.

Ronald Dale Barassi had been born at Castlemaine in 1936 and he spent his early years living in Guildford with his grandfather, Carlo, because of the untimely death of his father, Ron Snr. He was to become more famous as a footballer than his dad.

The Coming of the Railways

The opening of the Bendigo/Melbourne railway in 1862 meant that young men like George Reed were able to travel by train from Castlemaine to Melbourne to watch Aussie Rules matches as the game became a state-wide popular conversation topic at the time. In 1880 George may well have been among the 13,000 enthusiasts who attended the contest reported in the *Australian Sketcher* as an occasion where "the excitement displayed over the match amongst spectators and players was really something wonderful to the outsider."

The writer also indicated that women were among the spectators:

> ... and so deep is the interest taken in the struggle of these respective clubs by the ladies of Melbourne and Carlton that it is not difficult to tell from the expression on their faces which side is winning.

It was on one such visit that George Reed met Annie Dempsey. who was living in Melbourne. Wishing to see more of Annie, George decided to work in the City and joined the Police Force.

Meanwhile William and Ann Reed, George's parents, moved to Echuca.

The year 1883 saw both Annie Dempsey and George Reed living in

Melbourne. George was stationed at Russell Street Police Station and, in his role as a policeman, officiated at some of the crowd-pleasing VFA games of that era. Policemen were certainly needed to control the large numbers in attendance.

George and Annie saw each other as often as possible in 1883 and they married on 26 February 1884.

Charles Brownlow

In the first year of their marriage the young couple was able to see a number of games in the VFA. They may well have seen **Charles Brownlow** in action for Geelong.

Brownlow, who had been captain in 1883, was elected to be in that role in 1884 but business duties caused him to hand over the position to his vice-captain Harry Steedman.

Brownlow was well known in football circles. As a backman, he was a very competent player and, as a captain, he had lifted his team's performance by giving careful attention to training. Geelong were premiers in the year of Brownlow's captaincy.

Although Brownlow relinquished the captaincy, he continued to play for the club until 1891. In addition he was Secretary of the Geelong Football Club from 1885 to 1923, the year before his death. The Geelong Club delegate to the VFL from 1897 to 1922, he was vice-president of the VFL from 1911 to 1916 and Acting President in 1918 and 1919. After his death the award for the Best and Fairest in the VFL (and now the AFL) was named the Brownlow Medal. The Geelong player Edward "Carji" Greeves was the recipient of the first Brownlow Medal in 1924.

Some Football Issues

A couple of issues that administrators of the game have had to tackle throughout its history are highlighted in Garrie Hutchinson's *The Great Australian Book of Football Stories*.

The first one was the fact that the Australian game was rough and the spectators were very vocal. Hutchinson quotes an English spectator who, on watching a game, commented that:

> one very objectionable feature (of the match) is that the decisions of the umpire are treated with little respect … He further writes that a neat trip up, or a violent fall is greeted with applause and laughter, as though the crowd took a savage sort of delight in the discomfitures of the players amongst whom the behaviour of the spectators encourages bad temper.

At that time, cricket was seen as a game to be played fairly by gentlemen. On the other hand, the Australian game tended towards violence and this, with the partisanship of the crowd, made it a challenge for the administrators of the game to get the right balance between the desire of the players and spectators for victory, and the participants' endeavours to play within the rules.

Should a player, when the victim of rough and unfair play, as a Christian gentleman, turn the other cheek or should he try to get even? And what penalty, if any, should be applied to the footballer who takes the latter approach? These questions have vexed the game's administrators since the game's inception.

Furthermore, to what extent should players be safeguarded by the rules and protective clothing, such as helmets, against injury? It could be argued that conclusive answers have not been found to these questions yet.

Another issue raised by the competitiveness of the teams was that of player payment. Initially, the game was a pastime to be played by amateurs. However it wasn't long before good players were enticed by money and other incentives, from wealthier clubs, to transfer to these clubs.

Again, the issue of player payments has bedevilled the game's administrators until this day. Should all players receive the same wage?

Should there be a salary cap on the amount teams can pay players? Or should the free market reign? This issue begs another question. If players are paid because they play well, will not some of them be tempted by money to play poorly? And if gambling is involved will not the stakes be very high? These situations have caused problems in other sports, even in the "gentleman's game" of cricket.

The fact that these questions were raised 100 years ago indicates the necessity of eternal vigilance by administrators of the Australian game if it is to maintain its credibility with its millions of fans.

Moving On

George Reed was transferred to Maryborough in 1884. The couple was pleased that Maryborough had a football club which had been formed in 1872 and played its first inter-club match in the following year against Dunolly. Surprisingly, the club continued to play intra-club and social matches until 1924 when it entered the strong Ballarat competition and won the premiership in that year and in the following year. This would suggest that some of the social matches were of a high standard.

George Coulthard

An article in *The Sunday Times* from Perth, dated 8 August 1937, indicated that Maryborough played a match against Carlton "at Prince's Park in Maryborough (Victoria) in the early 1880s". The article, written by W. H. Nichols, formed part of a series of articles reminiscing on Aussie Rules footy.

In his article Nichols agrees with a previous writer in saying that **"George Coulthard**, of Carlton … (was) the greatest footballer ever". The writer added "that to this day I remain impressed with what a wonderful player he was in whatever place he played in." Coulthard won the VFA goal kicking on three occasions and was a member of Carlton's top team in 1877.

He was inducted into the Carlton Football Club Hall of Fame in 1990 and into the Australian Football Hall of Fame in 1996. Also a top cricketer, Coulthard played for the Melbourne Cricket Club, Victoria, and in one Test match for Australia. Sadly he had an untimely death, passing away from tuberculosis at the age of 27, leaving behind his wife and daughter.

Echuca

George and Annie Reed moved to Echuca in 1888 where George worked with road-making crews. There was a football club in Echuca and "scratch" games were played within the town and sometimes inter-club games against other towns. In 1876 Echuca played Rochester defeating them two goals to one. This was before behinds were counted in the score. Around that time Echuca also played matches against Deniliquin and Cummeragunga.

In 1909, Echuca joined the Goulburn Valley Football Association, which began officially in 1896 (before the VFL was established) with six teams, although it had dropped to as few as two teams prior to Echuca joining. Echuca was runner-up to Murchison in 1910.

In 1893, the Reeds made yet another move. This time it was to Costerfield, a somewhat depressed antimony and gold mining town in Central Victoria, between Heathcote and Nagambie. The attraction there was that rented housing was obtainable and that there were positions available in road making, timber cutting and farm labouring. There was also the possibility that more land might be opened up in the district and George and Annie might obtain a farm of their own.

2
The Jubilee Carnival and Jack Worrall

Social Matches, The Jubilee Carnival; St Kilda FC, Geelong FC, Melbourne FC, Carlton FC, Essendon FC, South Melbourne FC, Costerfield FC, Heathcote FC, the HDFL; Henry Young, Dave McNamara, "Joe" Pearce and Norman Clark.

George and Annie's enthusiasm for their move to Costerfield grew when, in 1905, with some of their boys then young men, Costerfield fielded its first team in the newly formed Heathcote District Football Association (HDFA). People around Heathcote had decided that the days of intra-club and "friendly" inter-club games were over and a local competition was desired and, as we have seen, the competition between the local teams was fierce.

With slight name changes and with breaks because of World Wars 1 and II, the Association has continued up to the present time. Over the next twenty years from 1905, 17 teams from around the district competed in the League.

Early in each year a meeting would be called and clubs that might have been interested in fielding a team would be invited to send a delegate to the meeting. It would then be decided if the competition would go ahead and, as this was usually the case, a draw would be made and the matches took place. A report of the meeting and the first few weeks of the draw was published in the *McIvor Times*. The season's draw wasn't published in its entirety but in parts throughout the season. However due notice would be given for games to be played. In the early years, up to five teams formed the competition.

Social matches only

It is understandable that Costerfield felt badly done by in losing the 1906 Grand Final to Heathcote with their VFL "imports" and they were probably well justified in showing their dissatisfaction by deciding not to field a team in the HDFL in 1907.

However as footy was a great love of the townsfolk and a key element of social life at the time there was still a great deal of football played by the club.

Social matches were arranged, for example, between Heathcote Married Men and Costerfield Single Men, played initially at Costerfield with a return match later in the year played at Heathcote.

According to the newspaper reports of these matches, the celebrations after the games were just as important as the matches. Usually the visiting team was hosted by the home team to a "scrumptious banquet" at the local hall or hotel. This was followed by a concert then a dance, to the music of a local orchestra.

Back in the Competition

Costerfield rejoined the HDFA in 1907 and the Reed family was represented in Costerfield teams in most seasons until 1924. My dad's older brothers (Bill, Kelly, Jack, and Ted) all donned the red, white and blue guernsey as well as Mick himself and younger brother Frank over that period. Mick played his first game of footy in 1918 but, as it turned out, it wasn't for Costerfield. The HDFA, later named the Heathcote District Football League (HDFL), was in operation in most seasons over that period but on two occasions there were breaks with the HDFL not functioning. Some notable events, both in football (in the HDFL and in the VFL), and in the wider world occurred over that period. The first of these was the Jubilee Carnival of 1908.

The Jubilee Carnival, 1908

Organised by the Australian Football Council, the Jubileee Carnival, held in Melbourne, commemorated the 50th anniversary of the beginnings of Australian Football. It was a great celebration in itself as well as an attempt to showcase the game to places other than the already football-loving states of Victoria, Western Australia, South Australia and Tasmania.

Outstanding players

There were three players in particular the Reed boys would have been keen to see in action at the Carnival.

The first of these was **Henry 'Tracker' Young** from Geelong who was the captain of the Geelong side. Tracker first played with Geelong in its VFA days. He was a superb athlete being highly skilled in Aussie Rules, cycling, rowing and boxing. He rode in the Melbourne to Warrnambool cycling event and was a sparring partner for the world heavyweight champion, Bob Fitzsimmons, when he visited Australia. Fitzsimmons later said that Young was the best amateur boxer that he had faced. But it was as a footballer that he really won his fame. A big man for his era, Young was tremendously fit and could ruck all day. He was adept at palming the ball to his rover.

An indication of Young's fitness is that when Geelong played in Melbourne, he would return to Geelong by taking a boat to Portarlington and then jog the 30 kilometres home from there. Young skippered Geelong from 1901 until 1909. He won the Geelong Best and Fairest award twice, is a member of the Cats' Team of the Century and has been inducted into the AFL Hall of Fame. Tragically Young died from a heart attack while swimming in the bay at Geelong. He was only 49 years old.

Unfortunately, despite its success in the VFA, Geelong had no luck in the early years of the VFL when Young was captain – Fitzroy, Essendon, Collingwood and Carlton being the dominant teams during that time.

Dave McNamara, the second player that George and his sons wanted to see, was generally regarded as St Kilda's best footballer up to that time. Arriving at St Kilda in 1905, he was one of the reasons for the Saints making the finals in 1907 and made such an impression at the club that the next year – the year of the carnival – he was made captain, at the tender age of 21. Playing at centre half-forward he was a strong high mark and a magnificent kick. He regularly scored goals when kicking from more than 60 metres out from goal. At 193 centimetres tall and weighing 92 kilograms, McNamara was a very big player in his era. He starred in the 1908 carnival and went on to play 122 games for the Saints and kicked more than 600 goals.

The other player that the Reeds wanted to see in action was **Arthur Mueller 'Joe' Pearce**, the dashing full back for Melbourne, who was famous for long clearing runs up the field. The son of the Principal of Bendigo Grammar, Pearce was recruited from South Bendigo. He had a well-paid position with the Australian Mutual Provident Society and was also very good at cricket, tennis and lacrosse. A strong Christian, he was a member of the Church of England (C of E) at East Melbourne and took an active role in his church community. He believed in playing the game fairly but that didn't mean that he wasn't a determined opponent. The great Collingwood full forward "Dick" Lee said of him that he was "by far the best full-back of his day". At a time when there was some money around for very good players, Pearce played strictly as an amateur. He believed that a footballer should not need money to give of his best.

The Jubilee Carnival was a great success although New Zealand and the non-Aussie Rules states were very inferior to Victoria, South Australia, Western Australia and Tasmania. It is interesting to note that half of the Western Australian team came from the Goldfields Football League including the captain Billy Trewhella.

Victoria was recognised as the winning team although it did not play Tasmania over the course of the event. However the Vics were not always

Dave McNamara (NEWSPIX)

superior to the other football loving states. On occasions in the first few decades of the 20th century when interstate matches were played, it was not unusual for Victoria to be beaten. In fact, given the population differences between Victoria and the other Aussie Rules committed states, the smaller states did quite well.

One well supported outcome of the Jubilee Carnival was the introduction by the AFC of the five-foot circle in the centre of the ground to prevent congestion. Players entering the circle at the bounce of the ball would be free-kicked.

Season 1909

The 1909 VFL season was interesting in that it was the first year in which Saturday afternoon was listed as a public holiday. It was expected that this change would result in larger crowds but this wasn't the case as it was a very wet winter. Attendance numbers grew in later seasons.

That year also saw the VFL altering the result of the match, a very rare occurrence in VFL football. In was common practice for country leagues to play mid-week games at that time and, on occasions, some VFL players appeared in those games with the permission of their VFL clubs, just as Franks, Casey and Gent had done in the Grand Final for Heathcote. During the 1909 season William Stewart, a fiery red-haired defender, who came from Kerang and played for St Kilda, turned out in a mid-week game between Eaglehawk and Bendigo in the Bendigo Football League. Unfortunately he was reported and received a one-week suspension for striking in that game. Despite this he played for St Kilda in their one point victory over Geelong on the following Saturday. When the VFL heard of Stewart's suspension, the four points were taken from St Kilda and given to Geelong.

To Moormbool West

Around this time the Victorian Government was looking at the possibility of opening up 40,000 acres of land in the Moormbool State Forest near Costerfield. This process of opening up State owned land for development in an orderly fashion happened from time to time across the State. In 1907 applications were called from people who were interested in obtaining some of this land. Annie Reed was a successful applicant for 305 acres of land in the Parish of Moormbool West.

One can imagine the celebration at the Reed household on hearing the result of their application. They called the property "Box Grove", an appropriate name for a farm to be carved from the Moormbool forest.

Jack Worrall – a Man from the Goldfields

Arguably the biggest name in football, if not in Australian sport, for 20 years either side of the turn of the century was **John "Jack" Worrall**. Like George Reed he was born in Central Victoria in the 1860s. His birthplace was Chinaman's Flat, a mining town near Maryborough, in Central Victoria. Chinaman's Flat had 30,000 people living in its locality shortly after gold was discovered there by some Chinese miners in 1854.

Born less than a year later than George Reed, Jack Worrall also played football at the local state school and in the open paddocks around his town. Unlike George, he also played and had a love of cricket. After moving to Ballarat he was seen playing football in the strong Ballarat competition and recruited by Fitzroy captain, Paddy McShane, a Test cricketer, to play both sports with that club. He moved to Melbourne in 1884. A high flying, solidly built rover, who could kick with either foot, Worrall captained Fitzroy, playing in the VFA at that time, for nine years and represented the Victoria in inter-colonial matches.

In the summer months he turned his hand to cricket, being good enough to represent Victoria, as an opening batsman, and to play 11

Test matches, with a batting average of 25. Touring England in 1899 he made 76 out of a team total of 172 in a Test match on a sticky wicket at Headingly. He once had an innings of 417 for Carlton, then an Australian record.

Notwithstanding his success as a footballer he had even greater success as a coach. After his appointment as secretary-manager of Carlton in 1902 he became the first official coach of a VFL team, revolutionising training methods. He donned his football gear and insisted on rigorous training, a clean lifestyle for his players and demanded unflinching courage on the field. Carlton, who had been cellar-dwellers up to this time rose to third in 1903 and then won successive flags from 1906 to 1908. Leaving the club in 1909 over money issues and his Spartan training methods, he coached Essendon to back-to-back flags in 1911 and 1912. The attendance at the 1912 VFL Grand Final was over 54,000. To that date, this was only the second time in VFL history that a Grand Final crowd had exceeded 50,000.

Worrall was a significant figure in the formation of the Australian Football Council in 1905. Late in his career he began a second vocation as a sports writer, a profession he followed more assiduously after 1920. With his background and expertise in both cricket and football he had great success. Although it is not certain that he coined the term "bodyline" with regard to the frightening fast bowling tactics used by the England touring team on their 1932 tour of Australia, he was the first to use it in a published article.

When the Reed boys were growing up, Jack Worrall was a household name for families interested in sport, particularly football and cricket. George Reed was able to tell his family, "Your mum and I saw Jack Worrall play. He was a great player and could kick with both feet. Came from up Maryborough way. Not far from Guildford where I was born. Learned to play on the goldfields, you know, just like me."

Although many thought that Carlton would be down for a long time after Worrall left the club, they once more became the powerhouse team of the competition in 1914, winning the flag in that year and again in 1915, under the coaching of **Norman Clark** a tough, unrelenting back pocket player who had been a member of the Blues' three premierships under Worrall and, although heavily built, was fast and capable of taking a very high mark. He won the Stawell Gift in 1899 and came from South Australia to the Blues in 1905. He later coached Brighton in the VFA and St Kilda and North Melbourne in the VFL.

It is noted in *The Encyclopedia of AFL Footballers* that Carlton teammate Rod McGregor wrote of Clark that "Speed and a powerful build and the courage to go through anything gave him all the ideal qualities of a back pocket player. He was a good kick and he took a mark now and then that was a revelation. We often wonder how he could lift his bulk so high. Norman Clark's particular type of play has not been duplicated, chiefly because no-one of his pattern has since appeared."

Norman Clark had a role as either a player or coach in the Blues' first five premierships.

Snippet

A key player in Essendon's 1911 premiership team was **Ern ('Ginger') Cameron**, a small and tenacious rover, who was twice the Essendon Best and Fairest award winner and a Victorian interstate representative on six occasions. It is said that in a match against South Australia at the 1912 Carnival, the South Australian ruckmen didn't try to hit the ball to their rovers, they simply tried to hit it away from Cameron.

Among the best players in Essendon's 1911 premiership win, Cameron broke his leg in the dying moments of Essendon's 1912 preliminary final against Carlton. Lying in pain on the ground he urged his team on and refused to leave the ground until the final bell sounded. (Injured players could not be replaced at that time.) The Melbourne Newspaper *The Argus* reported that "everybody deplored his absence from the Grand Final".

Still recuperating in Mrs Garlick's Private Hospital on Grand Final Day, Cameron had written a letter to his coach John Worrall saying, according to *The Argus*, that "all he wanted was for his team to win". And he asked for his team to oblige him. His letter was read out to the team before the match and greeted with great cheering. No doubt, Jack Worrall, brilliant orator that he was, used that letter to inspire his team and asked them to give everything to win the game for their courageous team-mate who was still in hospital. Probably this was a factor in Essendon's win.

Cameron, who was the recipient of a goodly sum of money as a testimonial from the Club, players and supporters, didn't play again. Still in his early twenties when he retired, "Ginger" had played 113 games with his club and had kicked 55 goals.

Cleaning up the Game

There was a down-side to VFL football in 1910 when a number of Carlton players were accused of taking bribes to 'play dead' in the semi-final against South Melbourne. The VFL investigated the charges and suspended two Carlton players for five years. This tough action was necessary as there were rumours that players in other teams may have also taken bribes in other matches. So as far back as 1911, a few players were willing to put their own interests above that of the team. It was written in *The Age* that it is "the duty of the responsible controllers of football to allay that suspicion (of players taking bribes) as promptly and effectually as possible".

Another measure was taken in 1911 to 'clean up' the game. Although officially amateurs, many players were accepting some form of reward 'under the lap', to play with their particular clubs. The rules were changed so that players were allowed to officially negotiate payment with the club committee. The question of player payment continues to be an issue up to the present time.

3
Footy at Costerfield and "Dick" Lee

A St Kilda Grand Final, Boom times disappear; The "Profs", Richmond FC, Fitzroy FC, St Kilda FC, Collingwood FC, Costerfield FC; the Cordners, Roy Park, and Vic Cumberland.

In 1908 Costerfield were back in the then four team competition and made up for its unfortunate loss in the 1906 Grand Final by finishing on top of the ladder and being awarded the flag. The competition comprised Costerfield, Heathcote, Toolleen and Knowsley.

Costerfield once again had a strong team in 1909 and won back-to-back flags. It should be noted that all teams didn't play each week and that match reports in the newspaper did not always include a description of the match and the best players. Often only the final scores were given.

In winning the premiership in 1909, Costerfield were the recipient of three trophies, donated by Messers E. Hood (a gold medal), J. Ring (a silver cruet) and J. Sangster (a silver ink stand). The trophies were given to the club at a gathering which took the form of a banquet and a dance on 22 September. In the spirit of democracy, a ballot was conducted to determine who from Costerfield would accept the trophies on behalf of the club. The winners were Mr G. Wood (player), Mr E. Brennan (patron) and Mr P. Finnigan (player).

I found no mention in the local paper of individual awards for best players from either the HDFL or the clubs.

The *McIvor Times* (26 August 1909) noted that the "Costerfield team have won the premiership by sheer merit, their system being superior to that shown by the other two teams, and (they) are to be congratulated on their achievement. They indulged in constant practice, and this got them into a way of playing to one another, which was the chief reason for their success."

So, serious training facilitated success on the football field in Central Victoria over 100 years ago.

Costerfield were runners-up to Knowsley in 1910. Costerfield did not field a team in 1911, as the HDFL was disbanded for the season probably because of extremely wet weather, but they were successful from 1912 to 1914.

Prominent Costerfield players over these successful years were Bradley, Wood, Finnigan, Reeves, Tattersall, Kirby, Gardner, Brown, Birmingham, Anderson and Phillips.

Mining Accidents and Community Spirit

The possibility of accidents is always on the minds of people working and living in mining towns. One such event occurred in Mt Lyell in Tasmania in 1912: a fire started in the mine and 42 men perished. Just over a decade into nationhood, Australia responded to the disaster and fund raising events were held to help those who survived, but suffered from the disaster.

A report in the *McIvor Times* dated 9 January 1913, tells of the Costerfield Sports held on 27 December 1912. It was held in aid of the Mt Lyell Relief Fund.

Also in 1912, a mining accident at a Costerfield mine saw loss of life and injury. A football carnival was held at the end of the season to raise money for families of miners who endured difficulties as a result of the tragedy. Four teams competed in the Carnival. In the first round Costerfield played Heathcote with Costerfield winning. This match was followed by a game in which Tooborac defeated Knowsley. The winners played off with Tooborac defeating Costerfield by 11 points.

The Carnival must have been taken seriously by the clubs involved as the report in the local paper indicated that "the friendly games which characterised the matches of late on the Heathcote ground did not continue (in the final game) and players and supporters gave way to bursts of passion which were not at all approved by the general body ".

Interest in the VFL

As early as 1911 VFA and VFL results were included in the *McIvor Times*, as many people had picked out their favourite teams and wanted to know the results of VFL matches. Kelly Reed, in particular, had an interest in Richmond from the time they were accepted into the VFL in 1908. He said it was because his mum was born there.

My dad Mick, an admirer of big brother Kelly, followed suit, and barracked for the Tigers. Annie liked Geelong while George Snr favoured Collingwood, as their colours were black and white – the same as Castlemaine's.

In 1908 the Richmond team moved from the VFA to the VFL and did reasonably well in their initial season, defeating Melbourne in their first game and winning six matches out of the 18 played. University (the "Profs"), the other new team to enter the competition in 1908, did better winning eight games. By this time the final series had changed to the system whereby the top team at the end of the season played the third while the second played the fourth side.

The two winners played off in the grand final. Carlton, under Jack Worrall, finished on top of the ladder and went on to win the flag. The Tigers again won six games in the following year and won about that number each year in their first decade in the competition.

After a better start than the Tigers in their first year, the Profs were never really a threat in later years and merged with Melbourne in 1915. That isn't to say that the University club hasn't made an impact on the football scene in Victoria. There is evidence that it was among the first football clubs founded as it played a match against Melbourne in 1863. It had a chequered career for the rest of the 19th century until it appeared in the strong Metropolitan Football League in 1905 where it became a powerful team winning the premiership in both 1906 and 1907 before it entered the VFL.

The Cordners

Leading lights in the University's early days in the VFL were the brothers, **Harry and Edward Cordner**. Both played with Melbourne before they went across to University when that club entered the VFL. Harry was a fine forward who was lost to the University club when he moved to Western Australia to practise medicine. He kicked seven goals in one game against Geelong. Edward, also a doctor, was a champion defender who played 60 games with the club.

Both boys also played District (Premier League) Cricket for University. Their father, Edward James Cordner was vice-president of the club. His wife began the University's days in VFL football by unveiling the club's 1907 Metropolitan League flag before the start of its first game in the VFL.

Edward Jnr was the father of four boys who played VFL football for Melbourne, including **Denis Cordner** who captained the Demons from 1951 to 1953 and won the club's Best and Fairest award twice. Older brother **Don** also captained the team and won the Brownlow medal in 1946. Other sons, **David** (53 games) and **John** (six games) also played. David's career was ravaged by injury while John's was cut short when he left Australia to study overseas as a nuclear scientist. John represented Victoria in interstate cricket. Few families have made such an impact on VFL football as the Cordners.

Denis Cordner

Tom Ogilvie was another Melbourne footballer

who crossed to the University side when it entered the VFL. Known as "Alick", he was a talented player who kicked 20 goals in the 27 games he played with the club. His ability was such that he was selected in the 1908 Carnival side.

Roy Park

A very successful goal kicker for the University team was **Roy Park**. Coming on the scene after the Cordners, he was a medical student who had three very successful seasons kicking 22 goals in 1912, 53 in 1913 and 36 in 1914 when his season was interrupted because of his studies. His 1913 effort was quite remarkable as he led the goal kicking at the end of the home and away season.

Jim Freake, the Fitzroy goal sneak, needed the finals to beat Park for the VFL goal kicking award that year. In all, Freake kicked 56 goals. Park's effort was even more salutary when one considers that University failed to win a game for the season and the whole team scored only 115 goals for the year.

Roy Park played with Melbourne after the University team folded. A very small evasive player and a deadly kick for goal, he played 13 games with that club and kicked 35 goals. When he was reported for striking he claimed his innocence and, despite three witnesses backing his version of events, he was suspended for four weeks.

Disgusted that his good name had been blemished, he retired from VFL football and turned his attention to cricket, another sport at which he was gifted. Park made 2514 runs in first class cricket at an average of just under 40 runs per innings with his highest score being 228. He played one Test for Australia.

St Kilda in the Grand Final.

Season 1913, when Roy Park was just beaten as the VFL top goal-kicker, was memorable for another reason – the rise of St Kilda. Wooden

Spooners in 1910, second last in 1911 and third last in 1912, few expected the team's dramatic rise up the ladder in 1913 when they finished second to Fitzroy.

In the finals system used that year, the second team played the third and the first played the fourth with the two losers being eliminated and the winners playing the "Grand Final". The team finishing top of the ladder had the right to challenge if it failed to win the first "Grand Final".

The Saints defeated South Melbourne in their semi-final and Fitzroy accounted for Collingwood. In the "Grand Final" the Saints were again in top form, defeating Fitzroy by 33 points. It appeared as if the Saints had overcome their finals' hoodoo. Of course Fitzroy challenged and a then record crowd of nearly 60,000 crammed into the MCG.

The Saints were favourites as few doubted that they could handle Fitzroy. But that wasn't the way it turned out. Incredibly nervous, the Saints could not get going at all and failed to kick a goal in the first quarter and repeated that effort in the next. They had failed to score a goal up to half-time, kicking only five points to Fitzroy's 4 goals 8 behinds.

The third quarter brought the Saints some success with rover Millhouse kicking a goal not long before the final break. Still just over four goals in the red at the beginning of the final term the Saints came out of the blocks with a rush and kicked four goals to be within a solitary point of Fitzroy. But the Saints again faltered – nerves again taking over as Fitzroy kicked two more goals to seal the game.

The best player for Fitzroy was half-back Jack Cooper, a Fitzroy born and bred lad who began with the club in 1908. Solid and persistent, he was a hard man to beat. It was said that he saved the game for Fitzroy when, at the time the Saints had momentum, he intercepted a pass from St Kilda forward Des Baird to **Vic Cumberland**, the St Kilda ruckman. Club Captain in 1911 and Best and Fairest in 1912, Cooper also captained the Victorian side in a match at Adelaide in 1912. On retiring from football in 1915 he joined the AIF, fighting in France and Flanders. After being gassed twice and returning to battle he was killed at Polygon Wood in 1917. His body was never recovered.

The Saints had to wait for over 50 years to win a Grand Final.

Snippet

Vic Cumberland is best known as the oldest man to play VFL football, playing his last game with St Kilda at the age of 43. However, he should be remembered for his skills as much as for holding that record. Around 180 centimetres tall, he was heavily built with a good leap which allowed him to palm the ball effectively to his rovers. He played football in Tasmania, South Australia, Victoria and in New Zealand where he helped to set up the game. He was a member of Melbourne's 1900 Premiership team and won the Magarey Medal for the South Australian League's Best and Fairest player when he played there before returning to St Kilda in in 1913. Upon the outbreak of World War I he joined the AIF and was wounded three times but survived the War to die in 1927 as a result of a motor cycle accident.

George Reed's Magpie Hero

One of the features of the game around this period was the goalkicking ability of Collingwood's full forward. **Walter Henry (Dick) Lee**, the son of Wal Lee, a Collingwood trainer who played a part in the founding of the club, was named by *The Encyclopedia of AFL Footballers* as one of the first of football's great full-forwards. Up until Dick Lee's time 30 goals were usually enough to win the VFL goal kicking award. Kicking over fifty goals regularly, including 66 in 1915, Lee won the award 10 times in the years 1906 to 1921. He was fast on the ground, a wonderful high mark and deadly accurate in kicking for goal. In all he played 230 games for the Magpies and kicked 707 goals.

Lee played in three premiership sides for the Magpies and for Victoria 17 times. George Reed had much pleasure lauding his hero, Dick Lee.

Football 'Don'ts'

On 16 July 1914, the *McIvor Times* had some advice of its own to young footballers under the heading "Some Football Don'ts". The list follows:

> Don't think that because you are good your club can't do without you. You never made a bigger mistake.
>
> Don't think that you are in the team to kick all of the goals – always play to a man in a better position, if he is on his own.
>
> Don't stick to your man if you are playing forward. Get on your own.
>
> Don't leave your man if you are playing back. Stick to him like glue.
>
> Don't run 10 yards and risk losing the ball when you can kick it 40 yards with safety.
>
> Don't give free kicks. They mean free goals.
>
> Don't turn your back on the field when you get a mark. Get rid of the ball quickly.
>
> Don't stop and appeal for free kicks. The umpire will see these.

These "Don'ts" could well have been written when Jack Worrall was the leading coach in the VFL and could well be helpful to young players, even in the 21st century.

At Home In Costerfield: 1910-1914

While the Reeds enjoyed settling into their new home at Box Grove there were a few features of life in the Costerfield area during the early part of the 20th century that can be commented upon.

Firstly, as most people were migrants, or descendants of migrants from Great Britain, there was a strong feeling for Great Britain in Costerfield and in the wider community during this period. British celebrations, such as Empire Day, were still enthusiastically enjoyed.

Secondly, everyone was aware that life in the mining/farming regions of Central Victoria was always problematic, at the whim of the weather and the prices of the products of the mines.

Thirdly, with some drought conditions during this period young people tended to leave home and try their luck elsewhere. In the case of the Reeds, two of the boys, Jack and Kelly, sought work in Western Australia, while, Mamie, the eldest daughter found employment in Melbourne where she met and married Bill Meadley in August 1914.

4
World War I and Bruce Sloss

World War I, Worrying times, Horrific loss of life, Footy at home, Footy abroad; Moormbool West FC, Costerfield FC, South Melbourne FC, Melbourne FC; George Hird, Fred Le Deux, and George Challis.

World War I began in August 1914 – the same month as George and Annie Reed's eldest daughter, Mamie Reed married William Meadley.

Although Australia had been a self-governing country since 1901, the Empire was still playing an obvious role in community life, fostering the old colonial ties with the "Mother Country". It was not surprising that Australia joined in the War. Support for Britain flowered in Costerfield as in other centres, both large and small, and encouragement was given to young Australians to join the army and fight in Europe.

For all Australians, the period of World War I was a tough time. Young soldiers went off to fight and were killed or maimed in large numbers and those at home waited anxiously for news. Many community activities, including sporting events, were abandoned. Fund-raising for the war effort took place while political debate about Australia's involvement occurred.

For the Reed family at Costerfield, with boys old enough to enlist, the War gave them the same worries as most other families at the time. Those eligible to enlist all had to ask themselves the same questions: "Ought I enlist?" and "What might be the outcome if I do?"

The best news for the Reeds during those years was that Mamie, living in South Yarra, gave birth in June 1915 to baby William (Bill) Meadley, George and Annie's first grandchild.

Footy and the War

The VFL played its part in the recruiting program for the Defence Forces in World War I. On 24 February 1915 (before ANZAC day) a meeting of 2500 people, sponsored by the VFL, the MCC and the Government passed a motion that "it is the duty of the sportsmen of Victoria to respond at once to the Empire's call by enlisting where possible". Forty-four enlisted on the spot.

The entry of Australia into the War meant that thousands of young men enlisted resulting in football clubs finding themselves short of players and unable to field teams, causing many football leagues to go into recession. The HDFL disbanded after the 1914 season as did the VFA for the 1916/1917 seasons. After completing the 1914 season with a full complement of teams, the VFL had a reduced number of teams for season 1915 before it returned to full strength in 1919.

From George Reed's perspective, as a Collingwood supporter, the pre-war years in the VFL were showing promise. Champion defender and member of the 1910 premiership side, Jock McHale, took over as coach. George was thrilled with the Magpies' 14 point victory over Carlton in the Grand Final in that year but disappointed by the Carlton defeat of Collingwood in the 1915 Grand Final. Although McHale was a believer in equal payment for all players, his great friend – wealthy business man John Wren – began a habit, in those years, of slipping a pound or ten shilling note to players who had performed well in a handshake after a game.

Joining Up

The Reed's wartime experience was much the same as thousands of other Australian families during those dreadful years. The first to join up was Ted Reed, who enlisted in Melbourne on 15 February, with Mamie's husband, Bill Meadley, next on 10 April, and Jack Reed enlisting in Perth on 7 October. George "Kelly" Reed also applied to join up but was rejected because of a hearing problem.

Annie's son-in law, Bill Meadley, and two of her sons, Ted and Jack, fought in France with Bill Meadley and Ted Reed being wounded and gassed while Jack Reed escaped being wounded but was gassed. The boys sent home letters and postcards as often as possible.

Annie Reed also had to face another tragedy as her husband George died from throat cancer in March 1917.

Three months after George's passing, Mamie gave birth to her second child, a little girl, Ann Maree Meadley. As was the case with many other wartime fathers, Bill Meadley had been sent overseas before his daughter was born.

War-time Footy – at Home and Abroad

The 1914 season in the VFL was the last "normal" season for a few years as the game was disrupted by the War. Victorians had weightier matters on their minds than football. Carlton hadn't won a flag since 1908. Coached by Jack Worrall, it finished on top of the ladder which comprised the normal 10 teams at the time. South Melbourne finished second. At the beginning of that season, Carlton had determined to do a lot better than they had been doing by recruiting half a dozen good players from the VFA and country leagues. Most likely the fact that players could be paid facilitated this process. Although defeated by South Melbourne in the Final, Carlton, as minor premiers, challenged and won the Grand Final by one goal.

Bruce Sloss of South Melbourne was best on ground in the Grand Final.

Jock McHale (NEWSPIX)

According to *The Encyclopedia of VFL/AFL Footballers*, "Sloss produced a solo performance of unparalleled excellence. The Swans trailed by 15 points at three-quarter time in a low scoring match but Sloss did everything in his power to haul his team to within six points."

Sloss later enlisted and while on service in England captained the Third Australian Divisional team which played the Australian Training Units team in the *Pioneer Exhibition Game of Australian Football*. It was played at Queen's Club, West Kensington, on Saturday, 28 October 1916. A crowd of 3,000 attended including the then Prince of Wales who later became King Edward VIII. All the gate money and profits from programs went to the funds of the British and French Red Cross Societies. The game probably lifted the morale of the servicemen involved as well as raising money for good causes.

War and the VFL

The 1915 season began on 24 April, the day before the Australian soldiers landed at Gallipoli.

When the news of this horrific event reached Melbourne there was great dismay and many thought that the season should be suspended because of the War. A meeting of the League Delegates was held at which it was decided that the season should continue. Carlton won the flag beating Collingwood in the Grand Final. **George Challis,** the courageous Carlton winger was seen by many as best on ground.

The VFL competition kept going during the War – with four teams in 1916, six teams in 1917 and eight teams in 1918. By 1919 there were nine teams competing with University having merged with Melbourne to rejoin the competition. In the latter years of the War the VFL allowed the competition to run because it was thought that it was good for community spirit. Players were not paid and profits went to the war effort.

On 4 January 1917, Lieutenant Bruce Sloss, the star of the 1914 Grand Final, was killed in action at Armentieres, in France.

Less than twelve months later Sergeant George Challis, the star of the 1915 Grand Final, was also killed in action at Armentieres.

In all, 89 ex-VFL footballers were killed in action in World War I, fifteen of those in the Gallipoli campaign, including Corporal 'Joe' Pearce who had represented Victoria in the 1908 Carnival. Pearce was among the first young men to enlist, doing so on 17 August 1914. He was promoted to the rank of Corporal on 6 April 1915, less than three weeks before he was killed. He was the first VFL footballer to die in action. A Life Member of the Melbourne Football Club and named among Melbourne's 150 Heroes at the 150th anniversary of the formation of the club, Pearce said the following in a speech at a farewell function given in his honour by the Melbourne Football Club:

> I have thought this thing over and I have considered it in every way. I am strong, healthy and athletic and I think I ought to go, and if I don't come back, well, it won't much matter.

The statistics of Australia's involvement in the War are horrific. More than 400,000 enlisted, with over 60,000 being killed while about 150,000 were wounded, of whom another 60,000 died prematurely after the War. All enlistments were volunteers. At the time, Australia's population was around 5 million.

Football Again – In the HDFL

The Heathcote and District Football League had disbanded prior to the start of the 1915 season.

At the time of writing, on a wall on the Costerfield Hall there is a Roll of Honour to ex-pupils of the Costerfield School (photo on next page by Marj Reed) who enlisted. There are 33 names on the plaque – sufficient to make it virtually impossible for Costerfield to field a team even if the competition continued during the War. Such tributes are on the walls of many schools and local halls throughout Australia with crosses beside

the names of those who didn't return. There is a cross beside W. Hill, F Robinson and J. Turnbull on the Costerfield plaque.

With the war situation improving towards the middle of 1918 and with better times at home, the HDFL was re-formed at a meeting held on 20 June 1918. One of the outcomes of the meeting was that the League would comprise four teams: Heathcote, Tooborac, Moormbool West and Costerfield.

The newer residents of the Moormbool West community, together with the teacher at the new local school, **George Hird**, had decided that they could form a team. For some players this meant leaving their Costerfield team of the past. Bob Oliver, a family friend from nearby Wirrate, was also a team member, as was Bob's neighbour **Fred Le Deux**, although the Le Deux family, like many farmers at the time, had not accepted the idea that Saturday afternoon was a time for recreation. Sometimes young Fred had to work on the family farm rather than play footy. "Football is a waste of good working time," his father used to say.

Moormbool West (sometimes called "Moormbool") lost its first three matches, but on 25 July it had its initial victory with M. Mewson, G. Hird and J. Tattersall being named as the best players for Moormbool West.

The 8 August report in the *McIvor Times* on the matches played on the previous Saturday indicated that Costerfield (6.6.42) had defeated

Moormbool West (3.3.21). The paper also commented that "Moormbool had all good men but perhaps the best were Tattersall, O'Connor (2), McCarty (2), Hird and Reed." From my research, this was the first time that my dad was mentioned among the best players in a footy team. I was thrilled to read it.

The rivalry between the Moormbool West and Costerfield must have been rather keen. It was reported, on 29 August, regarding the next contest between the two teams that "it was anticipated that the match would be fairly willing ... (and it was) ... for the game was varied on this occasion by a couple of stoushing competitions".

There was no mention as to who won the fight, but Costerfield won the game.

Moormbool West's next match against Costerfield was a month later and played at the Costerfield ground. Ever confident Mick Reed believed that his team could turn the tables on their rivals. Bob Oliver, the family friend from nearby Wirrate, was also in the team and young Frank Reed donned the Moormbool West colours for the match.

Mick successfully encouraged his whole family to watch the game. The Reed women enjoyed the footy too. There was also good representation from the Hird and Le Deux families in attendance. And the large Moormbool West contingent at the match wasn't disappointed.

The report in the paper tells the story:

> The Moormbool West footballers journeyed to Costerfield on Saturday and achieved the height of their ambition by defeating Costerfield on their own ground. It is many years since the tri-colours have suffered a defeat at home and it is decidedly a feather in the cap of the baby team of the association to have succeeded as they did. (*McIvor Times*, 26 September 1918).

My dad didn't figure in the report of the match against Costerfield. This was not the case for the last match of the season. In that game Tooborac defeated Moormbool West. I was pleased to see that Mick

Reed was mentioned three times in the write-up of the game.

It was reported that early in the match that:

> from the kick off Moormbool got possession and quickly had Tooborac on the defensive, a behind resulted from a scrimmage in front, to which a second was added by M. Reed and a third by Hird from a snap from the ruck.

Shortly after, "Tattersall passed along to Reed, who was allowed a free and sent the ball well in to McKenzie who had an exceptional chance for a 'sixer' but only secured a behind."

Yet further into the game "Connors registered a minor to which another was added by Reed. Hird was next to score from a difficult angle."

In 1918, my dad Mick decided, as a 20-year-old, to study for his Merit Certificate in the evening at Moormbool West State School under the guidance of the head teacher George Hird, whose family had been in the district as gold miners from as early as 1864. Mick was successful in obtaining his Merit Certificate and did some further classes with George with the view to becoming a student teacher.

5
Peace and Frank Maher

Home from the War, a Costerfield Flag, Features of footy; Heathcote FC, Richmond FC, Collingwood FC, Essendon FC, Geelong FC, Footscray FC, Hawthorn FC, North Melbourne FC; Vic Thorpe, Barney Herbert, "Checker" Hughes, Dan Minogue and the Rankins.

The end of the War saw soldiers gradually returning home from Europe and going back to normal life as best they could after their harrowing war-time experiences. While Jack and Ted Reed resumed life at Costerfield, Bill Meadley was suffering from neurasthenia and was put on a pension for life as it was believed he would be too ill to work again. He and Mamie purchased a house in Ivanhoe because it was thought that the fresh air in this outer Melbourne suburb would be beneficial to his health.

Footy with Costerfield again!

Football was back on the agenda again in 1919, but in that year Moormbool West did not enter a team. Many of the former Moormbool West players including George Hird, Jim Tattersall, Joe McKenzie, my dad Mick, and at times his brothers Frank and Ted, played for Costerfield that year. Only three teams entered in the competition: Costerfield, Heathcote and Tooborac. Tattersall, Finnigan, Bolitho, Wood (Costerfield's captain) Hird and Connelly were good players throughout the season. Costerfield won the Grand Final defeating Heathcote by four goals.

Despite the four goal victory by Costerfield, the game was not without interest for the spectators, particularly if they enjoyed a rugged affair, as the following paragraph, taken from the *McIvor Times* report of the Grand Final, indicates:

> Generally speaking the match was a good one, play being exceptionally fast, and the result being in doubt practically up to the last few minutes. It would be stretching the word a bit to call the game a friendly one, as on more than one occasion there was a display of fisticuffs.

Despite the toughness of the encounter, the reporter was happy with the performance of "Umpire Harris, who maintained full control of the game and gave impartial and honest decisions."

Costerfield Football Team, Premiers 1919

Back Row: C. Jones, J. McKenzie, G. Brown, **G. Hird**, D. Brown, W. Phillips, C. Ryan, A. Sexton, W. Gardner, N. Jenkins

Centre Row: G. Medhurst, **M. Reed**, M. Tobin, J. Tattersall, G. Wood, L. Griffiths, M. Burrows, V. Carroll

Front Row: G. Wallis, C. Wallis, J. Tattersall, W. Bolitho, T. Harvey

(*Courtesy Anne Bradley*, Pioneers of Costerfield)

Snippet

The rivalry between Costerfield appeared to be fierce and perpetual. It was witnessed as early as 1906 and again in 1919 and it reared its head once more in 1926. On 1 July that year Costerfield played Heathcote Blues at Costerfield. One incident resulted in court action taken by one player against another. It appears that T. Wright of Heathcote king-hit Costerfield's E. Hendry and broke his false teeth. In the legal case that followed Hendry claimed 50 pounds in damages to cover costs incurred in hiring a car to get to Heathcote, consulting with Dr Bull and a visiting dentist who mended the teeth, and missing six days of work. Wright won the case but received only a total of around eight pounds in damages as well as seven pounds, four shillings and sixpence in costs.

There were no mouthguards in those days.

The 1920 Grand Final was a close encounter throughout the game with only seven points separating the two teams at the first two changes and Costerfield leading by just three points at the next break and at the final siren.

The last quarter was an intense battle with Costerfield scoring the first goal for the quarter when (according to the *McIvor Times*) "on the wing Bradley was allowed a free from which he sent it close up to the sticks (which) was followed by Griffiths annexing a goal".

Another free kick, this time to Heathcote, resulted in a goal for Heathcote who were then only four points behind.

Again, according to the paper, Heathcote "commenced a determined fight for victory, and they looked very much like scoring when the bell rang, leaving Costerfield the 1920 victors with four points to spare".

Wallis, Jim Tattersall, Ryan, Griffiths, Phillips and Brown were the best for Coster with Tanian, Allsop, Anderson (2) Watkins and Elsbury doing very well from Heathcote.

Heathcote had their revenge on Costerfield in 1921 by winning the

Grand Final by two goals in a low scoring game. No players were singled out as "best" in the report which concluded that it "would be unfair to pick out the best players as every man in both teams did his utmost to win".

Two Flags for Costerfield

In 1924 times were so good in Costerfield that the club fielded two teams in the competition, Costerfield Rovers and Costerfield Ramblers. The Rovers wore red, white and blue colours. Efforts appear to have been made to make the teams as even as possible with G. Brown being appointed captain of the Rovers and C. Ryan vice-captain while the captain of the Ramblers was J. Tattersall with T. Harvey vice captain. Ted and Frank Reed were included in the Rovers' team.

Both Costerfield teams proved to be very strong with the Ramblers winning the minor premiership, but the Rovers, who hit their straps in the finals, won the flag.

Country Footy in the HDFA: 1905 to 1924

An examination of the Costerfield Football Club from its formation in 1905 until 1924, when a son of George and Annie Reed donned the tricolor guernsey of the club for the last time, illustrates a number of important aspects of the Australian game and the HDFL competition in the early 20th century. Other clubs and competitions across the country would most likely have had these similar features.

(i) Scratch matches

Before a competition was formed, scratch matches were played by different teams in a district.

(ii) Family game

Firstly, footy is a family game. A glance at team photos and newspaper reports across the years shows that often a number of members of the one family played with the team. In the instance of the Reed family five of the six Reed boys played with Costerfield, with three of them regularly in the senior team and the remaining two in the junior team. And, of course, the women folk followed the game too.

(iii) Few teams in competition

The HDFA varied in strength over the first couple of decades of its existence. The number of teams in the competition varied from two in 1905 to as many as six in 1924. However the smallness of the competition didn't dim the enthusiasm of the teams nor the rivalry between them.

(iv) Need for strong leadership

For a team to be successful, the need for strong leadership, both on and off the field, was notable at Costerfield. Jack Lally was captain of the team's first team in 1905 and continued in that role for many years. He was a fine footballer and had an administrative role with the club and the HDFL

(v) Support from the press

Another feature of the HDFL was that games were given good publicity in the local district newspaper, the *McIvor Times*. Not all games were reported on, nor were all selected teams published – most likely because team secretaries were unable to make them available in time for publication. However the games that were described were written about in great detail and often comments about the crowd and the umpire were included.

(vi) Differing finals systems

Different approaches were taken to awarding premiership honours in the HDFL in its early years.

If there were only two teams in the competition the team that won the most games (the minor premiers) was awarded the premiership. When there were more than two teams, two approaches were taken.

For example, in 1919, with three teams in the competition, a Grand Final was played between the two leading teams.

In 1924, with six teams in the competition, the second and third teams played each other for the right to challenge the minor premiers for the flag. There was then no right of challenge for the minors premiers if they lost the Grand Final.

The question of the best way to organise final series has been an ongoing challenge for football competitions, including the VFL/AFL.

(vii) Changes in Award Systems

Over the period 1905 to 1924, Costerfield won nine premierships. Photos were taken of those successful teams and players were given or purchased copies. Dad sometimes talked about the good players in those teams but he never mentioned terms such as "Best and Fairest" winners or "Leading Goal Kickers". It appears that individual players were not specially singled out. Footy was a team game and a photo of the whole team was all that was needed to recognise success.

This situation of little recognition being given to outstanding players changed a little in 1926 when the *McIvor Times*, following the introduction of the Brownlow Medal for the Best and Medal in the VFL, introduced the idea of a best player award for the HDFL. The newspaper donated a trophy to the winner who was decided by popular vote.

A coupon appeared in the newspaper which read "I desire my vote for … as being worthy of the McIvor Times Trophy for 1926."

The player's name was to be inserted in the appropriate space. Voters had to sign their names and give their addresses, then submit the coupon in a specially marked envelope to the *McIvor Times* office, where votes could be inspected.

In the year of its inception, Charlie Tanian of Heathcote, with 305 votes, won the *McIvor Times* silver cup for Best and Fairest in the HDFA.

As well as recognising the best player this was a very useful marketing device as people had to purchase the paper to vote. In times to come, as elsewhere, the HDFL awarded a Best and Fairest trophy based on central umpires' votes.

Snippet

The Taniens must have been a talented football family. Charlie and Jack Tanien were selected to play for the HDFL in the inter-league contests which were held at Bendigo in 1926. J. Tattersall of Costerfield was captain of the side which was beaten rather easily by the Korong District League Team. Other Costerfield names in the side were L. Phillips and J. Tobin.

In the VFL – The Tigers Come Good

The football seasons from 1919 to 1924 were good for Costerfield and for my dad, who was doubly blessed over those years as Richmond, his team in the VFL, also tasted success at that time.

In 1919, the VFL competition comprised nine teams. Richmond finished fourth on the ladder with 10 wins and six losses with Collingwood was on top with 13 wins. The Tigers defeated second team South Melbourne in their semi-final and then defeated Collingwood in the final. Collingwood, as minor premiers, challenged and won the Grand Final by twenty-five points. Dick Lee kicked three goals for Collingwood.

The Richmond 1919 team photo (on next page) was treasured by my dad. It was found in his possessions after he passed away. The photo had no names on it except to mention that D. Don, F. Huggard and G. Parkinson were absent.

From another source I was able to identify Barney Herbert, Hugh James and Vic Thorpe in the photo.

Barney Herbert is centre in the back row, with Hugh James on his right and Vic Thorpe on the extreme right in that row.

Richmond Team 1919

(Private possession and out of copyright)

The Richmond team that was runners-up in 1919 was as follows:

Backs: Bettles, Thorpe, Abbott;
Half-backs: Parkinson, Hislop, Huggard;
Centres: Morris, Hughes, Hede;
Half-Forwards: Maybury (capt), Bayliss, Harley;
Forwards: Smith, James, Don;
Rucks: Herbert, Moffatt, Hall.

There were no reserves at that time.

In 1920 the Tigers went one step further than in the previous year and won its first flag under captain **Dan Minogue**, who had transferred from the Magpies to the Tigers in that year. Richmond made it back-to-back flags in 1921, by defeating Carlton in a low scoring game.

Minogue was one of the all-time greats of the game. He captained three VFL teams (Collingwood, Richmond and Hawthorn) and coached five VFL teams – more than any other coach. Coming from Bendigo to Collingwood, after a near fatal mining accident, he proved his toughness by playing the whole match with Collingwood in the 1911 Grand Final after breaking his collarbone in the first few minutes of the game.

Minogue served with distinction in World War I and played, under Bruce Sloss in the Services match in London. He has been inducted into both the Richmond Hall of Fame and the Australian Football Hall of Fame. Many of the 1919 runners-up Tiger players were in the two premiership teams.

Mick Reed often spoke about some of the great Tiger players of the era including Vic Thorpe, Barney Herbert, Hugh James and Frank Hughes.

Vic Thorpe was an outstanding full-back regarded by Dick Lee as the best he had played on. Scrupulously fair, he was a great mark and a beautiful drop kick. He played 263 games with the Tigers and represented Victoria 14 times.

Barney Herbert was the leading ruckman for the Tigers in that era, playing 192 games with the Tigers and, although he derided his own kicking ability, he kicked 90 goals for his team. He had great understanding with his tiny and clever rover, Clarrie Hall, who played 150 games with the Tigers and was one of the best in the 1920 premiership team.

Snippet

According to *The Encyclopedia of AFL Footballers*, Barney Herbert reflected on the ecstasy of the Richmond players on winning the club's first Grand Final in 1920 when he wrote the following in the *Sporting Globe* on 2 May 1936. "Little Clarrie Hall, overcome by the triumph, made a wild rush for Dave Moffat and me. We just got a neck hold on each other and I am not afraid to admit that we actually KISSED each other in the excess of our joy."

Perhaps one of the most famous Tiger players of that era was centreman **Frank 'Checker' Hughes**. A clever ball handler, he was an excellent stab kick. Coming from Myrtleford, as a player he was good enough to represent Victoria. His playing career was interrupted by four years of service in World War I where he won a DCM. But it was as a coach that he later made his mark, coaching the Tigers to runners-up for four years before claiming the flag in 1932. This was at the time that Collingwood won its record four flags in a row. In 1933 he was appointed as coach of Melbourne and subsequently coached them to four premierships, the last being the 1948 flag. He was instrumental in changing Melbourne's nickname from the "Fuchsias" to the "Demons".

Half-back flanker in the Tigers' 1919 side, Frank Huggard, also served with distinction in the War winning a Military Medal in Europe.

Hugh James was the other leading big man in the side. Playing 188 games for the team he was regarded as one of the gentlemen of the game. A bricklayer and builder by trade he rarely trained because of his work commitments. He won the Military Cross in World War I and was one of the organisers of the Services football match played in London during the War.

Snippet

Centre half-forward in the 1919 Tiger team was George Bayliss, a quick thinking left footer. One afternoon, when the football was returned to the ground from a behind in a match against Essendon, it was found to be punctured. The full back gently kicked the ball to the umpire to show him that it was going flat. Bayliss quickly intercepted the ball and kicked a goal. Ruckman Hugh James, fair man that he was, argued that the goal should not be allowed. As the ball had not been kicked out from the goal square, the score wasn't counted, much to Hugh James' satisfaction.

However Bayliss went on to win the League goal kicking in 1920 with 60 legitimate goals.

Unusual Final Series

Attracted by the excitement of living in the City and no longer wanting to work on the land or be a teacher Mick Reed moved to Melbourne in

1924. The Tigers finished fourth on the ladder in that year and ended the season as runners-up. The VFL experimented with a new finals system that year with each of the four finalists playing each other over the finals series. Thus six games were played overall, with each team playing three matches. The team that was on top after this final series was granted the premiership if it had also been on top at the end of the season (minor premiers). Essendon, Richmond, South Melbourne and Fitzroy comprised the final four.

Essendon were minor premiers at the end of the season and on top of the ladder after the finals. Like Richmond they won two games and lost one in the final series but Essendon had the better percentage in the final series so Essendon were premiers.

The irony was that in the last match of the final series Richmond defeated Essendon by 20 points. Some said that Essendon didn't try too hard in the match against the Tigers because, with their excellent percentage, they were virtually certain to win the premiership even if they lost. The VFL reverted to the previous system in the following year.

At the end of the 1924 season there was a match between the VFA premiers, Footscray, and the VFL premiers, Essendon, which was won convincingly by Footscray. There was a suggestion that some Essendon players were bribed to "lie down" in this game and there was conflict in the Essendon rooms after the match.

Frank Maher

One Essendon player who certainly gave of his best in all matches was Essendon rover and Military Medallist **Frank Maher** (at right) who began his football career only after he returned from the

Frank Maher

World War I. He had shown little interest in football as a youngster, but enjoyed the game when playing with fellow soldiers in France.

On being discharged he played with Shepparton and then Lilydale, proving to be a nimble-footed and skilful rover. He was signed by Essendon and played a big role in his team's flag-winning victory against Fitzroy in 1923, and was made vice-captain in 1924.

During the 1924 final series, Maher was outstanding, displaying great ability at reading the play and being in the right place at the right time. He was appointed captain-coach of the club in the following year and, as a regular interstate performer, he had that role for Victoria at the 1927 Interstate Carnival. He later went to VFA club Oakleigh where he again displayed his football and leadership skills.

The Rankins

The next season was a momentous one for Geelong. Although the Pivitonians were the leading side in the VFA competition before the formation of the VFL, Geelong had not won a premiership until it broke the drought in 1925, by defeating Collingwood in the Grand Final before a then record crowd of over 64,000 people. Captain-coach of the side was forward Cliff Rankin, who had served on the Western Front during World War I, and was the Cats' (as Geelong were then called) best player in the Grand Final, slotting five of his team's 10 goals. Rankin, who used place kicks when shooting for goal, was remarkably accurate in doing so. He was part of a great Geelong footballing family. His dad, "Teddy" Rankin and his uncle, Tom Rankin, played around the turn of the century and his older brother Bert played around the same time as Cliff. Between them, "Teddy", Tom, Cliff and Bert played over 500 games with the Cats. Teddy, who was the first Cat to play 100 games for the club worked as a groundsman at Geelong College, a position taken over by his son Bert when he retired. Bert also followed his dad as a centreman for the Cats. The Rankins certainly served Geelong very well indeed.

Snippet

Season 1925, also saw three clubs from the VFA (Footscray, Hawthorn and North Melbourne) enter the VFL. The 12 team competition, comprising Melbourne suburban teams, plus Geelong, was to last for over 60 years. Older people in 2013 still hark back to those days of tribal football when the first question that was asked of a new acquaintance was, "What team do you barrack for?" The question might still be asked in 2013, but not as early in the conversation.

6

The Depression and Bob Pratt

The Depression, Heading West, Excellent umpiring, Shepparton Imperials, Living in "Tigerland"; Collingwood FC, Richmond FC, South Melbourne FC; the Colliers, the Coventrys and the "Foreign Legion".

In 1924, Mick Reed was employed by Victoria Railways at Richmond station, and living with his sister Mamie, and her husband Bill Meadley, at Ivanhoe. He played footy with the Ivanhoe Football Club alongside the then-young and later-famous Collier brothers.

Albert and Harry Collier played with Ivanhoe in 1924 before they joined Collingwood. Harry Collier was Best and Fairest for Ivanhoe in 1924. Albert ("Leeter") Collier joined Collingwood in 1925 while Harry waited until 1926. Although he began his career at Collingwood as a full forward, according to *The Encyclopaedia of AFL Footballers*, "Leeter" was "Strong and extremely vigorous, (and) later developed into a champion centre half back, who took great care of his smaller team mates, especially brother Harry." Harry Collier was a tough and skilled rover.

Both went on to play in premiership teams and each won a Brownlow Medal – the only two brothers to do so.

Multi-premiership player and coach of the Demons, Norm Smith, a Magpie supporter in his youth, thought very highly of Leeter Collier as a footballer. According to Ben Collins in his biography of Smith (*The Red Fox*), the legendary Demon said in 1962, that "if he had to select his greatest ever team, Leeter Collier would be his Number One pick ... not so much for his brilliance as for his protective play". Smith is quoted as saying, "I can still remember his great pace, soaring high marks, his wonderful kicking ... His team work made him one of the greats of football." It would be difficult to find a player from that era who would be given a better accolade than that of Smith's for Leeter Collier.

Both Collier brothers played in six premiership teams, equal second to Hawthorn's long-playing Michael Tuck who played in seven flag-winning sides.

Ivanhoe Football Club was formed in 1912 and played in the Heidelberg District Football Association until it joined the Sub-District Football League in 1922 where it remained until 1934 when it joined the Victorian Amateur Football Association (VAFA). At that time Alan Killigrew, a renowned St Kilda coach in the '50s, played with Ivanhoe. Many say that Killigrew laid the foundations for St Kilda's premiership in 1966.

Ivanhoe had an interesting start when it joined the VAFA. In its first three years the team won 60 consecutives matches and three premierships as it moved up through the various grades in the Association.

Another Set of Brothers

Recruited from Diamond Creek, **Gordon Coventry** kicked 1299 goals in his 306 games with the Magpies. He was Collingwood's leading goal kicker 16 times and the League's top goal kicker on six occasions. It was said of him that once he was in the front position he was so strong that it was almost impossible to beat him for a mark or on the ground. He was member of the Collingwood Team of the Century and has been inducted into the Australian Football Hall of Fame (Legend sta-

Gordon Coventry
NEWSPIX

tus) and the Collingwood Hall of Fame. He passed away in 1968 at his Diamond Creek property.

A regular opponent of Gordon Coventry in matches against the Tigers was backman **Joe Murdoch** who was inducted into the Richmond Hall of Fame in 2011. Members of his family attending the ceremony said Murdoch was tough both on and off the field. He drove his car around Castlemaine, his home town, until he was ninety because no-one was game enough to ask him not to do so before then.

*Joe Murdoch
'Richmond Weekly', 1923*

Joe was involved in a famous incident with Gordon Coventry in 1936 when they allegedly exchanged blows and both were reported. Coventry claimed that Murdoch had hit him on boils on the back of his neck. In an interview with Rhett Bartlett for his book *Richmond F. C. "The Tigers" A Century of League Football,* Murdoch said that one of the Wrens (either John or a son – he couldn't remember) offered Joe 50 pounds to plead guilty at the Tribunal. He rejected the offer and told the Tribunal that, "He never hit me. I never hit him." Obviously he wasn't believed as Coventry was given eight weeks and missed the Grand Final, while Joe got four weeks. Joe came back for the last game of the year and then retired. Murdoch played 180 games for the Tigers and was a member of two premiership teams.

Coming to Collingwood later than Gordon, older brother **Syd Coventry** had a shorter playing career with only 227 games. As a ruckman he was at his best when the going was toughest. He was the best player on the ground in the 1927 Grand Final.

That particular Grand Final was a significant match for a couple of reasons.

Firstly, it was the first of four successive flags won by the Magpies: all under the coaching of Jock McHale.

Secondly, the weather conditions both before and during the game were dreadful. Heavy rain fell all day and the ground was in an atrocious condition. Jock McHale told his players not to attempt marking with their hands but to only take marks on their chests. He also told them to kick the ball off the ground wherever possible.

The game became a hard slog with a total of only 3 goals 20 behinds being scored by the two teams. Collingwood won with 2.13.25 to the Tigers' 1.7.13. The combined score of 38 points was the lowest score kicked in a VFL match since 1900 and no lower score has been registered in a VFL/AFL game since 1927. The Collingwood captain, Syd Coventry, was regarded as best afield for the game and his brother Gordon kicked Collingwood's two goals. Richmond rover Jack Fincher kicked the Tigers' only goal.

Syd Coventry (NEWSPIX)

Syd's leadership skills were recognised in that he was named captain of the Collingwood Team of the Century. He won the Brownlow Medal in 1927 and was twice Collingwood's Best and Fairest. He acted as non-playing coach of Footscray for two years before returning to the Magpies to act as vice-president and later president of the club.

Shepparton Imperials

Mick Reed's next move was to Traralgon in 1925. He didn't play footy there, probably because he was committed to doing shift work with the Railways.

When Dad was transferred to Shepparton in 1926 there were two football competitions around Shepparton, one that played on Wednesdays (the Goulburn Valley League) and a district competition that played on Saturdays.

The Wednesday competition was regarded as the major competition and included teams from Shepparton, Rushworth, Mooroopna, Kyabram, Tongala, Tatura and Murchison. Perhaps this competition was played mid-week as the district farmers, who would have made up many of the footballers, might not have wanted to play on a Saturday. With Sunday being seen as a day for church attendance and rest, these men may not have wished to have two days in a row away from their farm.

The Saturday competition comprised Undera, Ardmona, Mooroopna, Dookie College, Shepparton Imperials, Shepparton East and Cosgrove. Perhaps the men who chose to play in this competition were those whose work commitments prohibited them from playing on Wednesdays.

Mick Reed played for Shepparton Imperials in the Saturday competition for seasons 1926 and 1927.

Not making the finals in 1926, the Imperials won the flag in 1927, defeating Dookie College to win the minor premiership. The report in the paper about that game noted that "everyone in the team did well but Mick Reed was best on ground". It was most gratifying to read this over 80 years later.

The 1927 Grand Final would have been Mick Reed's last game of competition football.

Although he didn't play in 1925, when he was at Traralgon, Mick played with four clubs over 10 seasons: Moormbool West, Costerfield, Ivanhoe and Shepparton Imperials. He was a member of four premiership teams, three with Costerfield and one with Shepparton Imperials. No doubt his success and enjoyment of the game were factors in his encouragement of his boys to become involved in football.

Comments about the Umpire

Just as the *McIvor Times* reported on the Heathcote competition, so the *Shepparton News* gave space to the competitions around Shepparton and it appears that a commentary about the umpire's performance was mandatory there too.

On 21 June 1926, the newspaper's report on the match between Shepparton East and Shepparton Imperials began as follows:

> Much rivalry exists between these two teams and though the game was willing at times, nothing of a spiteful nature was apparent which was no doubt owing to the capable umpiring of Darcy who always had a firm hold on the game.

Doubtless, umpire Darcy would have been very pleased with the report on that game, but the situation was not so comfortable for him in the next match between Shepparton Imperials and Ardmona.

Under the headline, *Umpire Laid Out*, the report continued as follows:

> In the third quarter J. Pearson, one of Ardmona's 6 footers, caused a diversion, when he accidentally laid out central umpire Frank Darcy. Pearson who was unaware of the proximity of the umpire suddenly raised his arm and his elbow connected with Darcy's chin … Darcy stopped down for two or three minutes.

However, never deterred, "Darcy umpired in his usual excellent style."

It appears that umpires can be "accidentally laid out" even when there is only one of them to get in a player's way.

MacIsaac and McCaskill

Playing with Shepparton Imperials in the 1920s, Mick Reed would have been well aware of the controversy concerning a couple of Richmond players, Angus MacIsaac and Bob McCaskill, who came from the Mooroopna/Shepparton area. As the Goulburn Valley competition was played on Wednesdays, MacIsaac and McCaskill played with their country teams mid-week and with the Tigers on Saturday. MacIssac's country team was Mooroopna while McCaskill's was Shepparton.

Angus MacIsaac (Richmond Weekly', 1923)

Both were playing with the Tigers when they defeated Collingwood in the final round of the 1924 season. Collingwood protested, claiming that the players had broken VFL rules in playing with two teams. The VFL reprimanded both players and told them not to do so any more. As the VFL season ended before the Goulburn Valley competition MacIsaac ignored the VFL's ruling by resigning from the Tigers and played a very impressive game for Mooroopna in its Grand Final win over Tatura. His action resulted in him being suspended from playing with any club in season 1925. However the ban was lifted in 1926 and MacIsaac returned to play two more seasons with the Tigers.

In 1927 Grand Final, MacIsaac was in the back pocket in the Tigers' losing team against Collingwood. From that position he had a run on the ball as he was a tall man with a very good leap and hence, an effective ruckman.

MacIsaac left the Tigers at the end of the 1927 season to take a position of playing/coach of South Bendigo for which he received seven pounds per week ($14) compared with the three pounds ($6) he was getting at Richmond. He later returned to Mooroopna to finish his career there.

MacIsaac is thought to be the first of many young men from Assumption College, Kilmore, to play VFL/AFL football.

Bob McCaskill left the Tigers at the end of the 1925 season after playing 36 games, mainly in the centre. He later coached Sandhurst in the Bendigo League to six consecutive premierships.

Moving on he then coached North Melbourne for over 100 games helping them to reach the finals for the first time in 1945 when they were defeated by Carlton in the first semi-final. McCaskill had less success as coach of Hawthorn during his stint there from 1950 to 1952.

Mick Reed in "Tigerland"

In 1928 Dad was transferred back to Melbourne and stationed at the Outwards Parcels Office at Spencer Street Railway Station – now known as Southern Cross.

Mick lived in Tanner Street which could be said to be in the shadow of the spire of St Ignatius Church and no doubt Dad attended that church on the first Sunday he spent in Richmond.

Dad had retired from footy but wasn't finished with sport. He had played tennis at Shepparton and given that the tennis courts of the St Ignatius Tennis Club were adjacent to the parish church, Dad decided that tennis would then be his main sporting activity. Besides, the Richmond Football Club had a decidedly Irish Catholic flavor at that time and a number of the players would unwind after Saturday's football match with a Sunday game of tennis. Amongst these players was a young Jack Dyer. Dad remembered Dyer as a shy young lad but he later had a great admiration for Dyer as a player and coach.

Jack Fincher, a rover for the Tigers, was another of Dad's mates from

Jack Fincher (private photo)

that era who played tennis at the St Ignatius courts. As we have seen, Fincher kicked the Tigers' only goal in the 1927 Grand Final. According to *The Encyclopedia of Footballers*, Fincher was "an extremely tenacious rover who played 69 games with Richmond and 39 games with Footscray. He had the misfortune to play in three losing Grand Final sides for the Tigers in 1927, 1928 and 1929".

Jackie Fincher and Dad lost touch with each other when Jackie left Richmond to play with Footscray in 1931. He spoke of him sometimes when I was growing up. There was a photo of him, along with Basil McCormack in a family photo album. McCormack was champion centre half-back for the Tigers.

A workmate of Mick's in the Railways at the time was Martin Bolger who was a premiership back pocket player for the Tigers.

Dad liked to tell the story of when Martin came to Richmond to try out with the club. Asked his age, he informed the club that he was 21 years old when he was really much older. "If I told the club my real age I would have been quickly shown the door," Martin would say to Mick. That strategy wouldn't work in the 21st century as players are earmarked as ALF potential almost from the time they cut their second teeth.

Another Richmond Tiger player who was spoken of as a good friend was Doug Hayes, a rover from Camberwell who played 82 games from 1922 to 1928. Dad took an interest in the career of his son, Alan Hayes, when he came to Tigerland in 1959. Alan played 23 games over three seasons before he went to South Australia.

The Great Depression

As well as a Magpie flag, the year 1929 saw the onset of the Great Depression beginning with the collapse of the New York Stock Market in October of that year. This crisis spread worldwide and Australia was hard hit with plummeting exports and high unemployment. Many who kept their jobs were forced to take a wage reduction or reduced working hours. Workers' strikes occurred, sometimes leading to violence. However success at sport kept the morale in Australia high through to the early to mid-1930s when the depression began to lift.

New South Wales born Don Bradman proved himself to be the world's best batsman in the late 1920s, a position he held for a couple of decades, and Phar Lap showed the world that Australia could produce great race horses by travelling to Mexico to compete in and win the Acqua Celiente Handicap with prize money bigger than any previously offered in the northern hemisphere.

The Smarts and Jack Symons

St Ignatius Parish Tennis Club, was a very fortunate venue for Dad as it was there that he met his future wife, Muriel Peace Smart. Muriel, the second eldest of seven children, was a typist/secretary for a Myer executive and lived in Dover Street, which runs parallel to Punt Rd south of the Richmond Railway Station. Muriel's family lived near the corner of Kelso Street in Dover Street and were Richmond supporters.

Mum's brothers, Harry, who was particularly keen on footy, and Noel, used to play kick-to-kick in Kelso St and sometimes walked down Kelso St, crossed Punt Rd and played scratch matches with their friends in Gosch's Paddock.. One of their friends was Jack Symons, a promising footballer, who later married the sister of Mum's neighbour and best friend, Della Hines.

Snippet

My Mum's second name was Peace because she was born on the day that the Boer War ended, 31 May 1902. It was an appropriate name for Muriel as she was a gentle, loving woman admired by all who knew her.

Although the VFL was very much in its infancy at the time the Boer War started, a number of players elected to serve the British Empire in that war against the Dutch colonial forces in South Africa. Two players who had played against each other in the 1898 Grand Final enlisted and were killed. Lieutenant Stan Reid, a back pocket player, was among Fitzroy's best in that game while Trooper Charlie Moore was a full forward who kicked one of Essendon's three goals in their 15 point loss. Moore had played 30 games with Essendon, while Reid had played 24 with Fitzroy.

Heading West

Before the onset of the Great Depression (which saw railway workers being asked to work part-time rather than lose their positions), Dad was able to obtain leave to accompany his brother, Jack Reed, on a visit to Perth. The reason for the trip is not clear but no doubt Jack wanted to catch up with friends he had made on his earlier visit. Perhaps there were mates from his army days still living in the West.

The "Foreign Legion"

The Reed brothers were not the only ones who went west around that time. A recruiting team from South Melbourne also took the journey.

While Richmond, Collingwood (under Jock McHale) and Geelong (with Reg Hickey captain and coach) won two premierships in the 1930s, the Swans were arguably the glamour team of that era playing in four successive Grand Finals from 1933 to 1936, yet winning only one. After winning the 1918 flag, the Swans went poorly in the 1920s and were determined to do better in the 1930s.

Under Club President, Archie Croft, a well-off owner of a chain of grocery stores, they began their recruiting drive. Still worried about inequalities in player payment, the VFL had passed in 1930 (at the instigation of a Melbourne club delegate, Gordon Coulter) the "Coulter Law" which limited player payment to three pounds per match.

South got around this new ruling during the depression by offering new recruits employment in Croft's stores. Johnny Leonard, "Bluey" Richards, Bert Beard, John Bowe, Brighton Diggins, Bill Faul and Jim O'Meara were recruited from Western Australia plus three South Australians and two players from Tasmania including Laurie Nash. It was because they had so many players from Western Australia that a football writer, Hec De Lacy, coined the name "Swans" for South Melbourne after the Swan River in Perth. The name has stuck and we now have the Sydney Swans.

Finishing fourth in 1932 the Swans then recruited, much to Dad's disappointment, the captain of the Tiger premiership team, Jack Bissett, as playing coach for 1933.

Bissett had immediate success with South beating the Tigers in the Grand Final in that year before a record crowd of over 75,000 at the MCG. Laurie Nash was best on ground having 29 kicks and taking 13 marks, many of them quite spectacular. Bissett coached the Swans until 1936 but they were beaten by the Tigers in the 1934 Grand Final and by the Magpies in 1935 and 1936. Bissett coached the Swans for 80 games of which they won 63. He was selected as coach of the Swans' Team of the Century.

Despite the brilliance of many of the imports, perhaps the most famous name in the Swans' team of those years was local lad, full forward **Bob Pratt** who kicked 109 goals in 1933, followed by a record 150 in 1934 and 103 in 1935.

During the 1934 season Pratt also kicked a double-digit number of goals in three successive matches when he kicked 11, 11 and 12 goals over rounds 13, 14 and 15.

In later days two other players have equalled this feat; John Coleman of Essendon, at the beginning of the 1953 season when he kicked 10, 11, and 10 in the first three rounds of that season and Tony Lockett, then with St Kilda, kicking 12, 10, and 12 goals over rounds 7, 8 and 9 in 1991.

In all, Bob Pratt played 158 games for the Swans and kicked 681 goals. Pratt had pace, courage, was an exceptional high mark and a long, accurate kick. Jack Dyer said of Pratt that "it would be difficult to convey Pratt's greatness to future generations of football fans who had not been privileged to see him in action".

Snippet

On the eve of the 1935 Grand Final in which the Swans were to play Collingwood, Bob Pratt was hit by a truck carrying bricks, as he was getting off a tram. He was unable to play in the match on the next day and the Magpies took the flag by 20 points. It was rumoured that the driver, in his remorse, gave Pratt a packet of cigarettes.

The accident to Pratt was a stroke of luck for Jack Regan, the Collingwood full back, who said of Pratt that he was his most difficult opponent and that he stood out from all the other forwards he played against, not only for his high marking, but because when the ball hit the ground he was after it like a terrier.

Both Pratt and Regan are in their respective clubs' Teams of the Century, although Pratt is in the forward pocket beside Tony Lockett at full forward.

Marriage of Mick and Muriel

My parents, Mick and Muriel, were married at St Ignatius Church in Richmond on 6 January 1934. Later in the year they were at the Grand Final when the Tigers defeated the Swans' "Foreign Legion". After an even first quarter the Tigers slammed six goals in both the second and third quarters. The Tigers were coached by Frank "Checker" Hughes who told his defenders, particularly Bolger, Sheahan and O'Neill, to crowd Bob Pratt. They successfully did this keeping him to two goals. However South's centre half-forward Laurie Nash kicked six goals for the Swans. Jack Titus was Richmond's best player kicking six goals in the Tigers' 39 point victory. Dad, when later recalling that match, used to say that "a champion team will always beat a team of champions".

Snippet

One of my parents' favourite players in the late 1920s and early 1930s was **Jack Baggott** who was recruited as a forward from Dimboola in 1927 and topped Richmond's goal kicking in 1927 and 1928. However he was such a versatile player that he was moved to the backline later in his career, being part of the Tigers' premiership defence for the club's premierships in 1932 and 1934. He later coached Essendon and South Melbourne without great success.

The Tigers were unable to snare Jack's younger brother Ron Baggott. When living with his family who had moved to Northcote, the younger Baggott was signed by the Demons as was his Northcote mate, Norm Smith. Both were triple premiership forwards in Melbourne's three 1939 to 1941 flag-winning teams. Baggott and Smith were outstanding in finals over those years.

Jack Baggott
(Richmond Weekly, 1923)

Ron Baggott won the club Best and Fairest in 1940 and joined the Armed Services after the 1941 season. Although past his best, he returned to play with the Demons in 1945. Ron Baggott then became well-known as a football commentator with radio station

3KZ. My dad also had great respect for him when he became General Manager of the Victorian Railways Institute, a body set up by the Railway Commissioners to provide educational, social and recreational facilities for railway workers. The Institute's facilities, at Flinders Street Station, to be renovated in 2014, were extensive and included a gymnasium, a billiard room and a ballroom.

7
World War II and John Coleman

World War II, War-time losses, A Fitzroy Flag, A Trip to Geelong, Following the Tigers, Finals' matches, the Cats' return; Fitzroy FC, North Melbourne FC; "Bluey" Truscott, Jack Symons, Alan Ruthven, Allan Hird and the Pannams.

Mick and Muriel initially lived in Armidale where Ramon was born. They moved to 55 George Street, Oakleigh, in 1937, the year before my birth. Maureen was born nearly two years later just before the start of World War II. Once again Australia stood loyally behind Great Britain and entered the War.

Although times were tough during the War, things improved steadily in the 1940s and 1950s as fridges, washing machines, motor cars and eventually television became more commonplace.

But one thing didn't change. Mick and Muriel, and subsequently their children, still barracked for Richmond who were runners-up in 1940 and 1942.

The Tigers won the premiership in 1943 and although I know that **Jack ("Captain Blood") Dyer** was playing coach of the team, I have no memory of that win. But I can recall the 1944 Grand Final and the discussion that went on about it. Mum and Dad were keen for the Tigers to make it two flags in a row and were confident that

Jack Dyer

they could do so as they finished on top of the VLF ladder at the end of the home and away matches. They also had a personal interest in the game. They knew one of the players quite well. Jack Symons was a Richmond lad, with whom my uncles played kick to kick in Dover Street where my Mum lived when growing up.

Rewarded at Last

Beginning his football career at Burnley Jack Symons was soon spotted by Richmond and was pleased to be invited to play there in 1934. A big man, **Jack Symons** had played 111 games with the Tigers to the end of the 1943 season as a follower or key position forward or defender. He was back pocket and second ruck in the team that lost to the Demons in 1940, and was centre half-forward in the Tigers' losing Grand Final side against the Bombers in 1942.

Symons was keen to play in a premiership team for the Tigers, but he missed selection in the winning premiership team in 1943. Nevertheless his services to the club were recognised in that year as he was made a Life Member of the Richmond Football Club. Still wanting to be in a premiership team Symons transferred to Fitzroy in 1944. He was picked to play against the Tigers in the Grand Final that year. Of course Dad, Mum and we kids hoped that the Tigers would win but Mum, in particular, felt sorry for Jack Symons and hoped he would do well in a losing side.

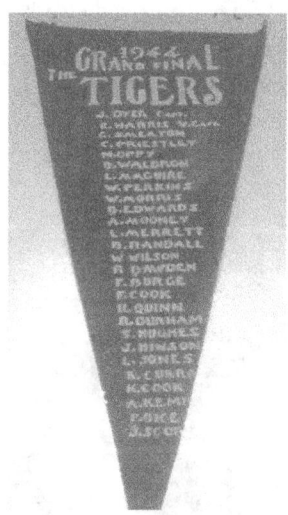

Private photo/Kevin Reed

Dad went to the game and I can remember him coming in through the back doorway, throwing his copy of the *Football Record* onto the kitchen table and saying sadly, with a deep sigh, "Well, the Tigers lost."

Our only consolation for the Tiger defeat was that dad brought home a Tiger flag (at left) with all of the players' names on it.

So, Jack Symons got to play in a premiership side. He played in the first ruck in the game, alongside renowned Fitzroy follower Bert Clay and rover Alan Ruthven, and kicked a goal.

Two of the Fitzroy team were good footballers themselves but their sons were to become bigger names as sportsmen. Keith Stackpole Snr kicked two goals in the Grand Final and played interstate cricket for Victoria. His son, Keith Stackpole Jnr was an outstanding cricketer, playing in many Tests for Australia over almost a decade, in the 1960s/70s, scoring seven Test centuries and 14 test half centuries as a courageous and hard-hitting opening batsman. He was also a legspin bowler.

Dan Murray was 19th man for the Fitzroy premiership side in 1944. His son, Kevin Murray, was to become one of the team's most decorated champions, playing 333 games with the club, winning the Brownlow Medal in 1969 after being runner-up twice and third once. He was named as captain of the Fitzroy Team of the Century. Murray would feel very much at home playing AFL football in 2013, not only because he was such a good player, but also because he proudly sported "tatts" on his arms – a rare sight on the footy field in those days.

Alan "the Baron" Ruthven, from the 1944 team, also won a Brownlow Medal, being successful in 1950. A brave rover, Ruthven was a beautiful left-foot kick. He was later a popular publican and one of the first panellists on *World of Sports* when that show hit the TV screens in the 1950s. He was also named in the Fitzroy Team of the Century.

Season 1944 was also of interest for two other reasons. Although Richmond was beaten by Fitzroy in both the second semi-final and the Grand Final, the Tigers were minor premiers for the year finishing on top of the VFL ladder. Both teams had 13 wins, four losses and a draw for the home and away games. But the Tigers finished on top with a percentage of 131.15 against Fitzroy's percentage of 131.09 – a difference of only 0.06 per cent. This is the closest that the two top teams have ever been at the end of a season.

Both of the Grand Finalists were led by playing coaches in 1944. This was the last time that this has happened, but it wasn't unusual for VFL teams to have playing coaches in the early seasons of the game. In fact up to and including 1950, flag-winning teams had playing coaches on 15 occasions. Since that date only three playing coaches have been successful: Charlie Sutton who won the flag with Footscray in 1953 and John Nicholls and Alex Jesaulenko who had success with the Blues in 1972 and 1979 respectively.

Snippet

The playing coach of Fitzroy in 1944, when they defeated Richmond in the Grand Final, was Fred Hughson who was famous for his extremely long kicking. In 1943 he drop-kicked a ball 76.18 metres in a competition against a US serviceman who threw a gridiron ball 63.39 metres. Hughson later coached South Warrnambool.

Cats' Return

Geelong had dropped out of the VFL in 1942 and 1943 because of difficulties as a result of WWII. They had lost a number of players to the Defence Forces and there were always the costs associated with travelling to Melbourne every second week. Although they made application to return to the VFL in 1944, their request was not readily accepted with some Melbourne clubs worried about the time taken, and the cost involved, in travelling the distance from the City to Geelong. There was also a fear that Geelong's team would be too weak to offer worthwhile competition. The Cats were eventually allowed back into the VFL but the decision was not a unanimous one.

Geelong did struggle for a few years, winning only seven of the 54 games it played from 1944 to 1946, but by the end of the decade it was to become a force once more. One wonders how different the history of the VFL/AFL might have been, if Geelong were left on the sidelines in 1944.

World War II and Football

Just as it did in 1914, Australia followed England into War against Germany in September 1939. However on this occasion conscription wasn't such a big issue, particularly after Japan entered the War and the danger was more imminent. At the beginning of the War, Prime Minister Menzies introduced compulsory military training for a three months period for all men when they turned 21. These conscripts (the militia) played an important role in defending Australia on the Kokoda Track in New Guinea and in fighting overseas, particularly at Tobruk in Libya. Just as in World War I, VFL footballers fought and died in the Second World War. Three young men, Len Thomas, Jim Park and Harold Comte, who lost their lives had played over a hundred games with their VFL clubs. Len Thomas had played 209 games, mainly with South Melbourne, before he joined up. He was a dashing centre man, quick off the mark, an accurate kick and was centre in the South Melbourne 1933 premiership team and Club Best and Fairest in 1931 and 1938. He represented his state on six occasions and was playing coach of North Melbourne in 1942. Len's father Bill was also a fine player for South Melbourne and Richmond, playing just short of 200 games of VFL football. He was a member of the 1909 South Melbourne premiership team and an interstate captain. When playing for Richmond he broke his leg in two places after flying for a mark. There was no stretcher available at the ground and he had to lie on the grass for a considerable time until a stretcher could be rounded up. Jim Park, a high-marking defender, played 128 games with Carlton. An interstate representative, he was given the job of guarding Collingwood's brilliant Ron Todd in the 1938 Grand Final, keeping Todd to three goals and playing a significant role in Carlton's victory. Harold Comte was an excellent utility player for St Kilda. Coming from Echuca to the Saints, he played 104 games for the club and won their Best and Fairest in 1933.

I can remember my parents talking of another famous war hero who also played VFL football. This man was **Keith "Bluey" Truscott**, a pilot who was shot down over the British Channel and whose deeds won him two DFCs.

A determined redhead, Truscott played 50 games with the Demons and was a member of their 1939 and 1940 premiership teams. He played one game for the club during the War, while home on leave, leading the side on to the ground. To the community's shock, he died in a target practice exercise over Exmouth.

Like Truscott, Ron Barassi Snr was part of the 1940 Melbourne premiership side. In 1941, during World War II while serving in at Tobruk in North Africa, he was the first VFL footballer to be killed in action. Tobruk, a port on the Mediterranean Sea, is where the Australians made a legendary stand during the North African campaign.

It was told on the television program *Who Do You Think You Are?* (featuring Ron Barassi Jnr's life) that with his last words to comrades he expressed his concern for his wife, Elza, and his young son Ron. When he first heard the story of his father's death on the program, Ron Barassi Jnr was deeply moved.

It is difficult to believe that along with Truscott and Barassi, two other members of the Demon 1940 side, Syd Anderson and Harold Ball, lost their lives in World War II.

Another VFL footballer, **Kevin Dynon** of North Melbourne, was in the RAAF and stationed at Exmouth during the War. Dynon began with the Shinboners in 1943 but played only a

Kevin Dynon (NEWSPIX)

few games as his career was interrupted by the War. He also managed four games in 1944, and had played three with the club in 1945 when it made the finals for the first time in its VFL history.

North, which finished third on the ladder behind South Melbourne and Collingwood, was able to bring Dynon from Exmouth to play in the first semi-final against Carlton. The game, played before a crowd of around 55,000 at Princes Park in Carlton, because the MCG was being used to house military personnel at the time, was virtually over by half-time as the Northerners had kicked 1.12.18 to the Blues' 8.4.52. Although they outscored the Blues in the second half, North went down by 26 points.

After the War, Kevin Dynon had an illustrious career as a centreman at North, being their captain for three years, a regular interstate representative and compiling 55 Brownlow votes in his 149 games with the club. He later took the position of playing coach with Moorabbin in the VFA.

The 'Bloodbath'

In 1945 Carlton played South Melbourne in the Grand Final, also at Princes Park. The Carlton ground was packed with 63,000 people and the gates were closed before the match started. The game became known as the "bloodbath" because of the violence of the play and because nine players were reported.

Martin Flanagan wrote about this match in his book *The Game in Times of War*. He attributes the violence of the game not only to the great rivalry between the clubs but also to the fact that many of the spectators were soldiers stationed in Melbourne at the time. They were "on for a good time" and urged the teams to use the violence that resulted. Rugged play on the football field was nothing to what they had experienced during the War.

Although finishing fourth on the ladder at the end of the year, Carlton defeated the Swans, who had finished on top, by 28 points. Winning the flag from fourth place was a rarity in those days, when four teams played in the finals

That 1945 Grand Final was the last game of Laurie Nash, one of the all-time greats of VFL football. Nash was the son of a Collingwood captain, Bob Nash. (According to the *Encyclopedia of AFL Footballers*, Bob Nash is said to have once jobbed a team-mate for "not playing straight" – a euphemism for being paid not to do his best.)

Despite not being tall, Laurie Nash was a wonderful high mark who could kick with either foot. As noted earlier, he was centre half-back in the Swans 1933 premiership team but preferred to play on the forward line. He proved his point later in his career when, moved to the forward line, he kicked many goals.

Nash also played Test cricket for Australia, taking 10 wickets at an average of 12 runs per wicket in the two Test matches that he played.

Snippet

Les Jones was selected as a Richmond follower for the 1944 Grand Final. His sister-in-law, Pat Jones, a Waverley resident, told me that Les was a member of a large family and that he later moved to Yallourn to coach there as many of his siblings including one of his sisters had moved to Gippsland. There, she married Vic Waite. The couple had a son Vin, a high marking, long kicking Carlton dual premiership defender. Vin's son, Jarred, in recent years has made a habit of foiling Richmond's attempts to defeat Carlton in big games such as the 2013 Elimination Final when he kicked four goals.

Uncle Harry's Shop

As is still the case in 2012, the highlight of the week for many young boys in the 1940s and 1950s was going to the footy, with other members of their family, to follow their favourite team. And this was the case for Ramon and me during those years. Dad did shift work so was available most Saturday afternoons to go to the football.

Sometimes Dad would come home to take Ramon and me to the games, but as we grew older we would catch the train to Richmond and meet him at Uncle Harry's general store in Dover St, Richmond. Uncle Harry was Mum's brother. We would have a quick lunch there and then head for a game. Often Harry would accompany us.

One Sunday in the '40s, when the Reeds were at Uncle Harry's, a young Richmond player came into the shop. He was John Nix a handsome, well built, lad from Trafalgar in Gippsland. Harry called the Reed boys who were very pleased to meet Nix, who was friendly to us. Nix was quite young, only 17, when he started with the Tigers and played mainly as a centreman. Wearing Number 1, he was also the Number 1 Tiger for us. We hoped that one day he would win the Brownlow. However injuries kept his tally of games, over his eight years with the club, to only 95.

It was easy to get to the footy from Harry's shop as many of the grounds were close by. We could walk to the Richmond and Melbourne grounds and catch public transport from Richmond to the North Melbourne, Collingwood and Fitzroy ovals. I can also remember sometimes making the long trip out to "Windy Hill" to watch the Tigers play Essendon (the Bombers).

Mick used to buy membership tickets for the Richmond Cricket Club. Two Ladies' tickets (at right) were given to members and children (Ramon and Kevin) could use these tickets to watch games from the Cricket Club Stand.

A Trip to Geelong

In 1948 Dad, Ramon and I went with Uncle Harry in his car to see Geelong play the Tigers at Kardinia Park. It was an exciting day for us.

On arriving at the ground and, having parked the car in a nearby street in South Geelong, we took up a position behind the goals at what I believe was the City-end of the oval. The Geelong full-forward, Lindsay White, was a standout player for the Cats. I remember White as a tall but not heavily built footballer, a fast lead, a sure mark and a good kick for goals. I can still see in my mind White moving this way and that in decoy moves before heading for a space, a couple of yards in front of the Tiger full-back to accept a neat pass from a Geelong player. And then he put it through.

Lindsay White began with the Cats in 1941 but played for South Melbourne when the Cats didn't play in the VFL because of the War. He won the League goal kicking with the Swans in 1941. On returning to the Cats in 1943 he again did well winning the League goal kicking in 1948 with 86 goals. He was also captain in that year.

I also remember **Bernie Smith** from West Adelaide who started with the Cats in 1948. A centreman, Smith had won West Adelaide's Best and Fairest in 1947 and was best on ground in the team's Grand Final win over Norwood in that year. Playing in defence for the Cats, with his wavy, blond hair and cool demeanour, he seemed to be able to wander across the back line and get kicks whenever he liked.

Bernie Smith (NEWSPIX)

In 1951, Smith, a member of the Cat's premiership team that year, won the Club Best and Fairest award and the Brownlow Medal. He was a member of both Geelong's and the AFL's Team of the Century and in 1996 was inducted into the Australian Football Hall of Fame. The Brownlow Medal count in 1951 wasn't the gala affair it is in the 21st century. The votes were counted at the VFL headquarters with the winner being informed later of his success.

Snippet

When Uncle Harry took the Reeds to see the Tigers play the Cats at Kardinia Park, that ground was still a relatively new home ground for the Cats. From the time that Geelong joined the VFL in 1897 until 1940, Geelong played at the Corio Oval in Eastern Park. Patrons could take the tram along Ryrie Street from the Central Business District to get to the Oval. However, in 1941, with World War II underway the Corio ground was taken over by the Army to be used for the training of soldiers. Consequently the Cats played their home games at Kardinia Park in that year. Because of the War, Geelong did not field a team in the VFL in 1942/1943 and when the club re-entered the League in 1944 they continued to play at Kardinia Park. Its proximity to the South Geelong railway station made it a handy location for patrons going to the footy by train either from Geelong suburbs or Melbourne. The ground which was initially used as a temporary measure eventually became their home. The old Corio Oval is no longer in existence as such. The years 2012/13 have seen yet further improvements being made to the Kardinia Park oval to make it a "state of the art" facility, including huge and powerful floodlights for night matches.

In the Outer

I remember watching the Tigers in a 1949 match against Carlton at Richmond's old Punt Road ground. The crowd was huge, about 46,000 – too many for the ground to hold. In one section of the ground, the crowd broke down the fence and spilled on to the oval.

I have two other vivid memories from that game. These were of discomfort that I and many other young supporters endured, in going to the footy at "Tigerland" in those days.

Occasionally, whenever I go to the toilets at the MCG with their tile-covered floors, ample toilet paper and warm air-blowing hand-dryers, my first Punt Road memory comes flowing back. I recall the lavatories at the railway station end of the Richmond ground on that day. A small

11-year-old at the time of the match, I went to the toilets with my dad at half-time and had to follow him, pushing my way through the mob to find a space at the urinal. The floor was a sea of urine; there was one cold water tap for hand washing and no towelling for hand drying. The smell was worse than anything I had encountered before. And confronting the in-coming crowd to tip-toe out of the place was even scarier than coming in. Tripping over was a constant fear.

Later in the same afternoon I endured the other horrific event. After the game, I barely managed to hold my feet as I was pushed along by the crowd to the Richmond station to catch the train home. The throng then entered a wide passage-way which led to the rather narrow ramp that was used to get onto the platform where passengers caught the Dandenong train. With such a huge crowd at the game I was crushed by people moving from the wider passage into the ramp. There was little light in the ramp and I was just carried along by the mass of people. Luckily I didn't fall over as I held onto my dad's trousers. I was never so pleased in my life as when we got to the top of the ramp and saw sunlight as we reached the platform. For years after that experience I had nightmares about struggling up station ramps and falling over amidst crowds of people.

To make matters worse, Carlton, whom all good Tiger supporters hated, won the match.

John Coleman

Around the same time Dad also took us to a game at Essendon. The great **John Coleman** was full-forward for Essendon. Coleman, recruited from Hastings was a football hero of rock star proportions when he played during the decade after World War II. He was capable of taking spectacular high marks which would be followed by long, accurate kicks for goal. So proud was Hastings of its favourite son that Stephen Glassborow was commissioned to sculpture Coleman marking over Fitzroy full-back, Tom Meehan. The work, which well captured Coleman's marking ability, was erected in the town. Meehan, who was playing his first game for Fitzroy after transferring from St Kilda said of the mark, "He was on the wrong side of me and I thought that was fine, but he was a spring whiz and he just jumped on me."

Mick Reed used to say of Coleman, "He seems to float in the air."

On the day that Dad, Ramon and I went to see the Tigers play at Essendon, Coleman had a very good day kicking eight goals from about 10 shots. At the other end of the ground Richmond had an excellent centre half-forward named Ray Poulter. One of my favourite players, Poulter played 170 games and kicked 351 goals for the Tigers. He represented Victoria in 1955. He was a very solidly built player and used long drop kicks when shooting for goal. However, because he was often shooting from a great distance he could be inaccurate on occasions. On this day he kicked two goals from a similar number of shots as Coleman. Essendon won quite easily because of Coleman's accurate kicking.

Coleman played in Essendon's 1949 and 1950 premiership teams but was reported for striking Carlton's Harry Casper in the last home and away match in 1951. Anxiously awaiting the result, a huge crowd gathered outside the League's headquarters on the night of the hearing. They were shocked to find out that Coleman was suspended for four weeks and would miss the finals. Many in the crowd, particularly the young women, broke down and wept on hearing the outcome which was headline news in the daily papers the next day.

Essendon, without Coleman, was beaten by Geelong in the Grand Final.

The career of the great Coleman ended prematurely in 1954, his sixth season with the Bombers, when he fell awkwardly and damaged his knee. He had kicked 14 goals in the match prior to the one in which he was injured and topped the goalkicking list in four of the five full seasons that he played, kicking 537 goals in his 98 games. Later

Coleman coached the Bombers, helping them to win premierships in 1962 and 1965.

In his mid-forties he died on the Mornington Peninsula from a heart attack. It was claimed that had there been better medical facilities on the Peninsula at the time, he may have been saved.

Snippet

In 1948 Essendon drew with Melbourne in the Grand Final kicking 7 goals 27 behinds to Melbourne's 10 goals 9 behinds. Melbourne won the replay.

In 1949, with Coleman in the side, Essendon defeated Carlton in the Grand Final kicking 18 goals 17 behinds to Carlton's 6 goals 16 behinds. Coleman kicked six goals bringing up 100 in his first season of VFL football. I was lucky enough to be there, and to see and hear the Bomber supporters go wild when he kicked his 100th goal.

Jack Douglas

Another player in that era was Dr John ("Jack") Douglas who played 14 games for Hawthorn. Later in life I became friends with him through tennis. In one of his games for the Hawks, Jack Douglas was centre half-back against Richmond's Ray Poulter. Jack told me that, as they shook hands at the start of the game, the more experienced Poulter greeted him with a comment along the lines:

"If you get in front of me, sonny, you'll be history. I'll flatten you."

As it turned out Poulter didn't flatten Jack Douglas who was too quick. Jack said it was one of the better games that he played for the Hawks. He later coached, for many years, St Kevin's Old Collegians Football Club in the the VAFA. Jack Douglas played veterans' tennis until well into his seventies. After he retired to Warrnambool, he had a heart attack while playing, passing away on the tennis court.

John O'Mahony

Another player in the tennis team at Holy Family Tennis Club, where Jack Douglas and I played, was **John O'Mahony**. John played 112 games with Hawthorn and came eighth in the 1956 Brownlow Medal. In the *The Encyclopedia of AFL Footballers*, John is described "As an instant star when he came from Camberwell Juniors. A clever and elusive centreman he marked and kicked well. A gifted player, he was an unselfish footballer and a creative team man who later became assistant coach and the Hawks' chairman of selectors."

John O'Mahony's grandson, **Jarryd Blair** (below with John) made his debut with the Magpies in 2010 playing in their premiership team. He was a member of the Magpies' losing Grand Final side in 2011. At the conclusion of the 2013 season Blair had played 81 games and kicked 64 goals. He also showed his value to the side by leading the club in tackles.

Snippet

Marj and I were invited to John O'Mahony's 70th birthday. I was playing competition tennis with John at the time. There were many ex-Hawthorn players present as well as tennis playing friends. At one point I was talking in a group that included John Kennedy, Graham Arthur, Roy Simmonds, Phil O'Brien, and Maurie Considine – all Hawthorn greats. (Kennedy, Arthur and Simmonds were named in the Hawks' Team of the Century.) Marj joined the group and I duly introduced her in turn to each member of the group. Not being 'spot on' with Hawthorn teams of the '50s and '60s, Marj asked a perfectly reasonable question, "Tell me, fellows, are you footballers or tennis players?"

Another well known full forward in the Coleman era was **Jack O'Rourke**, the Tiger champion. O'Rourke was a high leaping player recruited from South Warrnambool. He played 44 games with the Tigers and kicked 144 goals. When Jack Dyer was sacked, O'Rourke left the club and returned to Warrnambool Many years later I played bowls with him at the Warrnambool Bowls Club. Jack was often seen walking along the beach at Warrnambool. Even as an older man he walked with a noted spring in his step.

More Finals Footy

Mick Reed and his boys loved to go to the Finals.

With high hopes we journeyed to the MCG to watch the Tigers play Fitzroy in the first semi-final in 1947. It was the first time that the Tigers had made the finals since 1944. Of course, they were led by Jack Dyer. A powerful ruckman early in his career, Dyer spent his last couple of seasons at full forward. He was very successful in that role and mastered the drop punt which is the preferred kick today when a player is kicking for goal. Ramon and I saw Dyer's last game when he kicked six goals against Geelong and was carried from the ground by his admiring fans after the game was over. Coaching was not a full-time career in Dyer's days. At one time he owned a very popular milk bar in Church Street, Richmond.

The 1947 team read as follows: **Backs**: Burge, Durham, Priestley; **Half-backs**: Perkins, F. Cooke, K. Roberts; **Centres**: Merritt, Stokes, Russell; **Half-forwards**: Mooney, Fraser, Phillips; **Forwards**: Curry, Dyer, Oppy; **Rucks**: Morris, Jones; **Rover**: Wilson.

(I can still recite the starting line-up and believe that Leo Maguire and a young Roy Wright were the reserves, but I am not sure).

In our chats about those times Ramon and I recall Brownlow Medallist Bill Morris who was a wonderful high mark, excelled at tapping the ball to his rovers and was an accurate left foot kick.

Don "Mopsy" Fraser also comes to mind. "Mopsy", who wore long hair before it was fashionable, was a wonderful key position player who lost his temper quite easily. It is said that he missed over 50 games through suspension during his career. Mopsy's father, Don Fraser Snr, also a fiery footballer, played with Richmond too. He later played with Oakleigh and kicked 12 goals for them in 1930 in a game against Brunswick. That tally was later equalled twice (by Alby Naismith in 1945 and Jack Watson in 1951) but it was never bettered. Don Snr's career ended when he sat on a ball and refused to move after a dispute with the umpire.

Max Oppy, who was named as forward pocket and second rover was also a tough player, reputed to be one of the toughest to ever play with the Tigers. He was a "stopper". Lou Richards, the Collingwood rover, had great respect for Oppy. In his autobiography *The Kiss of Death* Richards had the following to say about Oppy:

> There was one man at Richmond who used to give me nightmares. Right through my career Max Oppy used to belt the living daylights out of me. Max played in the back pocket and was built like a pocket battleship – made of muscle and having huge forearms, the bloke was put on earth to make a rover's life hell.

To the Reeds' disappointment the Tigers lost that 1947 final against Fitzroy quite easily, probably because a number of the players, who had played in the 1943 premiership team, were "getting a bit long in the tooth".

Snippet

In his 2012 publication, *An Incredible Race of People – A Passionate History of Australia*, Senator Bob Katter points out that in 1947 a great majority of Australians could trace at least one line in their family trees back to the gold rush period. This was because there was very little migration to Australia between that period and the post-WWII intake. As most of the gold rush people who remained in Australia were of Anglo/Celtic origin, this is reflected in the names of players in football teams. The names in the 1947 Richmond team illustrate this.

Allan Hird or the Tigers?

In those days the League reserves (or seconds, as they were then called) played their Grand Final before the main match. Dad showed particular interest in the second's Grand Final in 1950. Richmond was playing Essendon. The Tigers were coached by Alby Pannam, a tough rover who had played with Collingwood, while the Bombers were coached by **Allan Hird**, a former senior player with Essendon and St Kilda. Both Pannam and Hird were playing coaches of their teams.

Dad wasn't too sure who to barrack for, as he always barracked for the Tigers, and yet, as we have seen, Allan Hird was born at Costerfield. Mick told his sons that he had played football for Costerfield with Hird's father, George, and knew him well. The Tigers lost but I think Mick wasn't too disappointed as he was pleased for his friend's son, Allan, to have had success.

With Coleman at full forward and Dick Reynolds as playing coach, the Bombers also won the flag in the firsts that year, beating North Melbourne rather easily. The Reed boys took North's defeat somewhat harder than the Tiger's loss in the seconds as they had a soft spot for the Shinboners who had not won a premiership since they entered the VFL, 25 years earlier.

North also had a couple of exciting

Les Foote (NEWSPIX)

performers in **Les Foote** and the already mentioned Kevin Dynon, a very talented all-round footballer who played in the centre. Foote was a real "twinkle-toes" who could weave his way out of trouble in the heaviest of traffic.

Snippet

The player recognised as best afield in the 1950 Grand Final was Norm McDonald, perhaps the best indigenous footballer in the years between the time when Pastor Doug Nicholls played with Fitzroy and Graham "Polly" Farmer was a champion ruckman for Geelong. He was tall for his era, somewhat in the mould of Adam Goodes in that he was extremely quick, capable of taking a strong mark and had the ability to carry and bounce the ball over great distances. His attacking play out of defence often resulted in goals for the Bombers. (McDonald was selected on the half-back flank, beside Goodes, at centre half-back, in the Indigenous Team of the Century).

Geelong's Bob Davis, one of the best half forwards of that era, believed that McDonald was the man who worried him most. In his *Football Stories,* Garrie Hutchinson quoted Davis saying of McDonald that although he "never seemed to mind you he was always alongside you when it mattered – and he would whip the ball away from me too." Davis went on to say that "I was 15 stone (95 kilograms), McDonald was 12 stone (76 kilograms). Pound for pound he had to be the best defender I met."

McDonald had enlisted, under-age, in the Army in 1942 where he initially served as an anti-aircraft gunner, before transferring to the RAAF to be trained as a paratrooper. However he didn't see action in this role as the War ended while he was still in training. McDonald was also a successful sprinter, coming second in the Stawell Gift in 1952, as well as a professional boxer. Unlucky not to be named in the Bombers' Team of the Century, Mc Donald was named number 32 in the list of Essendon all-time greats.

The Hird and Pannam families

Although the football prowess of my dad's friend George Hird, is not generally well known, it was passed on to his son, Allan, his grandson, Allan Jnr, and his great-grandson, James.

Recruited from Williamstown in 1938, Allan Hird Snr played 14 games with Hawthorn, 102 games with Essendon (without a break) and 38 games with St Kilda. He was a fast moving tall man playing either in a key position or in the ruck. He played in the Essendon 1942 premiership team and was captain-coach of St Kilda in 1946-47. He later became prominent in the administration of Essendon Football Club, being on the Committee from 1955 until 1958, Club Treasurer in 1959-60, Vice-President in 1965 and President from 1969 until 1975. An inaugural inductee in the Essendon Hall of Fame he was made a Club Legend in 1996. A grandstand at "Windy Hill", Essendon's former home ground, is named after him.

Allan Hird Jnr played four games with Essendon during the 1966-67 seasons before he moved to Canberra where he coached Eastlake for three years from 1969 to 1971. Like his father, he was interested in working in football administration and was President of AFL Canberra from 1989 to 1991.

James Hird, the son of Alan Jnr, later proved to be a great player for the Bombers from 1992 to 2007 and was appointed coach of that team in 2011.

Alby Pannam, the coach of Richmond reserves in 1950, was also part of a great Aussie Rules family. His father, Charles Pannam Snr, played with Collingwood in 1897, the inaugural season of the VFL. A cheeky winger and forward he was the first man to play 100 games of VFL football. He was a premiership player with the Magpies and later coached the Tigers. Two of his sons, Alby Pannam and Charles Pannam Jnr, also had successful VFL careers. Alby, a Best and Fairest winner with the Magpies, coached the Richmond seconds, as we have seen, and like his father coached the Richmond senior side. He later had success as a coach of Oakleigh in the VFA. Charlie Jnr played in the centre in Collingwood's 1919 flag-winning team and later played with and coached South Melbourne.

Charlie Pannam Snr also had two grandsons who played very successfully for the Magpies. Lou and Ron Richards, sons of Charlie Snr's daughter, were both premiership players for the Magpies, with Lou captaining the 1953 premiership team and Ron being regarded by many as Best on Ground in that win. Lou later became particularly well known as a media personality.

Albert Pannam Snr, the brother of Charlie Pannam Snr, also played with Collingwood. In the first decade of the 20th century he had 28 games and kicked 12 goals.

Between them the Pannam/Richards dynasty notched up 878 games for the Magpies from 1897 to 1955.

8
A Fitzroy Flag and Fred Fanning

Post-War footy, the Oakleigh Districts, the "Rec", A Goal-kicking record; South Melbourne/Sydney Swans FC, Richmond FC; Stan Le Lievre, Harry "Soapy" Vallence, Warwick Capper, Stephen Wright and Laurie Fowler.

Our house in Oakleigh was on a corner block with Edward Street running alongside the property. Across the road in Edward Street was a big vacant wedge of land, bounded by Box Hill Road (now Huntingdale Road), Edward Street and the railway line which ran between East Oakleigh (now Huntingdale) and Oakleigh railway stations.

At the narrow Oakleigh end of the vacant land, in Edward Street, was a timber yard, beside which was a large area of recreation reserve (the "Rec"). This became three cricket grounds in the summer and a sizeable football oval in the winter. There was a change shed in one corner of the land. During World War II, both the Rec and the remaining land were occupied by the Army with coiled razor wire around its perimeter keeping the Reed children and their friends out of the camp.

Oakleigh Districts Football Club

Immediately post World War II, apart from the Oakleigh Team in the VFA, there was no other senior football club for players not good enough to play VFA football. Led by Jack Hogan and "Pop" Holmes, a committee was set up in late 1949, to successfully form a new club – the

Oakleigh Districts Football Club (the "Districts"). They received little help from the Oakleigh VFA club in doing so. The Districts' Website tells more of the story.

> Former St Kilda back man Stan Le Lievre was appointed the Districts inaugural coach for 1950 at four pounds per week. Stan was famous for his Plymouth ute, often seen on match days carrying more than its legal allowance. What could not fit in hung over the sides. "One day I had 17 blokes in the ute" said Stan. The reason was (that) in the club there was only one ute and two motor bikes.
>
> The first home ground was the Police Paddocks – where the Oakleigh swimming pool and sporting complex is now situated. ... The change rooms (pictured below), if you could call them that, were approx five by four metres, the walls were full of holes with old cricket mats helping to keep the wind out ... there was no hot water or electricity. Jackey Peake would put the headlight of his motor bike through the doorway to light up the room.

With permission from Oakleigh Districts Football Club

A big moment in footy

In the last round of the 1947 season, **Stan Le Lievre** was full back for St Kilda against Melbourne. His opponent on that day was **Fred Fanning**. In the 15 September 2012 edition of the *Sunday Age* the encounter between Stan and Fred was recorded as one of the top 50 "biggest moments in the history of the game". It came in as Number 17 and read as follows:

Fred Fanning's record 18-goal haul for Melbourne against St Kilda at the Junction Oval is a landmark which has now stood for 55 years, and will probably never be beaten. Perhaps equally remarkable is that it was also his last game of league football. Fanning had kicked 10.4 the week before against Footscray, and in the last round of the season, managed his 18 from just 19 shots at goal. St Kilda defender Stan Le Lievre recalled the nightmare 50 years later. "Nobody wants to put their hand up to playing on him but it doesn't worry me," he said. "The ball was coming down quickly from blokes like Norm Smith, and Fred was a very big man, hard to get around. Somebody said I should grab hold of his footy nicks and pull them off every time the ball came down, but they would have run out of nicks." Fanning finished the year with 97 for the season, still the Demons' record, but at just 25, immediately left the club to coach Hamilton for 20 pounds per week. Melbourne had been paying him three.

Fred Fanning

Success for the Districts

Joining the strong Caulfield and Oakleigh District (COD) competition which included nearby teams such as Murrumbeena, Carnegie, Glenhuntly and more distant teams such as East Sandringham and Glen Waverley, the Districts had their first win on 1 July 1950 when they defeated East Brighton. The website includes the following about the win:

Oakleigh Districts in Brilliant Win

Oakleigh Districts overwhelmed East Brighton at the Oakleigh ground with fast systematic football. Stan Le Lievre captain and coach of Oakleigh shadowed Brighton full forward **Harry ("Soapy") Vallence**, past League and Association star. Stan's long driving kicks, high marks and spoiling tactics were a delight to watch. Oakleigh centre line of Kight (best on ground), Anderson, Atkins was a match-winning factor frequently kicking their team into attack. Best Players: F. Kight, S. Le Lievre, B. Anderson, B. Atkins, R. Rees, H. Ashton, B. Cunningham, G. Barnfather.

Stan Le Lievre obviously had a better game on Soapy Vallence than he had on Fanning although Soapy was arguably just as talented in his prime. Vallence had a remarkable career in both the VFL and in the VFA. Coming to the Blues from Bacchus Marsh, Vallence took a couple of seasons to settle in before he became a champion full forward, winning the club's goal kicking award eight times and playing in the Blues 1938 premiership side. In 1939 he moved to the VFA club, Williamstown, where he kicked 133 goals. Former Collingwood star, Ron Todd, kicked 199 goals in the same year and Willy won the flag. After World War II Soapy played three seasons with Brighton, before transferring to East Brighton where he played on Stan Le Lievre. He later played for Caulfield until he was around 50 years old – still able to mark and kick well.

Harry 'Soapy' Vallence was named as full forward in the Blues' Team of the Century. In 1987 he was one of the first inductees into the Blues' Hall of Fame.

Back row V Richardson B Robertson B Cunningham R Davies G Barnfather R Rees F Kight
2ⁿᵈ B Row P Burns P Farrell I Lee J Camm G Collins I LeGriffen J Peake E Burns B Podesta
3ʳᵈ B Row B Dowd P Richardson S LeLievre R Brewster T Camm B Walsh Pop Bruce
Front Row A Bell J Fizgerald B Atkins D Beard B Timms J Bruce B Andersons

With permission from Oakleigh Districts Football Club

Gerry Collins, who is fifth from the left in the second Back Row in the photo of the Oakleigh Districts' 1951 team, played for Richmond in the VFL and was then a premiership ruckman for Oakleigh in the VFA. The Camm brothers were excellent big men. Both played for the Oakleigh VFA side. Frank Kight who lived in the next street to us was an excellent small man and won the Club Best and Fairest in 1952 and 1955.

The Rec

With the end of the War, the Rec reverted to a sports ground with its footy oval and cricket pitches. In the early '50s, the Oakleigh Council gave the Districts permission to vacate the Police Paddocks and take over the Rec.

This meant that two different football teams played on the ground.

The Oakleigh Districts Football Club used it of a Saturday afternoon. The Oakleigh Young Christian Workers (YCW), a Catholic team, also formed after the War, used it for their Under 18 team on Sundays. The Oakleigh Districts Under 15 team played on Saturday morning. The Districts also had an Under 18 team which shared the ground with their senior team on a Saturday afternoon..

Because of its closeness to the Reed's home, the Rec became an adjunct to the Reed backyard. With mates from school and the local district, Ramon and I spent hours playing football and cricket there.

Bob Johnson, Jack Darcy, and Gordon Peake were among those who played at the Rec from time to time. All three later played VFL football. Jack and Gordon played only a few games for Richmond but both were members of 1960 premiership team for Oakleigh in the VFA. Bob became a champion premiership ruckman/forward for Melbourne.

Gordon Peake played with the Districts before he went to Oakleigh in the VFA. He had a number of brothers, including Ken, Ron and Jack who also joined in at the Rec; Jack not so often as he was much older than the others. Another family represented in "pick-up" matches at the Rec was the McGowns. Peter ("Pip") McGown was a clever rover for the Districts over a number of years

Other lads who were seen at the Rec from time to time were Normie and Don Thornhill who also lived in George Street. Norm was probably the better footballer of the two. Don won the seconds' Best and Fairest in 1958. But the player I most remember was Ferdie Thomas, a brilliant and tough footballer who really didn't make the best use of his ability. So tough was Ferdie that if a dozen or so boys were playing kick-to-kick, Ferdie would be at one end shooting for goal with the rest of the lads contesting his kicks. The successful lad would kick the ball to back to Ferdie.

Boys chose not to compete with Ferdie not only because he was an outstanding footballer but also because he enjoyed a bit of physical competition.

Cricket too

Of course, in the summer we played cricket matches at the Rec. I joined the East Oakleigh Cricket Club who also used the ground in the summer. Playing with me there were Alan Wing and "Bluey" Peddle who also played footy with the Districts. A big man, Alan was a tough competitor as a footballer and a talented all rounder as a cricketer. Bluey showed class as a batsman and as a clever footballer.

It wasn't too long before the Districts formed a cricket club of their own. Peter Burns, who won the Club Best and Fairest award in 1953 and is in the footy club photo, was a leader in this area. Another footballer who loved his cricket was George Tuddin who was Best and Fairest in the footy club's seconds in 1962, 1963 and 1964. A wily off-spin bowler, he was also a determined winger on the footy field. But then again being determined was the name of the game for the Districts on both the football and cricket fields.

Playing with the Districts

As the Oakleigh Districts Under 15 team played at "the Rec" in 1951, when I was in Year 9 (Proficiency) at De La Salle Malvern, I joined in training there one afternoon and was picked as 19th man for the team on the following Saturday morning. I played only a couple of games there because, as a small lad still Under 13, I found the bigger Under 15 opponents a bit overpowering.

Despite the fact that I no longer played with the Districts, I still kept in contact with the club and often played kick-to-kick with some of the boys at the Rec and watched their under-age games occasionally. Team members that I remember were Max Ferguson, a talented centre-man, the Baird twins, very good rover/forwards as well as Jimmy Wilson and Brian Smith who went to primary school with me. Jimmy's uncle, "Warby" Wilson, played with Oakleigh in the VFA. John Gilder was also an excellent centre-line player.

Many of the team, particularly Jimmy Wilson, Brian Smith and Max Ferguson went on to give excellent service to the Districts' senior team over many years. Brian, noted for the way he wore his cap on the back of his head, went to school at De La Salle. A very solid defender, he was vice-captain of the De La Inter-College Under 15 side and was Best and Fairest for the Districts' Firsts in 1958. Max Ferguson also won the club's top award two years after Brian.

New Ground

After their senior team had used the Rec for a relatively short time, the Districts were granted the full use of a newer ground on the Princes Highway. This could accommodate all of the Districts' teams while the Catholic teams could use the Rec on both Saturdays and Sundays for open-age and under-age football.

From the Districts to the VFL

Three well known VFL players, Warwick Capper, Steven Wright and David Rhys-Jones began their careers at South Melbourne after being recruited from the Oakleigh Districts. Another ex-Districts player to make a name for himself as a VFL player was Laurie Fowler who went from the Districts to Richmond in 1971.

i) Warwick Capper

A flamboyant full-forward who played for the Sydney Swans and the Brisbane Lions, Warwick Capper was famous for his long blond hair, his tight shorts and his high-marking ability.

Because of his penchant for obtaining publicity, not always related to football, his outstanding football ability is often overlooked. In 90 games with the Swans he kicked 317 goals. He won their goalkicking award from 1984 to 1987, the year in which he became the second Swan player to kick a ton with 103 goals. The legendary Bob Pratt was the first. Capper was at Brisbane from 1988 to 1990 playing 34 games there and kicking 71 goals. His quest for notoriety was still evident in 2011 when he took part in the Channel Nine show *Celebrity Apprentice* as a 1980s icon. Unfortunately he was one of the first apprentices to be "sacked".

ii) Stephen Wright

A tough red-headed rover, Steven Wright began his career with South Melbourne and then crossed to Sydney with the club, being a solid performer over many years and winning the Best and Fairest award in 1985 and 1990. This meant that in 1985 ex-Oakleigh District players won the Swan's goal-kicking and Best and Fairest awards. Wright was in the New South Wales side which in 1990 had a win over Victoria. In 2003, he was included in the Swans' Team of the Century and has been inducted into the Swans' Hall of Fame.

Since retiring he has had a busy coaching schedule as playing coach of Claremont in Tasmania and with coaching positions in New South Wales, Canberra and South Australia. In Victoria, he has coached North Ballarat in the VFL and Old Grammarians in the Victorian Amateur Football Association (VAFA). In 2011, he used his vast knowledge of the game as assistant coach at his old club, Oakleigh Districts. No doubt he received a warm welcome home. In 2012 he was coach of the side when it was Runners-Up in B-Division of the Southern Football League.

Despite his apparent success with Oakleigh Districts in 2012, readers of the *Waverley Leader*, on 4 December 2012, were surprised to find that Stevie Wright and the Oakleigh Districts Football Club were to "part company". It appeared that a number of the players, believing that Wright had poor communication skills, had orchestrated a coup. Wright said, "I don't feel like I've been sacked or asked to resign. I feel like I've been assassinated."

The Club President said that "Steve's return to the club of his junior playing days ... was sincerely appreciated," and "his integrity was without question." Wright indicated that despite the experience he would coach again. Such are the ways of footy clubs!

iii) David Rhys Jones

One of the most controversial players of all time, David Rhys-Jones also went from Oakleigh Districts to South Melbourne and then to Sydney Swans. In 1985 he was recruited by Carlton and won the Norm Smith Medal for being best afield in the 1987 Grand Final in which the Blues defeated Hawthorn. There is no doubt that Rhys-Jones was a great player, but he is also remembered for his willingness to be involved in altercations on the field. He appeared before the Tribunal on 42 occasions, 25 of these being on charges, with 17 of them being as a victim. He was suspended for a total of 22 matches in his VFL/AFL career which isn't too many for so many appearances before the Tribunal. Perhaps he was easily riled and the incidents were not always his fault. Once, when he attended the Tribunal as a victim, it was allegedly that he was struck by a player who was later to become a high profile and very well paid AFL administrator.

iv) Laurie Fowler

In 1973 I attended the Grand Final between the Tigers and Carlton. The Tigers had been badly beaten by Carlton in 1972 and wanted revenge. They were given an inspiring talk by coach, Tom Hafey, before the game and began with a determination to stop at nothing to get the ball. One of the most talked about incidents of the match took place early in the game when Laurie Fowler, from Oakleigh Districts, with his eyes fixed squarely on the ball flattened the much, much bigger Carlton captain John Nicholls, slowing him down for the rest of the game. The Tigers went on to win by five goals.

To celebrate their Centenary Year in 2008, the Tigers decided to announce their "100 Tiger Treasures", consisting of 10 awards, each with 10 nominees. The awards were chiefly given to players but also to club moments and club campaigns. The first award, given to the "Best Individual Performance of the Century", went to Kevin Bartlett for kicking 21 goals in the 1980 final series and winning the Norm Smith Medal in the Tigers' successful Grand Final that year. Amongst Bartlett's

21 goals were the seven goals he kicked against Collingwood in the Grand Final. Other nominees for "Individual Performances" included Jack Dyer, **Jack Titus**, Bill Barrot, Doug Strang, Roy Wright, Tommy Hafey, Michael Green, David Cloke and Matthew Knights. Bartlett and the nine other nominees comprise 10 of the "100 Tiger Treasures".

One category was called "Brave Acts of the Century". This was won, not surprisingly, by Francis Bourke, who was nominated twice, with two brave acts. Laurie Fowler's clash with Nicholls was also one of the 10 brave acts nominated. Hence Laurie Fowler is one of the "100 Tiger Treasures". Fowler played 49 games with Richmond before transferring to Melbourne where he had an outstanding career, winning two Best and Fairest awards and representing Victoria twice. He played 140 games with Melbourne but is most remembered for that one incident in the 1973 Grand Final. The Oakleigh Districts Football Club has certainly made a notable contribution to VFL football.

Jack Titus (NEWSPIX)

Snippet

The 1950s saw Australia at war again, this time in Korea. Once again potential, then-current and former VLF footballers joined the services. Perhaps the most notable of these was **Geoff Collins**. A tough half-back flanker, he played in the 1948 Demon premiership side before he served in Korea as a pilot in the RAAF. He flew over 100 missions and was cited for bravery. He returned to play with the Demons and captained their losing Grand Final side in 1954. He was listed in the Demons' "150 heroes" – the award instituted to commemorate the 150th Anniversary of the Club's founding. His father Jack, a talented wingman of an earlier generation, was also listed among the 150 Heroes.

9

School Footy and John Kennedy

Footy at De La Salle College; Melbourne FC, Carlton FC, Richmond FC, Hawthorn FC, St Kilda FC, Geelong FC, Claremont FC; the O'Connells, the Johnsons, the Russos, the Kennedys and Jack Dyer.

The two games I played for the Districts' Under 15 team in 1951 were my only games, other than at school, until I left school on completing Matriculation in 1954. However there was inter-House football at school every year. Ramon and I had some success playing in House football with Ramon being captain of his premier House team on one occasion.

De La Salle Under 15 Football Team, 1950

(Courtesy 'Blue and Gold')

Front Row: M. Watkins, B. Tobin, J. Varcoe; **Second Row**: J. D'arcy, M. Brown, M. Brick, R. Johnson, B. Slattery, P. McCormack, J. McCarthy; **Third Row**: D. Congues, B. O'Dea, N. Carrick, R. Reed, D. Hardiman, D. Melrose, T. Connors; **Back Row**: J. Donovan, P. Archibald, R. Horrigan, R. O'Toole, B. Lefoo, B. Mullaney

Although not stars, both of us played for the school at the Under 15 level. Melbourne premiership player **"Big Bob" Johnson**, with whom the Reed boys had played football at the Rec, was captain of the College Under 15 XVIII in the year in which Ramon was in that team. Leaving school after Intermediate (Year 10) Ramon didn't play with the First XVIII; however I managed to play every game with the Firsts when I was in Matriculation.

Perhaps the most memorable game for the De La Salle ("De La") team in 1950 was the first match of the season against the Christian Brothers (CBC) Parade team. As that school was located in East Melbourne, the Parade boys who came from the inner suburbs were far too tough and skilled for the more gentle types from the eastern suburbs. The match was played at the muddy Fitzroy oval and the next day the De La Principal, Brother Oswald, called the team aside to vehemently criticise the boys for their performance saying that many of them "didn't even get their shorts dirty".

Three of the Parade team, including Carlton champion, Sergio Silvagni (father of AFL Team of the Century full-back, Stephen Silvagni) and his cousin, John Bennetti, ended up playing League football. Bennetti later coached Oakleigh. A late 1970s publication entitled *Australian Rules – 100 Greatest Players* (in *The Murray Sports Nostalgia Series*) says of Sergio: "The son of Italian migrants, Silvagni played his junior football with Christian Brothers' College, Victoria Parade, East Melbourne. He was a gutsy schoolboy footballer with an advantage of great strength over his rivals." Much the same could be said about his cousin.

Brother Oswald's talk had its effect and De La did not lose another game for the year, finishing second to Parade on the end of the year table.

Three boys from my grade at De La Salle played VFL football. Laurie O'Toole played 13 games with Richmond before moving to Sandringham where he was a star in a premiership team there. Les Eldering had an eight game career with St Kilda in 1960. Eldering, a tall ruckman, obtained three Brownlow medal votes in his brief stay with the Saints. He had a stellar career with the Commonwealth Bank in the VAFA. Peter Barry, after beginning his career at centre half-forward, was the regular full-back for Carlton in the early '60s after coming to the club as a forward from Bayswater. He played 77 games and kicked 24 goals for the Blues.

Snippet

Peter Barry figured in one of the most controversial incidents in the VFL in the '60s. The match was a tense Carlton-Geelong preliminary final in 1962, with the winner to play Essendon in the Grand Final. Barry was playing on Geelong champion full-forward, Doug Wade, when, with Carlton holding a narrow lead late in the final quarter, Wade, after jostling with Barry, took a mark well within his kicking distance. A goal would have put the Cats in front. However to everyone's surprise and the disappointment of Geelong supporters, umpire Jack Irving, from a distance up the field, awarded a free kick to Peter Barry. Barry cleared the ball and the siren sounded shortly after. Carlton won by five points. Irving later said that Wade had been holding on to Barry's shorts before the ball reached them.

The stars of the De La First XVIII in that year (1954) were Brian Cash and School Captain Bernie Teague.

Brian Cash was one of four Cash boys who went to De La. His brother Michael was captain of the Firsts, a few years before Brian. Another brother, Pat Cash (at right) was an outstanding sportsman and scholar a little earlier. Pat was captain .of the College First XVIII and a member of the First XI.

Later Cash went to Hawthorn in the VFL, playing 58 games for 75 goals. He played mainly at centre half-forward and won the Hawthorn goalkicking with 26 goals in 1951, his first year with *Courtesy 'Blue and Gold'*

the club. His son, Pat Cash Jnr, managed by his father, was a champion tennis player, winning at Wimbledon and being successful for Australia in a number of stirring Davis Cup battles.

Bernie Teague also studied Law having a successful career in that profession. He became extremely well known after the horrific 2009 Black Saturday bushfires, as the Chairman of the Bush Fire Royal Commission.

De La Salle First XVIII, 1954

(Courtesy 'Blue and Gold')

Front Row: P. King, T. Sheridan, K. Reed, P. Shiel, B. O'Regan, M. Cadden, V. Noone

Centre Row: J. Brown, T. Duggan, P. O'Brien, M. Brown, B. Cash, R. Faul, B. Teague, R. Clarke, J. Noseda

Back Row: M. Kellock, L. Allen, J. Samon, J. Kelly, F. Worcester, L. O'Toole, P. Malally, G. Larratt, W. Toogood, J. Flanagan, P. Rankin, J. Pelligrini

Although not tall, Bernie Teague was a very successful centre half-back in the school team. As he was the school sprinting champion his speed was one of his assets as a footballer. Great courage was another. His weakness was that he wasn't a natural kick often attaining height with his kicking rather than distance.

More Stars from De La Salle

While Bob Johnson and Peter Barry were the most well-known VFL players from the Reed boys' years at De La Salle, different eras have seen other De La boys make names for themselves in senior football.

Jack Dyer came to the College after attending St Ignatius College at Richmond, another school run by the De La Salle Brothers. It is said that Brother Peter who taught at St Ignatius encouraged the very promising young footballer to move to De La Salle when he himself was transferred to De La. In fact, Dyer won a Sports Scholarship to change his school. Such a scholarship would have been a rarity in the late 1920s. He won a number of sporting trophies while he was at the College. Dyer was a very successful schoolboy footballer and later became a Richmond champion. He was the playing coach of the 1943 Richmond VFL premiership team and, for a time, his 312 games for the Tigers was the record for the most number of VFL games played. He was six times the Club Best and Fairest. A noted hard man, Dyer also became a well-loved and very successful media personality on his retirement from the game. In the latter role he sometimes amused his listening public by his misappropriate use of words or phrases. Among his most remembered examples are the following:

> "Yes, we had an enjoyable time on the French Riverina (Riviera)."
>
> "I won't say anything in case I say something."
>
> "Bartlett's older than he's ever been before."
>
> "Johnston missed one from the 10 yard square – it was impossible to miss that."
>
> "That's the beauty of being small – your hands are close to your feet."
>
> "Bamblett made a great debut last week, and an even better one today."
>
> "It's as dark out there as the Black Hole of Dakota (Calcutta)."
>
> "That player spends too much time where the ball ain't."

A paragraph in the 1952 *Blue and Gold* (the Annual College magazine) congratulated **John Kennedy** (at right) on obtaining his Bachelor of Arts degree at The University of Melbourne. It also mentioned that while at De la John had been prominent on the football field and that "as a ruckman in his last year at school (1941) he has been a tower of strength in a premiership side". The article went on to say that "John had chosen teaching as his profession."

John Kennedy went on to become one of Aussie Rules' most notable figures. He was a very successful player, coach and also highly respected as man of great honesty and integrity. The latter quality was also recognised in the teaching profession where he became Chairman of the Teachers' Tribunal as well as a successful School Principal. While much has been written about his football career, in particular about his toughness and his oratory, it would be difficult to improve on the following words inscribed beneath the statue of him at Hawthorn Football Club's training facility at Waverley:

> John "Kanga" Kennedy played 164 games for the Hawthorn Football Club in 1950-59, including its first ever finals appearance in 1957. In 1960 aged just 31 Kennedy became coach and transformed Hawthorn and led the club to its first three premierships in 1961, 1971 and 1976. Kennedy's Hawthorn teams became known as "Kennedy's Commandos". Wearing his trademark overcoat, his booming voice and stirring words inspired generations of Hawthorn players, taking them from easy beats to the most respected and revered club in the League. He epitomised and taught all the values and attitudes that the Club cherishes. These were overwhelmingly a sense of TEAM, total DISCIPLINE, total INTEGRITY, and WILL to WIN at all costs. They are now core values, part of the club's character and as we compete in the 21st century this legacy as defined by John Kennedy will never be forgotten.

John Kennedy's son, **John Kennedy Jnr**, attended De La and went on to play with Hawthorn. Although not as well known as his legendary dad, he had an enviable record as a footballer, playing in four premiership teams in the '80s when the Hawks were coached by Allan Jeans for two flags and Alan Joyce for two. A versatile footballer he was capable on the ball, up forward or in defence. In a career spanning 13 seasons he played 241 games and kicked 211 goals including five he kicked in the first quarter in a 1984 match against Carlton.

Snippet

Through John O'Mahony I have had the pleasure of meeting John Kennedy Snr socially a couple of times. On one occasion John Kennedy mentioned to a small group that he had a split fracture in his index finger and it was quite sore. He had caused the injury by frequently spraying plants in his garden. He said that when he was coaching he didn't give much credence to players "split" fractures. "If a bone was properly broken, the player was rested. Otherwise he could play". He went on to add that he had now changed his mind about the severity of such an injury.

He then commented that he was treating his finger and, to the amusement of the group, showed them his finger 'splints' made from two parts of a clothes peg bound by insulation tape. No doubt his finger recovered.

John Coffey was a student at De La in the '40s. On leaving school he played for West St Kilda before he was signed by St Kilda. A brilliant mark and a stylish left foot kick, Coffey was very successful as a half forward flanker. He was embroiled in a clearance wrangle when he wanted to transfer to Morwell. Eventually he did play with the country team and after five years there he returned to play once again with the Saints. A Victorian representative, in all he played 89 games with St Kilda and kicked 52 goals.

As most football followers know, St Kilda has won only one flag. That was in 1966 when they defeated Collingwood by one point. With only a short time to go in the final quarter, that winning point was kicked by ex-De La Salle boy, Barry Breen, who later captained the Saints and played a then-record 300 games with them.

In more recent times Hawthorn 2008 premiership player Trent Croad was an ex-De La boy. Born in New Zealand, Croad grew up in Narre Warren in Victoria after his family migrated to Australia. His grandfather was an All Blacks Rugby Union player. Drafted to Hawthorn in 1998, he played 84 games there before transferring to Fremantle for seasons 2002-2003 where he won that club's goal kicking award in 2002. He returned to the Hawks in 2004 and became a key position back man – a position he relished, using his size and athleticism to great effect. An injury suffered in the 2008 Grand Final eventually led to his retirement in 2010.

Croad was an All-Australian in 2005 and represented Australia in International Rules games in 1999, 2000 and 2005.

Modern day Carlton champion Andrew Carrazzo was also educated at De La Salle. Playing his early football at St Simon's Rowville, Andrew had a relatively slow rise through junior football starring with East Burwood and Oakleigh Chargers (where he came second in the Morrish Medal) to be drafted by Geelong in 2002 as a Rookie. Although he won the Cats' Best and Fairest in the VFL he was unable to make it on to their senior list. Carlton picked him up as a rookie in 2004 and after good performances in the VFL he was selected for his first senior game with the Blues in 2004. Since then he has played as a midfielder and a rebounding defender, winning the John Nicholls Medal for Carlton's Best and Fairest in 2007. He played his 100th game with the Blues in Round 1 in 2010 and, in the absence of Chris Judd, was named acting-captain. To the start of the 2012 season he had played 140 games for the Blues. He has been made a Life Member of the Club.

The Kennedy/Russo Dynasty

For a period in my years at De La Salle, **Felix Russo** was my Physical Education teacher. A beautifully built athlete, Russo was recruited from

Elwood CYMS to play with St Kilda where he played 14 games. He later coached Sandringham in the VFA. He married Joy Johnston, the sister of famous Australian writer, George Johnston, the author of the classic novel, *My Brother Jack*. Three of their children have had an impact on VFL/AFL football.

Their son, **Peter Russo**, was a premiership player for Hawthorn in 1978 and 1986, missing out on the 1983 flag-winning side with a knee injury. A very versatile footballer, he played 162 games with the Hawks for 102 goals. He finished his career with his dad's old team, St Kilda, where he had 33 games before a knee injury ended his career.

Felix and Joy had a daughter, Jenny Russo, who married ex-St Pat's Ballarat boy, Ray Ball, a defender who, in the late '60s and early '70s, played a dozen games with the Tigers before he moved to South Melbourne where he wore the red and white colours 43 times in VFL matches. He later made coaching contributions with both Carlton and the Sydney Swans.

Ray and Jenny's sons, Luke and Matt, played AFL footy, with Luke Ball, initially a star with the Saints and later a Collingwood premiership player being the better known. Matt Ball played 17 AFL games with the Hawks and twice won the Best and Fairest award for Box Hill Hawks in the VFL. He is a 100 game player with that club. In 2010 he played with Old Xavierians in the VAFA and captained that side to a premiership.

Bernadette Russo, another daughter of Felix and Joy, married John Kennedy Jnr and their son **Josh Kennedy** also played for the Hawks before moving to the Sydney Swans. Josh was in brilliant form with the Sydney Swans throughout the 2012 season and a member of their premiership side. The Hawks, as well as his dad and grandfather, may have regretted letting him leave their club.

So, my Phys Ed teacher at De La had a son and two sons-in-law, as well as three grandsons who played VFL/AFL football. Together, ex-De La boys Felix Russo and John Kennedy Snr, who had a son and a grandson who played VFL/AFL footy, began a glorious Kennedy/Russo football dynasty.

"Old Bob" Johnson and "Young Bob"

Football and cricket weren't the only sports that my parents, Mick and Muriel, encouraged their three children to play. Dad ensured that Ramon, Maureen and I joined him as members of the Sacred Heart Parish Tennis Club. The Reeds and other families usually played their tennis on Sunday mornings, particularly during the summer months. They were often joined by Ramon's school friend, **Bob Johnson Jnr,** and his father **Bob Johnson Snr** ("Old Bob" as he was known at Oakleigh). I had heard that Old Bob Johnson had also played for Melbourne but his career was never talked about by Old Bob himself.

From later research I found out that he was the best player on the ground for the 1926 Grand Final in which Melbourne beat Collingwood by nearly 10 goals, after leading by only nine points at half time. The hero of the match for the Melbourne side was Old Bob who in a great display of forward work kicked 6.7.43.

Winning their first premiership since 1900, Melbourne's season was neatly rounded off when their centre-man, Ivor Warne-Smith, won the Brownlow Medal. Old Bob tied, with "Cargie" Greeves of Geelong and **Allan Geddes** of Richmond, for second place in the Brownlow in that year. Geddes was a class winger for the Tigers, captaining the team for three years and a member of the 1932 and 1934 premiership sides. He was a regular interstate player.

Further research into Old Bob's football career indicated that he came originally from the wheat-growing district of Quambatook in the Mallee and that he played initially for Northcote in the VFA winning the Recorder Cup for the Association's Best and Fairest in 1924.

Alan Geddes (NEWSPIX)

Snippet

The Johnsons, father and son, were often seen playing table tennis in the Sacred Heart Parish Hall. Of course they were both very good players. However I used to be amused watching them play. Because of their height, the table wasn't much higher than their knees as they pounded the ball across the net to each other.

John O'Connell

Among my dad's keepsakes there was a telegram (below) from Mary O'Connell, of Claremont, Western Australia, sending "Best Wishes for your future happiness", on Dad's and Mum's wedding day.

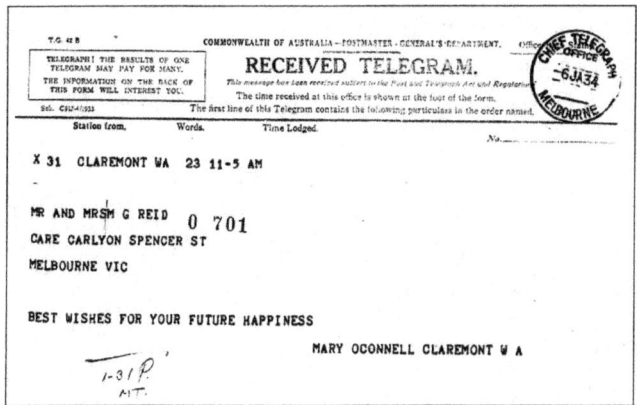

Mary was a friend whom my dad and his brother Jack met when they went to Perth before World War II.

One day when I was a student at De La Salle and our family was living in Oakleigh, Mary O'Connell visited us. On her visit Mary spoke of "her boys", John and Frank, who were good at sport.

A few years later, one of her boys, **John O'Connell**, was transferred in his employment to Victoria and was recruited to play for Geelong in the VFL. John, who had played for Claremont in Western Australia, was a ruckman and played 81 games for Geelong, kicking 65 goals during the years 1955 to 1960.

When I was writing this story in the second decade of the 21st century, I wondered what happened to John O'Connell when he returned to Perth after the 1960 season. On a more personal front, I was also interested to know if the present-day O'Connells knew anything of the Reeds.

John O'Connell

I found out via the internet that John, when back in Perth had played for and had been assistant coach of Claremont and was still associated with the club. I wrote to him at the Club. My letter included questions such as: How much more footy did he play? Did his brother continue to be involved in sport? Did he have family members who had sporting talent? I also asked him if he knew Big Bob Johnson, who had played footy for East Fremantle in the '60s. I was thrilled when, shortly after, I received a hand-written response to my letter.

Firstly, John pointed out that Mary O'Connell was not his mother (as I had assumed) but his aunt – the sister of his father. John attached a hand-written page of information – a "rundown" about his family and their sporting involvement. He then added, "Screw it up if you like."

The attachment is a pretty good "rundown" of what must be one of the best family sporting resumes you could find. John clearly made a great contribution to Aussie Rules as a player, a coach, an assistant coach, and an administrator at the club, and the Western Australia Football League (WAFL) level, as well as with the Claremont Past Players' Association. His work has been recognised in that he was made a Life Member of all three organisations and a stand at the Claremont Football Ground has been named after him.

John's wife, Pam O'Connell, who came across to Victoria with him, was a Victorian and Australian champion athlete as well as a hockey player for Victoria. Pam didn't run at the Melbourne Olympics because her main event, the 400 metres, wasn't an event for women until eight years later when it was won by Betty Cuthbert at Tokyo.

John's brother, Frank, was the Australian 880 yards track champion in 1956 but an injured hamstring prevented him from competing in the Games.

And what's more, two of John's sons have both played AFL and WAFL football. In fact, **Michael and David O'Connell** were the first set of brothers to play for West Coast Eagles in the AFL, although they did not play at the same time. Michael was in the inaugural West Coast Eagles squad and played 10 games in 1987. In the opening round of the 1988 season he was moved forward when playing against his dad's old club, Geelong, at Kardinia Park, and, in a match-winning effort kicked five goals.

I certainly didn't "screw up" the attachment! John concluded his letter by saying that he knew Big Bob Johnson well "when he was starring for both Melbourne and East Fremantle. Loved the bloke".

The internet was a handy tool for me to obtain even more information about the O'Connells. I found that when John was transferred over to Victoria in his employment, a number of teams sought his signature as he had been one of Western Australia's best players in a game against Victoria played at Subiaco in 1951, his second season in the WAFL. John was picked to represent WA when he was only 19.

Geelong became his destination because at the same time Claremont was interested in signing the Geelong centre half-back John Hyde as playing coach. Hyde was Best and Fairest for Geelong in 1950 and had been in the Geelong 1951 and 1952 premiership teams. Although not a direct swap, John's willingness to go to Geelong made it easier for the Cats to let Hyde go to Claremont.

I also found out that John had a successful career as a playing coach for Maddington in the strong South Suburban Football League in Perth. Maddington had been premiers and runners-up over the three years that O'Connell was coach and had won the club Best and Fairest award while he was there.

John had also omitted to mention in his "run down" that he had a two decade career as a successful sports commentator in the media, retiring from that role to become General Manager of the WAFL at the time when the West Coast Eagles were to come into the AFL.

In another internet article, entitled *Where Are They Now ? – John O'Connell* by Ron Head, the writer commences by saying that no-one "has contributed more to West Australian football than John O'Connell". Head pointed out that another feature of O'Connell's stay at Maddington was, in Head's words:

> the visit of his old club, Geelong, who agreed to play against a combined South Suburban side, bolstered by some WAFL stars including Barry Cable ... at the Gosnells oval.
>
> With local legend "Polly" Farmer in the visitors' line up the ground was packed. O'Connell captain/coached the locals, and set the scene for a lively encounter with an early piece of biffo with a young Sam Newman. "Sam was a cheeky bugger even then," John commented. "It was a great time."

O'Connell also reminisced, for the article, about the great times the Geelong boys had on their bus going to and returning from their games in Melbourne, with a stop for lunch at Werribee on the way to the game and much singing and entertainment on the return trip.

Ron Head concludes his article by noting that the "O'Connell name is a well respected one at Claremont, Geelong, and Maddington, as well as the WAFL and the media. An outstanding exponent of the game, as ruckman, forward, and coach, his lifetime of service to all facets of football in Western Australia has been outstanding. The game is the richer for the contributions of John O'Connell." John O'Connell was inducted into the WAFL Hall of Fame, which happened around the time of his 80th birthday – a time of great celebration for his family.

Snippet

One of John O'Connell's grandsons, John Williams, played with Claremont in the WAFL in 2013. He came fifth in the Club's Best and Fairest award.

10

The "Oaks" & "Chooka" Howell

The "Oaks", A disappointing loss – then success, YCW footy, teachers' college Footy; Northcote FC, Fitzroy FC, St. Kilda FC, Williamstown FC; Bob Skilton, Pastor Doug Nicholls, Jack McAlister, George Rudolph, and George Smeaton.

With the population explosion that had taken place after World War II there was a need for more schools and teachers. As an aspiring teacher, on leaving school in 1954, I started studying to be a primary school teacher at Burwood Teachers' College (BTC). There I was pleased to catch up with Jim McKenna (a neighbour of my cousins, the Fergusons, in Yarrawonga), whom I had played college footy against when he had attended Assumption College, Kilmore.

To begin our post-school footy careers Jim and I joined my Oakleigh friends and played (at the Rec) for the Oakleigh Young Christian Workers (YCW) team in the Catholic YCW Under 18 competition. The coach of the team was Jack McAlister, a well known former Oakleigh player.

As the YCW games were played on Sunday afternoon, the games were well attended by players from other local teams who had played on a Saturday, as well as family members from the opposing sides.

Big Bob Johnson, who later in that year played in his first premiership with Melbourne, often came along to watch. He brought some friends with him. One mate who was a regular spectator was Kevan Hamilton who had played with Big Bob in Melbourne Thirds (Under 19) sides. Unable to break into the strong Demon line-up, Hamilton moved to

Oakleigh YCW Under 18 Team, 1955

(Courtesy 'Oakleigh Amateur Football Club)

Back Row: Mr Jack McAlister (coach), B. Greely, J. McKenna, T. Healy, R. Clarke, G. Honan (V. Capt), E. Bryant, J. Tindley, J. Kennedy, B. McArthur, Mr Le Broq (Patron);

Centre Row: B. Kirwin, P. Rohan, B. McAlister, B. Woodhouse, P. Cox (Capt), B.McCarthy, M. Wiseman.

Front Row: J. Miller, K. Reed, J. White, B. Marshall, K. Gardiner

Carlton where he played 11 games in 1956 and kicked 22 goals, winning the goalkicking award for the Blues in that year.

Another footballer who attended on occasions with Big Bob was Frank Dunin, an Ormond lad who played with Richmond. Frank, recruited from University Blacks played 69 games as a ruckman for the Tigers from 1953 to 1959 – with a break in 1954 when he was studying at Dookie Agricultural College as part of his Agricultural Science degree from the University of Melbourne.

Team Chaplains

The YCW organisation ran three Under 18 competitions across Melbourne at that time, each embracing a different area of the City.

Oakleigh played in the south-east section. Opposition teams included Malvern, East Melbourne, Richmond, Surrey Hills and Middle Park among others. Each team had a young curate who followed the team and was the team chaplain. Father Maurice Sheehy, who sadly passed away in 2012, was the chaplain of the Oakleigh team while Fr John Brosnan looked after the St John's East Melbourne boys. Fr Brosnan later became well-known for the work he did for prisoners when chaplain at Pentridge Prison, giving great support to Ronald Ryan, the last man to be hanged in Victoria, in Ryan's final days.

In 1985 Tom Prior wrote a biography of Fr Brosnan ("Fr Bros") entitled *A Knockabout Priest: The story of Father John Brosnan*. In the section where Prior writes about Fr Brosnan's days as the YCW chaplain at East Melbourne, he quotes ex-Collingwood player Barry Donegan who said the following about YCW football in those days:

> We had a good team, a tough team, but you have no idea how many good teams and tough players were around in those days. ... a number of boys ... used to play VFL Under 19s of Saturdays and YCW football on Sundays. ... We just couldn't get enough football.

Jim McKenna and I didn't play VFL Under 19s on Saturdays but we had our second game each Wednesday playing with the BTC team. There was no teachers' college competition, as such, but football-loving lecturers from each of the half dozen or so teachers' colleges arranged the weekly matches. Games were also played against police trainees and large secondary schools such as Scotch College and Melbourne High School.

So, for two years we had a football feast, playing both Wednesdays and Sundays, and improving our skills quite a bit as there were very competent footballers in most of the opposing teams.

I particularly remember playing a game against Middle Park YCW at an Albert Park Oval. It was a windy day and the opposition had a brilliant player who played centre-half forward when they were kicking with the wind and centre-half back when we had the wind. We couldn't handle him at all. He was totally courageous and kicked equally well with either foot.

At the end of the 1955 season, the delegates from each club had to attend a meeting at the competition's headquarters next to St Francis' Church in Melbourne, to hear the result of the vote counting for the Best and Fairest awards for each of the sections of YCW footy. Jim McKenna and I went along for our club.

The votes had already been counted. There was no building of tension as the night progressed. The organisation's secretary simply read out the leading vote-getters. I wasn't surprised to hear that the winner of the South-East Section's award was the brilliant Middle Park YCW player, Bob Skilton. He polled 21 votes. However I was surprised and flattered to hear that, with the assistance of ruckmen Pat Cox and Gary Epstein, I came second in the voting with 18 votes. However the three votes' margin between Skilton and me was not the only way our seasons differed. I played all 18 games whereas future triple Brownlow Medallist, **Bobby Skilton**, played in only seven games. He obtained three votes in every game that he played!

In the following year, Bob Skilton began his long and successful year with the Swans – sharing the roving with 1955 vice-captain and interstate representative Gray "Mickey" Sibun and later with Brian McGowan, a small courageous player who was the first to wear a helmet consistently in VFL fooball – his was a bike helmet. McGowan played 118 games with the Swans before heading to South Australia. He won the Swans goalkicking in 1961.

Other good players in the YCW competition that year were Paddy Guinane who later played 146 games with Richmond and Ron Johnson who had 19 games with the Tigers.

A number of players from opposition sides in the Wednesday games made it to the VFL including Ian Hinks (59 games with Hawthorn), Geoff Howells (16 games with Hawthorn) and Ray Allsop (54 games with Richmond). But the best of all was interstate wingman John O'Neill who played 136 games for Geelong. O'Neill, like Skilton, was well known for his courage. In 1958 he played five games with a broken wrist and still won the Geelong Best and Fairest award.

The Oaks

Like most football-loving boys growing up in post-World War II Oakleigh, Ramon and I barracked for VFA team Oakleigh ("the Oaks"), who played at the Warrawee Park oval in Warrigal Road. The Oaks joined the VFA in 1929. Before that they had played in the Metropolitan Football Association (MFA) since 1908. The MFA began as a football competition at a meeting held at the Salvation Army Headquarters in Bourke Street, Melbourne, in 1892, pre-dating the formation of the VFL. Initially it was called the Metropolitan Junior Football Association with the "Junior" being dropped from the title in 1912. In that year the MFA played their finals as curtain raisers to the VFL finals at the MCG.

At that time some of the MFA clubs were linked to VFL clubs including Carlton Districts, Collingwood Districts and Fitzroy Districts which were associated with Carlton, Collingwood and Fitzroy respectively. However the MFA functioned as an organisation independent of the VFL, making its own regulations as it grew.

By 1927 the MFA had three sections playing with players required to wear numbered jumpers and visiting players to wear white shorts. A *Football Record* was available for the supporters. In 1930 the "Order Off" rule was introduced. This meant that an umpire could tell a player to leave the field, without a replacement, for a period of time if the umpire thought the player was guilty of grossly unfair play. In 1933, with four sections of competition, the MFA changed its name to the Victorian Amateur Football Association (VAFA), the body which still exists today.

Not long after Oakleigh left the MFA it had success in the VFA.

The Oaks were premiers in both 1930 and 1931. This was largely the result of a recruiting campaign which saw them sign three outstanding players: **George Rudolph**, a ruckman from Richmond, Eric Fleming, a ruckman/forward from Geelong and Frank Maher mentioned earlier, a clever rover from Essendon who later played for Fitzroy. All three were still in their prime when they transferred to Oakleigh.

Rudolph played for Victoria on seven occasions; Fleming had been a member of the 1925 Geelong Premiership team and was later to coach the Oaks, while Maher played for Victoria nine times, and was captain and coach of the 1927 Carnival team. Maher was appointed captain and coach of Oakleigh and after success there he returned to VFL football as captain and coach of Fitzroy in 1932-33 and of Carlton in 1935-36.

Although it only lasted two years the ruck-roving combination of Rudolph, Fleming and Maher was legendary around Oakleigh when the Reed boys were growing up. Despite this, the Oaks didn't easily win their Flags. In both years they defeated Northcote by only narrow margins.

George Rudolph (NEWSPIX)

Pastor Doug Nicholls

Sir Douglas Nicholls played for Northcote in those years when Oakleigh had success, as well as in the Grand Final in 1929 when Northcote won the premiership.

Doug was born in 1906 on a Christian mission station in NSW. At thirteen he worked in shearing sheds and lived with shearers. He was a natural athlete and an outstanding footballer. In 1927 he was invited to train with Carlton but left because of racial comments made about him. He then went to play with Northcote and was there until 1932 when he joined Fitzroy playing there until 1938. In 1935 he became the first indigenous player to represent Victoria in an interstate team. He was also a successful professional runner.

Nicholls, who was a strong Christian, worked as a lay preacher before undertaking the role of a social worker helping people with problems in the Fitzroy community. In 1957 he became a field officer for the Aboriginal Advancement League (AAL) and edited the AAL's journal *Smoke Signals* helping to draw Aboriginal issues to the attention of government officials and the general public.

Pastor Nicholls was knighted in 1972 and appointed Governor of South Australia in 1976. Dying in 1988, he was buried in the cemetery at the mission station where he was born. Sir Douglas Nicholls was a truly great Australian. He is quoted as saying, "All we want is to be able to think and do the same things as white people, while still retaining our identity as a people."

Jack McAlister

Another Oakleigh player during this era was Jack McAlister, the coach of our YCW team. Born in England, Jack played soccer as a youth and didn't play Aussie Rules until he was 17, but he quickly learned the game. Jack was recruited from the public service team to play with Oakleigh before it joined the VFA. He was full back in their 1930 premiership team and back pocket in the following year.

The Oaks slumped after their two premierships but were back on their feet by 1934, when Jack became captain mid-season and represented the VFA in a match against the VFL.

Interested in coaching, he coached Glen Iris in 1935. Jack then coached a couple of other local teams until 1941 when, at the age of 37, he returned to play with the Oaks, taking his total number of games with the club to 146. One windy day at Port Melbourne his soccer skills came to the fore when, as full back, he used the place kick 26 times to put the ball back into play after the opposition kicked behinds. The gale force wind made it impossible to control any other type of kick. When the VFA went into recess for World War II, Jack played for St Kilda seconds for three seasons before he finished his career as playing coach of Oakleigh CYMS at the age of 43.

After retiring from playing he devoted a lot of his time to coaching local junior teams.

Jack became a legend in the district and it was only fitting that the roadway off North Road, near Metropolitan Golf Club, leading to one of Oakleigh's well-used cricket and football grounds was named Jack McAlister Avenue. Jack was awarded the Order of Australia in 1979.

The Oaks, after World War II

Although Oakleigh had early success in the VFA it was not until after WW II, when the competition resumed, that the Oaks had further success.

My earliest memory of following Oakleigh was in 1946, immediately after the War. **Eric Beard**, a local lad and outstanding full-back, was my earliest Oakleigh hero. So good was Beard that he won the J. J. Liston trophy for Best and Fairest in the VFA in 1946. He was the first winner of the trophy as, prior to World War II, the Recorder Cup was awarded to the VFA Best and Fairest player.

Eric Beard

The coach of Oakleigh immediately after the War was Herbie Matthews. Once again Oakleigh had sought an outstanding player to lead the team. Matthews came from South Melbourne and was a Brownlow Medallist, tying for the award with Collingwood's Des Fothergill in 1940. Matthews was a solidly built centre line player who anticipated future trends in the game by moving far and wide making it difficult for an opponent to keep up with him. His father and son also played VFL football but Herbie was the star of the family. Oakleigh failed to win a premiership under Matthews, but had success under **George Smeaton**.

George Smeaton who had played 149 games with the Tigers and became the next playing coach of Oakleigh. Smeaton, an interstate representative, was an outstanding and tough full-back playing in three Grand Finals with Richmond. So courageous was he that, like Laurie Fowler, he is one of the "100 Tiger Treasures", for being nominated for one of the Tigers' "Brave Acts of the Century".

George Smeaton (NEWSPIX)

The years following George Smeaton's arrival were halcyon times for the Oaks. As we grew older we probably shared our time equally between following the Tigers and Oakleigh. We could ride our bikes to the Warrigal Road ground for home matches and were allowed to play kick to kick with our friends on the oval at half time. If the team was playing away, even as far as Northcote, Yarraville or Preston, there were furniture vans with portable wooden bench seats in the rear to make the journey a little more comfortable.

What's more, in those days, Oakleigh, with a population of around 16,000, was still a little like a large country town and, as not everyone had cars, people walked or used a local bus to get around. Consequently "everyone knew each other". Rovers Jim Edwards and Tommy Rawlings walked past our home every day, to and from work at Ogden's factory which was built on the site of the earlier army camp. Half-back flanker, "Warby" Wilson, had a nephew, Jim, who was in my grade at Sacred Heart School and Ted Ryan's photo, as captain of a school football team in the

'30s, adorned a wall in that school. Ted was a champion key position player for the Oaks. Roy Boswell, the Club's head trainer, had a daughter, Joyce, in my grade at Sacred Heart. Ron Jory, a fast moving ruckman and a lovely long drop kick, lived in Edward Street and my dad, knew Ron and his father well. Jack Murphy, a keen Oakleigh supporter, owned the barber shop opposite the Junction Hotel in the main shopping centre. Football was always the talk in the barber shop and sometimes I would see an Oakleigh player there having a haircut.

The Reed family enjoyed supporting the Oaks over the period that Smeaton was there. He was the man for the job. An excellent speaker, he had good inter-personal skills, maintaining the players' respect at all times. He was also a good mixer and an excellent "party singer". Ramon and I remember going to the *Kia-Ora Sports Parade* shows, held in the Plaza Picture Theatre in Oakleigh where Smeaton, much to everyone's enjoyment, would demonstrate his singing talents.

The *Kia-ora Sports Parade*, sponsored by the soft drink brand Kia-Ora, was a little like the *Footy Show* today in that it mixed talk about footy with some clowning about. The venue moved from one Club to another for each week's performance. Both VFL and VFA clubs were involved. Players were interviewed and dressed up for "little entertainments".

The show was broadcast over the radio with Norm Banks as the Master of Ceremonies and Max Reddy, the house comedian. Reddy's daughter, Helen, became famous for her singing of *I am Woman* – an anthem for the feminist movement.

Smeaton was getting a little old to play for very long when he came to Oakleigh but a number of players who, though not champions had played VFL football, were recruited to help. Among these was courageous Arch Baxter, a centreman, who had played 23 games with South Melbourne. Both Smeaton and Baxter had served during World War II. Also included in the group of ex-VFL players were Jack and Clive Watson (from Richmond), Max Howell (from Carlton), Beau Lambert (from Hawthorn), local hero Ted Ryan who played a few games with

Footscray and Alby Naismith, a centre half-forward who had 68 games with Hawthorn, kicking 68 goals. Naismith's father, Wally Naismith, played over 150 games with Fitzroy and Melbourne, being a member of the 1904 and 1905 Fitzroy premiership teams. He was a determined and popular back pocket player. Wally's twin, Charles Naismith, also played for Fitzroy, being one of their best in their losing 1906 Grand Final side.

Snippet

Max Howell, the Carlton recruit mentioned above, passed away on 3rd October 2012. A tribute to Max was placed in the *Herald Sun* from the "Oakleigh Football Club Past Players" regretting "the passing of former premiership player, 1950, 1952".

The names Alec Boyle, Norm Tindall and "Beau" Lalbert appeared at the foot of the notice; still comrades 60 years after their premiership days.

These experienced recruits blended well with home-grown Oakleigh locals like forward Alan Scott, ruckman Bill Williams and rover Jim Edwards as well as recruits from other leagues and clubs not too far distant from Oakleigh. Centre half-back Norm Tindall and ruckman Bernie Perkins were in this category. Perkins' brother, Bill "Polly" Perkins was a solid back flanker for the Tigers.

In 1949 the Oaks played Williamstown (the "Seagulls") in the Grand Final at the St Kilda ground (the Junction Oval). The teams had been great rivals throughout the year. Dad, Ramon and I went along to enthusiastically support the Oaks. **Ron Todd** was playing coach of Williamstown. It was a fine day with a crowd of 38,000 in attendance. VFA Grand Finals were played a week after the VFL Grand Final in those days, and with many people having an appetite for more football, usually attracted good crowds.

Ron Todd (NEWSPIX)

Vic Hill (left) was a talented Oakleigh half-forward flanker in the '50s. He was a left-footer who had played three games with Richmond and 20 with South Melbourne before coming to Oakleigh. He was handy around goals.

The Grand Final against Williamstown was close with the Oaks a couple of points in front late in the last quarter. Vic Hill took a mark about 50 metres out from goal almost straight in front. Hill could well kick the distance if he "got onto it".

He decided to be a little clever and thought he would waste a bit of time (run down the clock) before he kicked the ball. When he was about to kick, he put down the ball and started to pull up his socks. He then bent over to check that his boot laces were properly adjusted. The umpire told him to hurry up, but Hill continued to delay his kick. Losing patience the umpire blew his whistle and awarded a free kick to Williamstown. With three kicks, straight down the ground, Williamstown kicked a goal, took the lead and then the bell rang. The Seagulls won the flag. Oakleigh supporters, including Dad, Ramon and I were devastated. Mick bought an Oakleigh team flag for the occasion (see right).

The Reed boys' hero at that time was centre half-forward Max Wenn who was recruited from Berwick. Oakleigh was lucky to pick him up as a number of VFL teams were after him. A fast moving, high marking player, Wenn was a beautiful long kick. He was recruited by Carlton after the Oaks won the 1952 flag, playing 23 games and kicking 38 goals with the Blues. A broken leg ended his career prematurely.

"Chooka" and "The Tank"

Oakleigh was only a middle-of-the-road team for the bulk of the '50s. However there was some excitement for the fans when Oakleigh signed up another famous AFL player as playing coach in 1955. This player, **Jack "Chooka" Howell** (at right) had been a premiership Carlton ruckman who was runner-up in the 1946 Brownlow Medal. He had also twice been Club Best and Fairest. Both Howell's father and son played VFL football; his dad, Jack Howell, playing 40 games with South Melbourne and his son, Scott Howell, playing 39 games with the Blues. The Howell family has the distinction of three generations of a family playing in premiership teams: Jack Snr with South Melbourne in 1918, Chooka with Carlton in 1947, and Scott with Carlton in 1981.

Howell was reasonably successful in his first year at Oakleigh but suffering from a knee injury he retired in mid-1956. His position was taken by Eric Guy who had come to the club from Carrum in 1952. Guy, a strongly built plumber, was nicknamed "The Tank". His attack on the ball was extremely aggressive, never deviating from his path once the ball was in his vicinity.

Guy captained the club, after Howell retired, for the remainder of 1956 before he signed with St Kilda at the age of 24. Murray Weideman the rugged Collingwood champion described Guy as the toughest fair player of his time. Guy was a little diffident about going to the Saints as he thought he wouldn't make it. He was to prove himself wrong, representing Victoria on three occasions and being St Kilda's vice-captain for three of his six year career.

Dr Paul Callery knew Eric Guy as they were both ex-St Kilda players. Paul told me that Eric, when doing draining work, would rather dig a trench himself than use a backhoe to do the job. Guy felt that by the time he got the hoe to the site and set it up he could have manually dug the trench himself. Besides the digging kept him fit and saved him money.

With the loss of Guy and other good players from the early '50s, Oakleigh had to wait until 1960 to win its next flag.

Snippet

As part of the Olympic Games held in Melbourne in 1956, an exhibition game of Aussie Rules was held between a team selected from the VAFA and players from the VFA and VFL who played as amateurs.

Notables in that team were Denis Cordner (Capt), Ray Gabelich, Brendan Edwards and Laurie Dwyer (all VFL champions). Lindsay Gaze (from Prahran), later of basketball fame, was an emergency. Two ex-De La Salle students were in the team: Des Tobin who had played one game with North Melbourne and Gerry Gill, a University Blacks player in the VAFA at the time. The VAFA beat the VFL/VFA by 26 points (12.9.81 to 8.7.55).

11
Lalbert, Lake Boga and the Finn Brothers

A Mallee Farm, a football pedigree, a footy club meeting, the MMFL, weekends of sport, "Back to Costerfield"; Lalbert FC, Lake Boga FC, Geelong FC, St Kilda FC; the Hardimans, the Metheralls, Reg Hickey, Greg Kelly, Dan Kelly and Graham Cornes.

Young people are often advised to travel to broaden their minds. It turned out that I did travel. But it was not of the type that many envisaged. I journeyed, not overseas, but to take up my first position as a teacher.

My experience as a graduate teacher was much the same as hundreds of young teachers who began their teaching careers in Victoria throughout a large part of the 20th century; I was sent to a one-teacher rural school as my first teaching appointment.

For the majority of the group this meant that they were sent to an unheard of faraway place where they boarded (often on a farm) with the parents of one or more of the pupils and they were given far more responsibility than they had ever before encountered. Furthermore, they played a significant role in local community activities and they had an experience that they would remember for the rest of their lives. The young males were made particularly welcome in their new communities if they had skill at any of the sports that were played where they taught, including cricket and tennis in the summer and particularly football in the winter.

I first heard of my imminent travel experience on the last Friday in January, when I received a telegram from the Education Department informing me that as a recent graduate I was appointed as head teacher of State School, Number 4296, Cokum Reserve, via Lalbert, and that I was to commence work there on the following Tuesday. The name, address and telephone number of the secretary of the school committee, Leo Hogan, was also included, although I had no idea where Cokum Reserve was!

After initially panicking, I realised that my dad, working on the Railways, would probably know the whereabouts of Lalbert and if there was a railway station there, even if he hadn't heard of Cokum Reserve – which he hadn't. Dad was able to inform me that "Lalbert was south of Swan Hill, on the Robinvale line, a couple of stations after Quambatook, before you get to Ultima, but well short of Chinkapook and Manangatang. You catch the Mildura train to Bendigo, where you change and catch the Kulwin train to Korong Vale, then the Robinvale train to Lalbert." So, I then knew where Lalbert was. It was about 200 miles (about 330 kilometres) north-west of Melbourne, in the very dry wheat-growing region known as the Mallee.

Over a frantic week-end, I packed all that I thought I might need, including teaching aids and sporting equipment, and telephoned Leo Hogan to inform him that I was coming on the Monday train. Leo told me that it was the Meehan family's turn to board the teacher and that Phonse Meehan would meet me at the train. I hoped that Leo had told Phonse that also.

On arriving at the lonely Lalbert station I was met by a very friendly, unshaven Phonse Meehan in a large white Humber Super Snipe.

His welcoming statement was followed by a question, "Do you play football?"

"Yes."

"Then you'll play with Lalbert."

I wasn't sure whether that was a question or a fact, but not knowing any better, agreed to do so.

Phonse's Football Heritage

Obviously Phonse enjoyed footy. He told me on the way to his farm that he had a couple of cousins who had played for Geelong in the '30s – the Hardiman brothers. His mother was a Hardiman. He also let me know that he had cousins on his father's side, Tom and Jack Meehan, who played for St Kilda. I hadn't heard of the Hardimans but I knew of the Meehans. Both had moved from the St Kilda CYMS team to play with St Kilda in the 1940s.

Tom, the more successful of the two, played 73 games with the Saints, mainly at full back before moving to Fitzroy and then to Brighton in the VFA. Although not a great footballer, Tom Meehan will long be remembered. Firstly, for the Hasting's sculpture of him being out-marked by John Coleman. Secondly, there is a frequently seen photo of him being knocked over by Jack Dyer; often called the "get out of my way" photo. The Hardimans were very good footballers. **Harry ("Peter") Hardiman** and **Les ("Splinter") Hardiman** had both played in the premiership winning Geelong teams of 1931 and 1937. Peter was an aggressive left-footed follower who gave good protection to smaller players. A Victorian representative, he played 160 games with the Cats.

Les "Splinter" Hardiman, taller than his brother, was a key position player who could kick with either foot. He had a great leap which he used to outmark or spoil opponents. A regular Victorian representative, he left for Western Australia after the 1937 Grand Final. In that match against Collingwood, Splinter began the game at full forward but was switched to play on Ron Todd at quarter-time. Hardiman's ability to curb Todd, who had been dominant in the first quarter, was a significant factor in the Cat's victory. Les Hardiman was named in the Geelong Team of the Century.

Geelong had a successful era in the 1930s. They made the finals six times from 1930 to 1938, winning premierships in 1931 and 1937. The driving force behind their success was **Reg Hickey** whose playing career lasted from 1926 to 1940 and who continued as non-playing coach until

1959, figuring in four premierships. A grandstand has been named after him at Kardinia Park, Geelong's home ground.

Other players who gave Hickey support in the1930s were centre-man and Brownlow Medallist "Carjie" Greeves, tough ruckman Jack Evans, who kicked six goals in the 1937 Grand Final, as well as the Metherall brothers from Subiaco. Older brother, **Len Metherall**, a strong follower, was in the 1931 successful side. The younger brother **Jack Metherall**, who played in the 1937 premiership team, won the Geelong goal kicking award three times in the 65 games he played with the Cats.

The Meehan Farm

Phonse's farm, a property of about 1400 acres (about 600 hectares) adjoined the Lalbert-Culgoa Road, west of Lalbert, about half way to Culgoa. At that time electric power had not been connected to the house, nor to the school as I later found out.

Gladys and Phonse Meehan (at right) had six children: David and Lucy who had left school, Ken, Denis, Helen, who would be pupils at my school, and Maurice who would start school the next year. The school itself was pretty old being brought, by wagons and horses, from Bungeluke North State School (also in the Mallee) in the mid '20s.

Phonse was the bearer of this information, but it was Mrs Meehan who then added, "There are eleven children in the school at the moment but there will only be ours for this week as the other four families are still on holidays after the harvest. We had a good harvest this year."

I also found out during this conversation that that the five families took turns at boarding the teacher and that I would be at the Meehans for six months before I was moved on.

Before I turned in for the night, Phonse told me that I would need to get up by half past seven to go to school. "David will take you all down there in the Humber. It's about three miles away." The fact that David, was about to turn 17 and without a driver's licence, didn't seem to worry him.

The Lalbert Township

David took me into the Lalbert township one afternoon to pick up the mail and the bread. This trip gave me an opportunity to have a look at the town. The main road through Lalbert was the Birchip-Swan Hill Road, which ran roughly north-south.

Situated along this road were a couple of churches, two banks, a general store, a number of houses and the Lalbert Hotel which was on the corner of an east-west running street. A garage, baker, a post office, another general store, a café and the public hall were found in this street. A couple more streets also ran west off the main road. These streets formed the main residential area of the town. As noted, electricity had not been connected to the town. I was surprised to see that a gravity-feed bowser was used to fill the tank of a car at the local garage. Local girl, Dot Power, an excellent basketball (netball) player kept the books and operated the bowser.

Across the railway line to the east of the shops were the football/cricket ground, four tennis courts with gypsum surfaces and a couple of basketball (netball) courts. There was a new timber and fibro cement change room, with showers and hot water, for the Lalbert team, while the visitors had to make do with the older corrugated iron shed, which also had showers and hot water. A kiosk was located next to the visitors' rooms. Of course there were toilets but at that time there were no changing rooms for the basketballers.

I was pleased with the football facilities as they were better than those at the Rec but the surface of the oval, although level, looked somewhat hard. A nine-hole golf course had been formed in a paddock next to the oval. I thought that Lalbert would be okay for a while.

Settling In

With all of the other families having returned from holidays there was a full school of eleven pupils on the next Monday. Helen Meehan was the only girl but she fitted in well, as she was good at sport. Two of the fathers seemed rather anxious to have a chat to me. The reason for this soon became obvious as the pattern of the conversation was similar to when I first met Phonse.

"Hello, I'm Jim Brennan and this is Bruce McLennan, I'm president of the Nullawill Football Club and Bruce is Secretary, do you play football?"

"Too late", was the cry. As it turned out the Meehan family was the only family who used Lalbert as their town centre, all of the others went to Nullawill.

Things soon settled down at the school, with me working long hours to prepare work for the six grades represented at the school including the Grade 7 boys, Ken Meehan and his friend Max "Axle" Smith. Every day Max drove his two brothers and a couple of neighbours' children to school in an old Dodge.

Although the Meehans had a clay tennis court at the farm, for my summer sport that year I chose to play cricket with the Lalbert team. Three boys from a neighbouring farm, Billy, David and Peter Free, played cricket and I journeyed the long distances to places such as Sea Lake and Manangatang for the one day games that were played in the competition. Lalbert didn't make the finals and before long everyone was talking about the sport that really mattered – football!

Lalbert Footy Club

Phonse was able to give me a good run-down on the Lalbert Football club. Like at Heathcote, Costerfield and many other country towns, Lalbert teams were formed for intra-club and inter-town matches in the late 19th century, with Lalbert entering its first team in a competition around 1912.

It was an interesting competition as the teams comprised towns along the Robinvale railway line: Chillingollah, Waitchie, Ultima, Meatian and Lalbert. Phonse told me that the train was utilised to get players to the matches but he gave me no details as to how the system worked.

The Lalbert Football Club web-site has no record of how long the "train line" competition lasted, however there is evidence that from 1922 until 1947, when it joined the Mid-Murray League, Lalbert had teams in a number of football associations that appeared in that area in the first half of the 20th century. These included the Northern District, the Quambatook District and the Southern Mallee Football Associations.

The web-site also suggests that in some years, probably drought years, the Club didn't field a team at all. Like at Costerfield, there would have been a meeting relatively early in the year to decide if it would be possible to field a team for the up-coming season. If so, a decision would have to be made as into which competition the team should be entered.

In 1957, the Mid-Murray League, centred on Swan Hill, comprised the following teams: Quambatook, Lalbert, Lake Boga, Swan Hill, Tyntynder, Woorinen, Nyah, Nyahwest, Tooleybuc and Balranald. The distance from Quambatook, the southern-most team, to Balranald in the north was over 180 kilometres. Of course road transport was used to get to the grounds for the matches and some of the roads were not then bituminised.

Lalbert won the premiership in that competition in 1952, defeating Woorinen in the Grand Final. There was no doubt that Lalbert would be entering a team in 1957. It was a strong club.

The Brothers Finn

Phonse also told me that a couple of teams in the competition, Quambatook and Lake Boga ("Boga"), were Lalbert's traditional rivals. I had heard of Lake Boga as the Finn brothers, Stan and Ray, who had played for Oakleigh in the '40s, made news at Oakleigh when they left the VFA team to play for "good money" at Lake Boga. **Stan Finn** was a forward while **Ray Finn** was a rover. Ray had played 10 games for Essendon in 1944-45, kicking 14 goals. They were regarded as good, tough footballers at Oakleigh.

I gave this information to Phonse who replied that although he hadn't seen them play ("too busy with a young family") he had heard that they weren't bad players but that they were "not as good as they thought they were" and also that they "sold out in a final in their last year", leaving the town in a new truck. To lack humility on the football field (or anywhere else) was a serious character blemish in Phonse's eyes and of course to "sell out" and "play dead" is totally unacceptable.

Over 50 years later, when researching for this book, I decided to make use of the internet and microfilm of the *Swan Hill Guardian* from the State Library, to see how good the Finns really were. I found that Stan Finn kicked 105 goals in 1950, winning the Mid-Murray goal kicking award, and was the first Mid-Murray player to reach "the ton" in a season.

In 1951 Lalbert played Boga in the second semi-final. Boga had been very successful during the season and finished on top of the ladder well clear of Lalbert who were second. Lalbert won the semi by over eight goals. The *Guardian* claimed that the form of Boga "was too bad to be true and not worthy of their position as MMFL leaders".

Ray Finn kicked three of Boga's five goals. On the Swan Hill ground on the same day, Woorinen defeated Tyntynder in the first semi-final. The experiment of playing the two finals on the one day seemed to be a success as 7,000 people attended. The town's population was not much more than 7,000 at the time.

Boga recovered to defeat Woorinen in the preliminary final, with Stan Finn kicking nine goals and both Finns named among Boga's best players.

Lalbert and Boga were to meet in the Grand Final. There was much expectation about the match. Could Lalbert repeat their drubbing of Boga in the Grand Final? It wasn't to be. Boga maintained their form, winning the Grand Final by over four goals. Both Finns were again named in the best players with Stan kicking eight goals and Ray three. Between them the Finns kicked 11 of Boga's 14 goals and more goals than the entire Lalbert team. Perhaps there was good reason for Phonse's informant to be somewhat lukewarm about the Finns.

The Finns certainly didn't "sell out" in the 1951 Grand Final. Perhaps they played dead in the second semi to lengthen their odds for the flag – a risky proposition. Perhaps they had been saving up for long time to buy the truck, in which they allegedly left town after the Grand Final. Perhaps the whole story was made up by a disappointed Lalbert supporter.

Who knows?

Lake Boga Football Club – Premiers 1951

(Taken by Arthur Baulch, Head Trainer – Lake Boga Football Club Website)

Back Row: C. Trinnie, C. Scown, L. Baulch, W. Tripcony, G. Carmichael, B. Emerson, D. Martin, J. Kelly, R. Finn, D. Kelly, S. Finn, E. Manns, W. Newton (Trainer)

Front Row: C. Judd, K. Fitzpatrick, R. Mitchell, P. Schintler, 'Yank' Codling, L. Baulch, R.Taylor, T. Matthews, (Mascot: Mickey Finn)

The 1951 season was the last for the Finn brothers with Lake Boga, who, without them, did poorly in the following year.

The *Swan Hill Guardian* also noted that for the 1951 Grand Final the

Boga team had an average age of 26 years, height of 5 feet 10 inches and weight of 12 stone 1 pound, while the Lalbert team's average age was 25 years, average height was 5 feet 9 inches and weight was 11 stone 7 pounds. Not very big by 2012 standards!

In the photo of the 1951 Lake Boga team, the Finn brothers are standing in the back row. Between Stan and Ray in the photo, is **Dan Kelly**, a multiple winner of the Mid-Murray League Best and Fairest award, who was still playing when I was in the Mallee. Gordon Carmichael, (third player from the left in the back row), a solidly built, very mobile centre-man, was also still a very good player for Boga ten years later.

Snippet

After a poor season in 1952 Boga were back-to-back premiers in 1953 and 1954. A great asset to their team in those years was full forward Dick O'Bree who kicked 118 goals in 1953. Over the years O'Bree played with Lake Boga, Euroa and Wycheproof. A legendary country full forward, O'Bree kicked over 90 goals in a season seven times, including topping the ton twice. In 1956 he was recruited to Collingwood and was badly injured playing in his third game for that club. He was out for the rest of the season and didn't return to the Magpies.

Footy Club Meeting

The first official Lalbert Football Club meeting in 1957 was held a few weeks after my arrival in the town with the main agenda item being the appointment of a coach. The position had been advertised both in country and city newspapers some weeks earlier. The club was reasonably well off as 1956 had been a La Niña year resulting with the plentiful rain coming at the right time. Around 50 millimetres (20 inches) had fallen that year compared with the average of around 30 millimetres (12 inches).

The Club secretary, **Greg Kelly**, announced that there had been a few applicants with one, John Lane, who looked "pretty good". The meeting settled on making an offer to Lane, only 23, who had played with Richmond seconds for a couple of years, and was a ruckman for Camberwell in the VFA in the previous season. Furthermore, he was a bank teller who had work and accommodation in Swan Hill. The motion moved by Greg Kelly that "the club offers the position of coach to John Lane at 20 pounds per week" (more than I earned as a teacher) was passed.

Training started about a month before the commencement of the season with one intra-club practice before the first game. I was pleased to hear my name read out, over 3SH (Swan Hill), on the half-forward flank for my first game in open age competition against Tooleybuc, coached by Reg Goodes, from South Melbourne, who had played one VFL game with that club.

Snippet

A new club house had been built at Lalbert shortly before I joined the club. While I was there, steps were taken to adorn the walls of the new building with photos of club members. Greg Kelly, whose son Barry Kelly was to become a star player for Lalbert, and who had been Club Secretary for many years was chosen to have his photo on the wall. I was around at the Kelly house shortly after the portrait of Greg had been taken. Greg's wife was a person who liked everything to be "just right". She commented to me that Greg's photo had been taken to go on the clubroom wall but she "wasn't very happy with it and I'd like it to be taken again". Greg, a laconic and much more matter-of-fact person, was heard to mumble, "Bugger it all woman, it's what I look like." The photo wasn't re-taken.

For Greg's services to Lalbert and football in the region, the goal kicking award in the Central Murray League (formerly the Mid-Murray League) is called the "Greg Kelly Award".

Saturday Routine

On the Saturday morning, prior to the first match of the 1957 season I began a routine which would be continued just about every Saturday in the football season for nearly three-and-a-half years. After a breakfast of two fried eggs on toast, washed down with tea and more toast, I cleaned my football boots and, as Mrs Meehan had washed my football gear, packed my bag. If Lalbert was playing at home there was time for a kick of a footy with some of the Meehan boys before a light lunch of sandwiches. We then headed to the ground.

At the same time as I was getting ready, David would be doing likewise for his game, initially in the seconds but, as he got older, in the firsts. Lucy would be getting dressed in her basketball outfit while Phonse made sure that he had his white goal umpire's coat on hand for he was the goal umpire for the seconds.

Meanwhile, Gladys had prepared some goodies which would be on sale at the kiosk, and naturally she would take her turn at serving in the kiosk. And of course the younger children, having had their weekly bath in hot water from the chip heater, would be neatly attired with Maurice, the youngest, in his Lalbert jumper, hand-knitted by his mum. David, Lucy and I would travel in my Morris Minor which I had purchased before Easter that year. The rest of the Meehan family went in the Humber. Phonse, arriving early at the ground, would park his car in the same spot every home game so that his wife could sit in the car and watch the match. But she was usually too excited to do so and, as soon as the seconds' game started, she was on her feet barracking.

The happenings at a country footy match such as at a Lalbert home game in that era is perhaps better described by **Graham Cornes** in his "Full Foreword" to A. and M. Madigan's' publication *Bush Legends – South Australian Country Footy Stories*. He writes:

> Country football is mateship; it's cars circling the oval, horns blaring; it's freshly baked pies; it's the smell of rain as it sweeps

across the land *(not so often at Lalbert)*; it's the locals gathering their cans and eskies; it's the social clubs working selflessly in the background to keep their team on the ground: most of all, it's the kids running, laughing and squealing as they play.

Many a country person would recognise that scene painted by Cornes. After the match, most of the players would adjourn to the Lalbert Pub to talk about the game while the women and the few non-drinkers, including Phonse and David, would have similar discussions at the Café. Gladys would buy meat pies for the evening meal and all would be home in time to hear the match reports from the other games at 7.30 pm on 3SH. In the evening David, Lucy and I would then go to a dance, sometimes at Lalbert but on occasions at Nullawill, Dumosa, Wycheproof or even as far as Charlton. (Some time later, both David and Lucy married Charlton people).

The above whole-day pattern remained much the same for games at Quambatook and Lake Boga, however for games at Swan Hill and further north there were slight changes. As these matches involved travelling through Swan Hill, meat pies were usually "the order of the day" for lunch at a café in Swan Hill, which was also the venue for the evening meal. The "watering hole" for Lalbert players after such matches was the White Swan Hotel. I would join other players there and drink tomato juice before venturing to the Memorial Hall in Swan Hill for a dance.

When Lalbert played at Balranald, a "wet-the-whistle" stop was usually made at Goodnight, a very small township on the Murray River, to obtain a drink to clear the dust from throats of the players and supporters. The stop often proved to be a "good night".

This routine of taking much of Saturday morning to get ready for the football and travel to the venue, followed by playing or watching the game in the afternoon, and then indulging in some social activity into the night had been enjoyed by my dad Mick Reed and his family at

Costerfield, and by many other Victorian families before that time and long since – up to the 21st century. It has been the heart of community life for many small and large Victorian country towns over that time.

The behavioural pattern for Sunday was much the same for the Meehan household for the whole of the year, with Mass in the morning, followed by the "Catholic Hour" at the pub or soft drinks at the café. Then there was a return to the family farm for a light lunch. In the afternoon it was golf at the home or on the Lalbert course. Social tennis replaced golf in the summer.

With such sports-saturated weekends in country towns it is no wonder that so many of our champions come from the bush. While I haven't done or seen any research on the subject, it is my impression that a disproportionate number of VFL/AFL footballers come from regional areas when compared with their metropolitan counterparts.

Demographic and Economic Changes

When Mick Reed left his Costerfield home to work for the Victoria Railways in 1924 he was part of a trend of people moving from rural areas of the state to Melbourne. In the gold rush days during the 19th century the bulk of the state's population lived in the country – that was where the gold was found. However as gold petered out and with the seasonal fluctuations that affected life on the land, many young people, seeking the attractions of city life and the possibility of employment there, moved to Melbourne.

In 1921 half of the State's population lived in Melbourne. By 1933 that portion had risen to 54 per cent, with it rising again to 60 per cent shortly after the end of World War II. By 2001 72 per cent of Victoria's population lived in Melbourne. The movement to "the Big Smoke" was mainly from Victorian rural areas before World War II, but after that War much of the capital city's growth could be attributed to migrants from overseas.

"Back to Costerfield – 1958"

Early in 1958, my second year at Lalbert, I heard from my family that there was to be a "Back To Costerfield" in March of that year. Dad, Mum and my siblings were to attend. So, accompanied by David Meehan, I travelled from Lalbert and stayed at a hotel in Heathcote, to attend my first "Back To". The program at Costerfield included a Welcome Dance on the Friday evening, a School Roll Call, read by teacher George Hird, on the Saturday morning, a cycle road race and sports meeting on the Saturday afternoon with an Old Time Dance following in the evening. Church services were scheduled for Sunday morning with the event winding up with a "pleasant Sunday afternoon" during which appropriate farewell speeches were made.

Perhaps the most memorable part of the "Back To" for me was meeting some of the men with whom Dad had played footy and hearing them talk and rib each other about their footy days. Men were introduced as "our star ruckman", "a fast wingman", "a rough backman", "a hot-headed individual" or some other appropriate description.

When I met **George Hird,** mention was made of the fact that Dad and he had played together at Mooroombool West and in the 1919 premiership team for Costerfield. Young Allan Hird's successful football career was also commented upon as was the fact that we had seen Allan play in a Grand Final when he was playing coach of Essendon seconds.

The success at Geelong of young Fred LeDeux, the son of another ex-Mooroombool West player, was also brought up in conversation. His dad, Fred Snr, had played with Mooroombool West when his father allowed him to have a Saturday away from their farm. I knew that young Fred had been a top athlete and footballer at Assumption College, Kilmore.

We all enjoyed the 1958 "Back to Costerfield". Dad looked very much at home in the Costerfield environment. It was the first of a number of such "Back To" and "Reunion" celebrations that I have attended.

Such functions, whether held for dying towns, closing schools, school anniversaries, sporting (particularly footy) clubs or other institutions, were a most enjoyable part of the social landscape for many people in the second half of the 20th century.

Snippet

When I was teaching in the Mallee I found that many towns held special events, often annually, to bring people and money into the town.

One such event was the Dimboola Regatta which I once attended with a couple of mates. I wore a new, big "farmer's hat" to shelter my head from the sun.

It was a fun day with a carnival atmosphere and boat races on the Dimboola River, followed by a dance in the evening.

There was artist there who drew, for a fee, sketches of anyone willing to sit for a while. My friends told the artist that I was the head teacher of a rural school and that I was a left footer who kicked the occasional goal. Above is the unsigned artist's impression of me.

Our popular Head

12
Country Footy and the Rose Brothers

Country Footy, the Cats in form, Lalbert stars, a Footy Trip; Rochester FC, Castlemaine FC, Lalbert FC, Collingwood FC, Geelong FC, Shepparton FC, Tatura FC; Keith Warburton, Ron Paez, Glen Bow, Geoff Cooper, Bill McMaster, Fred Flanagan, Bill Ryan, Colin Rice, Jack O'Connor and Noel McMahon.

Lalbert won their first game of the 1957 season against Tooleybuc as they had a good team. John Lane was an impressive ruckman but a couple of the Lalbert boys, **Jack O'Connor**, the head teacher at the nearby Meatian school, and Ian Michel, a local farmer, were at least as talented as Lane. There were a number of experienced players from the 1952 premiership team still playing including defenders Arch Alexander, Bruce Jobling and high marking Rob Allen, wingman Max Nalder, forwards Max McGregor and Maurie Power as well as rovers Pat Power and Don McGregor. Younger players, John Curthoys. Gordon and Ken Allen also showed a lot of promise.

Rob Allen, a left footed centre half-back was similar in style to Geelong's Harry Taylor. He was rarely beaten in a contested mark and usually seemed to be in the right spot for an uncontested mark. One day at Nyah on their large oval beside the Murray River, Rob took nine marks in a closely contested final quarter to save the game for Lalbert.

A few weeks into the season Lalbert played Swan Hill at the Swan Hill oval. This was an important game for me as it was broadcast live over 3SH which meant that Dad and Mum in Oakleigh could pick up patches of the play despite the poor reception on the radio.

It was also a thrill for me as I was switched to the centre, just before half-time, to play on the Swan Hill centre-man, Graeme Kerr. I had seen Kerr play for Melbourne in the VFL seconds finals in 1956. Melbourne had won the premiership and Kerr, who played a few senior games with Carlton and Melbourne, won the Gardiner Medal for Best and Fairest in the VFL seconds that year. He had moved to Swan Hill to practise Law. Trying to keep up with Kerr was certainly a challenge.

Blisters

One of the problems with playing footy in the Mallee in the 1950s was the fact that as a result of the dry climate and the lack of watering facilities at football grounds, the footy ovals were very hard. As the season progressed I had problems with blisters. The pressure on my stops from the hard ground caused them to make indentations in the sole of my boots which in turn led to the blisters.

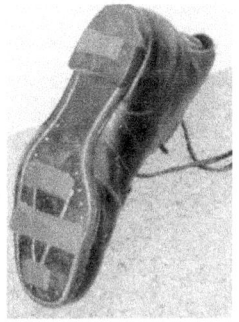

Phonse advised me to put bars, rather than stops, on my boots. Bars were strips of leather something like the lugs on large tractor tyres which went right across the sole of the boots. The above photo shows some imitation bars (made from Play-Doh) on the soles of an old high sided boot designed to protect the ankles The bars were about 1.5 centimetres high and they spread the pressure more evenly across the boot forming no indentations in the base of the boot. I replaced my stops with the bars and there were no more blisters.

Bobby Rose (NEWSPIX)

Bobby Rose, the great Collingwood player, once said that he used the same strategy to prevent blisters when he was playing with

Nyahwest where the four Rose boys, who played for Collingwood, grew up. Bobby Rose was an all-time Collingwood champion, playing 152 games with the Club and kicking 214 goals. He won the Magpies' Best and Fairest award on four occasions. Regarded by many as Collingwood's best post-World War II player, he was selected as centre in the Magpies' Team of the Century and inducted into the Australian Hall of Fame in 1996 and, as a tribute to his fearlessness as a player, the AFL Players' Association's Annual Award for most courageous player is named after Bob Rose.

A memorial statue in honour of Bob Rose was unveiled outside the main entrance of Melbourne Sports and Entertainment Centre, the home of the Collingwood Football Club, in 2006.

One of the first players to go to the country, to coach Ovens and Murray League (O&ML) team Wangaratta Rovers in 1955, Rose returned to coach Collingwood from 1964 until 1971, being the unlucky coach when the Magpies lost the flag to St Kilda by one point in 1966.

Snippet

Another footballer to coach in the county around the same time as Bob Rose was Fitzroy's **Bill Stephen** who went to Yarrawonga. A safe mark and an excellent kick he was an outstanding back pocket player. He had been club Best and Fairest twice and had represented Victoria 14 times before going to Yarrawonga. He also later returned to Melbourne to coach both Fitzroy and Essendon.

Bill Stephen

Times were different in those days for VFL footballers. The fact that such good players left Melbourne, to play and coach in the bush, was a sign of the times. VFL footballers were very poorly paid compared with players of today. A country job which often included employment and free accommodation, as well as a good coaching fee, could give a footballer a worthwhile reward for his efforts on the football field. Furthermore, if he were successful he might be able to obtain a better paid and higher status position with a VFL club.

Robert Rose Jnr, Bobby's son, also played football for Collingwood and interstate cricket for Victoria before he was left a quadriplegic as a result of a road accident. Bobby's brother, **Kevin Rose**, had more games for Collingwood than his more famous sibling, playing 159 games and kicking 47 goals. A rugged utility player he later coached Prahran to two flags in the VFA and was subsequently president of the Magpies.

Another brother, **Bill Rose**, played 40 games with the 'pies and, like Bobby, was member of the 1953 premiership side. Bill with Bobby and Neil Mann, formed their first ruck combination. **Ralph Rose**, the baby of the family, played 23 games with Collingwood. Both Bill and Ralph played for Nyahwest when I played with Lalbert against that club in 1957. Ralph, still on the way up, did very well on that occasion.

There was a controversial incident the 1953 VFL Grand Final in which both Bob and Bill Rose played. Geelong had an outstanding ruckman, **Bill McMaster**, who had been a key player in their 1951 and 1952 premiership teams. McMaster, who was playing very well, was felled in the third quarter, badly injured, taken from the ground and then to St Vincent's hospital. He was suffering from concussion and a bruised kidney. Football writer for *The Sun*, Kevin Hogan, wrote of the incident as follows:

> In an all out effort to win no Collingwood man spared a backward glance for Geelong's best ruckman, Bill McMaster, lying obviously badly hurt in the centre of the ground. The fact that McMaster had gone down in a pack from which the ball had already been swept away was only another spur to make certain the advantage was not wasted.

In a low scoring game, the Magpies kicked five goals to two in the third term to build on their small half-time lead to ensure their two goal victory.

In an article in the *2011 Toyota AFL Grand Final Record*, Bill McMaster said of the 1953 Grand Final:

> I got injured in the 1953 Grand Final. To this day I don't how it happened. I had no idea where I was until I woke up in hospital and Father Brosnan was standing over me; I didn't think that was a very good sign. I had bleeding kidneys.

Ever generous Collingwood patron, John Wren, was so pleased with the Magpies' victory in the 1953 Grand Final that he contributed 500 pounds to the Players' Fund on their victory. This was on top of the 500 pounds that Wren's sons Joseph and John Jnr, had given prior to the finals for the team's efforts throughout the year. In the days when VFL footballers received only single digit match payments these were very generous amounts. And, of course, Wren was still slipping money in a handshake to individual players who played well in a particular game.

On one occasion Lou Richards was on the receiving end of a handshake only to find that it contained only one pound instead of the expected £10. But Wren noted the mistake and gave Richards the ten pounds when he next saw him. Wren declined Richards' offer to return the original pound.

Co-incidentally, both John Wren and his great ally Jock McHale died within a month of that great 1953 victory. McHale suffered a heart attack after the game, passing away on the 6 October. Wren, who may have over-taxed himself struggling through the huge crowd to get to the end to which the Magpies were kicking in the last quarter, passed away on 26 October. Both men had seen the Magpies' first premiership since their back-to-back flags in 1935-36 when McHale was coach.

Early Retirement

Bill McMaster played 61 games and kicked 75 goals for Geelong and retired at the young age of 24 to return to his farm and take on the position of playing coach of the struggling Mortlake team in the Hampden League. In his seven years in that role he lifted his team to compete, without success, in four Grand Finals. However, while at Mortlake, he had success as a coach of the inter-league side. Over the years that McMaster was involved, that team included some very good players such as former Essendon premiership big man Ken Timms, ex-Geelong players Stuart Lord, Glen Bow and John O'Neill, as well as legendary Warrnambool goal-kicker Stan Noakes. The Hampden team had victories over the Ballarat League, the Ovens and Murray League and the Peninsula League.

McMaster returned to Geelong as coach in 1970-71, a period during which Geelong were team-building after some success in the mid to late '60s. Years later I had the pleasure of meeting Bill McMaster. He is a man about whom one never hears a bad word. Bill has another claim to fame in that it was he who signed up Gary Ablett Snr when Ablett was playing for Myrtleford. Former Geelong player, Greg Nicholls, was coach of Myrtleford at the time, and McMaster is said to have asked Nicholls if "he would mind having a talk to him (Ablett) and see if he's at all interested in playing League football again?" Ablett was; Nicholls lost his leading player and Ablett became a superstar.

Fred Flanagan

While the Magpies had the two Roses from the Mid-Murray League in their team for that final, Geelong also had former Mid-Murray players in winger Bert Worner and captain Fred Flanagan. Worner's cousin, Keith Worner, played for Lalbert during my time there.

Fred Flanagan, who once kicked 13 goals for Swan Hill as a teenager, became a champion for the Cats. A high marking, long kicking centre half-forward he captained the all-conquering Geelong flag-winning teams in 1951-52. He was the club Best and Fairest in 1949, runner-up in the 1950 Brownlow Medal, centre half-forward in the Cats' Team of the Century and a member of the AFL Hall of Fame. He was a member of the Victorian side in each of the nine full seasons he played with the club, representing his state 21 times and was captain and coach in a game against South Australia in 1952.

A soldier in World War II, he fought on the well-known Kokoda Track where a comrade was shot dead by a Japanese sniper as he was moving through the jungle beside Flanagan. Fred was later decorated for his actions in the swamps of Bougainville including his solo charging of an enemy gunner. After the War, Fred was a tireless worker for Legacy for 34 years, taking his turn to be President of the Geelong branch.

It is said of Flanagan in the *Geelong Advertiser* that one of his favourite football stories was when he tossed the coin with Lou Richards, the Collingwood captain during the 1950s finals. After shaking hands with Flanagan, Richards said to Fred, words along the lines of "Right. You come near me again you big bastard and I'll dropkick your bloody head over that grandstand."

Lalbert's 1957 season

Lalbert's form was a little up and down during 1957 but they came with a rush towards the end of the season, winning the last seven games and ending the season in second place, behind Swan Hill with Nyah in third position.

Lalbert lost the first semi-final against Swan Hill and went down against Nyah in the preliminary final. **Jack O'Connor,** Lalbert's Best and Fairest winner that year, played both games with a broken bone in his wrist. Swan Hill went on to win the flag. Swan Hill's best player in the final series was Neville Martin who went to Geelong in the next season, playing every game in their senior side, before returning to play for Swan Hill in the following year. Martin was an example of a player, of which there were many in those times, who could have had successful VFL careers but who did not persist at that level, usually because they were happy following their chosen careers at home, at a time when playing for an AFL team was less lucrative than it later became.

Best Player Awards

Unlike at Costerfield a generation earlier, where I found no evidence of players being singled out to receive trophies, the Lalbert club did give two trophies – the Best and Fairest and Best in the Finals awards.

However, from to time to time trophies were donated by supporters or businesses to players for their efforts in individual games. Dick Makeham, a local farmer, always donated a trophy to the best Lalbert and Quambatook players, in the firsts and the seconds, when the match was played at Lalbert. That year I was awarded the trophy in the seniors and David Meehan was successful in the seconds, while his sister, Lucy, picked up a trophy in the basketball (netball) match. As can be seen in the above photo, five-year-old Maurice, in his Lalbert jumper insisted on being in the photo.

Representative Games and the Ryan Brothers

In 1957, during the split round in the VFL, Carlton visited Swan Hill and played a representative Mid-Murray League team. As a curtain-raiser to the main game, a match between two Mid-Murray teams was played. One team was picked from the five teams north of Swan Hill and one from the five teams south of Swan Hill. I was one of the Lalbert representatives in the "South" team while Andy Ryan from Tyntynder was in the "North" Team. I mention Andy because of his high marking ability. Tall and somewhat heavily built, his ability to fly for a mark was quite surprising but he was surpassed in this skill by his brother Bill Ryan who was recruited by Geelong playing his first game with the Cats in 1963.

Capable of playing either centre half-back, centre half forward or in the ruck, Bill Ryan was a genuine high mark – one he took against St Kilda in 1965 is still regarded as one of the best ever. In 1971 he was 5th in the Brownlow Medal with a highlight that year being the winning goal he kicked after the final siren against Collingwood. In all he played 220 games for the Cats and kicked 220 goals. On leaving the Cats in 1973, Bill coached in Queensland at Coorparoo and Southport appearing in five premiership sides. In 1974 and 1975 Ryan captained the Queensland interstate side, leading them to a win against Tasmania, the first time that a Queensland team had beaten one of the southern Aussie Rules playing states. Ryan's five goals helped towards the victory.

The best two players for the Mid-Murray team against Carlton were **Glen Bow,** the Quambatook captain and coach, and **Geoff Cooper,** an indigenous player from Woorinen who kicked seven goals. Cooper played with the skills and vision of the many indigenous men playing AFL football today. He moved to Shepparton in the following year – a great loss to Woorinen and the Mid-Murray League.

Glen Bow, a beautifully built ruckman, was a great country footballer. Coming from Western Australia, he played about 20 games for Geelong in 1954-56. Still only 22 years old, he was offered the position as captain and coach of Quambatook. The position also had another job plus a house going with it. He sought advice from his Geelong coach, Reg Hickey, as to whether he should take the position. Hickey asked, "How much will you get?" To which Bow replied, "£25 pounds a week plus a job and a house to live in, rent free". Hickey's response was, "Crikey, take it. I'm getting only £12 ten shillings here."

So Bow took the job. He played two years with Quambatook, winning the club and competition Best and Fairest awards in both years. He then

A One-Eyed Look at Aussie Rules 159

moved around the country as a professional footballer, winning many other club and competition Best and Fairest awards. He passed away on Boxing Day in 2007 after a battle with cancer.

Other Mid-Murray Stars

Fred Flanagan, Bill Ryan and Neville Martin were not the only Swan Hill players who went to Geelong in the '50s. John Thomas, a half-forward who played with Neville Martin against Lalbert in 1957, joined Martin there in 1958 and played 35 games for the Cats.

Just the year before, **Colin Rice** played his first game with Geelong. Colin Rice, a rover or back pocket player was extremely hard at the ball and was a member of their 1963 flag-winning side. He was Best and Fairest in 1959 and in the following year he acted as captain in place of the injured Ron Hovey. In 1964 he transferred to Glenelg in the SANFL.

Colin's brother, John, was also a very good player for Swan Hill but John's football career was different from that of Colin. He made a name for himself as a journalist writing about football for the *Sporting Globe*. John's son Dean Rice was a very successful player for both the Saints and the Blues, playing over 100 games with each club after he had initially been rejected by the Cats. Injuries caused him to leave the Saints but the Blues were willing to take a punt on him and as a tough player he added strength to their half-forward line in their 1995 premiership year.

A thirteen-year-old left footer was an outstanding junior footballer at Tooleybuc, in the Mid-Murray League when I was at Lalbert. He won the Best and Fairest in the Mid-Murray league in 1962. The lad was later to make a name for himself in VFL football, playing 94 games with Geelong and kicking 109 goals, including four in the 1967 Grand Final. He was a member of the 1963 premiership team and was third in the Brownlow Medal in 1966, playing both in defence and in attack.

One of the classiest footballers of his era, John Sharrock, the lad from Tooleybuc, had to retire at age 24 as a because of a knee injury.

Footy Trip

Lalbert took an end of season footy trip as did most clubs at the time. In this instance it was to Shepparton. The weekend of the trip coincided with the Goulburn Valley League Grand Final which was played at Shepparton.

Along with 9,000 fans, the Lalbert boys went to the Deakin Oval to watch the match between Shepparton and Tatura. This was of particular interest to the Lalbert lads because Peter Collins, an ex-Mallee boy, known to many of the group, was in the centre for Shepparton.

Both clubs were captained and coached by well known ex-VFL players. **Keith Warburton**, a centreman or forward, from Brighton in the VFA and Carlton in the VFL, coached Tatura, while **Ron Paez**, a strongly built ex-South Melbourne utility player, coached Shepparton. The game turned out to be a cracker with no more than three goals separating the teams throughout the afternoon.

In the last quarter the match was even, with both coaches making Herculian efforts for their teams who went goal for goal. Warburton, moved from the centre to full forward, was especially good at that time. Three times he goaled to wrest the lead for his team during that quarter, once after a brilliant mark and another from a snap after a very clever piece of play.

In the report of the match on the following Monday, the *Shepparton News* claimed that "the match produced what must have been 'the goal of the year and the mark of the year', both to Warburton in an inspired last quarter".

But never to be denied, Shepparton were in front with only seconds to go when Warburton had one more opportunity, easier than any of the earlier ones, but this time he scored only a behind from his shot at goal. The bell rang and Shepparton were in front of Tatura by two points. They deserved the flag but I felt sorry for Tatura and for Warburton whom I had admired from the times he had played for Brighton against the Oaks.

The paper also reported that Collins, North and Howlett (of

Shepparton) took the honours across the centre, while Paez, James and McManus were in the ascendancy across the first line of attack.

The value of ex-VFL players, not yet past their prime, to country teams was demonstrated in this match.

For the rest of the footy trip, as I didn't drink at the time, I was able to sit back and watch the others enjoy themselves – and enjoy themselves they did!

I was moved to write the following verse about the excursion when I returned home. (I wasn't game to pin it on the notice board at the Lalbert pub).

The Footy Trip

The season continues after finals are won.
The best part of the year is yet to come.
Off go the boys and the well-wishers too,
To some far off town, where friends are few.
From the local pub the trip begins
A few beers for the road, or maybe a gin.
The road is dry, and this flamin' dust
Makes the next town with a pub, a must.
They only stop at a pub or inn,
Soon few boys know just where they've bin.
The weekend passes, for most too quick.
What's this I see? A young lad sick.
"His first footy trip," his mate reveals,
"The bugger's brought up all his meals."
On Sunday night the return is made.
The lad can boast for the next decade,
"Best footy trip I've ever had,
But please don't tell me Mum and Dad."

Snippet

Jack O'Connor, the Lalbert ruckman, married on the first Saturday of the May school holidays in 1957. He didn't play for Lalbert on that day. His bride was Fay Mooring. Fay's brother, Jim Mooring was a rover/forward for Carlton in the 1945 "bloodbath" Grand Final between Carlton and South Melbourne. Don Grossman, the Swans defender was disqualified for eight weeks for striking Mooring in that Grand Final. Coming to the Blues from Bendigo, Jim Mooring was a beautiful mover and won the Carlton Best and Fairest award in 1942.

Season 1958

The next season saw Lalbert a weaker team.

Coach John Lane had been transferred elsewhere in the bank and 1957 Best and Fairest Jack O'Connor had taken up a teaching appointment near Rochester. I had a very high opinion of O'Connor. A tall, well built and very strong ruckman/forward he could use both sides of his body to kick, handpass or palm the ball. He was a good high mark and excellent on the ground for a big man. And the tougher the game, the better he liked it. However Lalbert's loss was Rochester's gain, as that club, playing in the strong Bendigo League, was quick to sign him up.

The Head Teacher of the Lalbert School, Don Mariager, an experienced ruckman from over Horsham way, took over the playing coach role and Jack Gilmore, a local player, who had been paid to play in the premiership team with Swan Hill in the previous year, returned to Lalbert. A talented, tough and talkative player, Jack was a good man to have on your side. He used to try to "get players in". One day when playing against Quambatook Jack was at full-forward. During the previous week his opposing full-back had paid a record price of £20 per acre for land near Quambatook. It was a very windy Saturday and Jack spent the afternoon stirring the full-back in a loud voice:

"Who'd pay 20 quid an acre for land at Quambatook?"

"Look it's blowing away!"

"You'll have to go to Wycheproof to put in your crop."

"Not many bags to the acre this year."

"You'll never pay off that block."

"You'd better pray for rain."

Jack was a skilled sledger and it usually put off his opponent. But not always.

On another occasion, when Lalbert was playing at Balranald and Jack was playing at full-forward he told me, when we were running onto the ground, to "watch me while I get this full-back in".

As soon as the ball was bounced there was a great kerfuffle in the Lalbert goal square. Goal umpires, being provided by the teams playing, couldn't report misdemeanours. However, sensing trouble, the central umpire stopped play in time to catch Gilmore throwing punches at the full back.

I wasn't sure who got whom in, but Gilmore was later given four weeks suspension by the Tribunal.

Even with Don Mariager and Jack Gilmore, the side missed O'Connor and Lane considerably and didn't make the finals.

Other Rural School Teachers

I was pleased in 1958 when two of my footballing mates from teachers' college, Kevin Jenkins and Paddy Rohan, were posted to schools in the Mallee/Wimmera region. Kevin Jenkins ("Jenko") was appointed to the Cannie School as Head Teacher. Cannie is about half way between Quambatook and Lalbert on the railway line. Jenko boarded with Ray Free and his family. Ray supported Quambatook so Jenko was signed up to play with that team. The two Kevins were to be rivals, but Kevin Jenkins had the luxury of roving to Glen Bow.

Paddy Rohan, the other friend, was appointed to be Head Teacher of the Wilkur South School, located between Watchem and Warracknabeal. Paddy, a solid back-pocket player was signed by Watchem-Corack in the North Central League. Bob and Rhonda Taylor, with whom Pat boarded, followed that team. The three rural school teacher friends were able to visit each other from time to time and were made welcome by the respective families with whom they boarded.

At the end of the season and with none of their teams making the finals, Jenko, Paddy and I went to Bendigo to watch the Grand Final in the Bendigo Football League between Rochester and Castlemaine. The match, at the Queen Elizabeth Oval in Bendigo, was played before a crowd of 18,000 fans. Rochester was coached by **Noel McMahon,** former premiership captain of Melbourne in 1955 and 1956, as well as being a member of the 1948 premiership side. He was a fearless centre half-back.

The playing-coach for Castlemaine was Ray Poulter, my former hero from the Tigers. I was really looking forward to seeing Poulter in action once more, but I was disappointed as Poulter was a last minute withdrawal because of an injury.

My ex-Lalbert team-mate, Jack O'Connor was picked as centre half-forward for Rochester. The game was rugged and close but didn't reach a high standard. Rochester won by seven points. McMahon was one of the best for Rochester while Jack O'Connor, using plenty of vigour, took six marks and kicked a goal. There was a great celebration in the Rochester camp as it was their first Flag since they joined the Bendigo League in 1915. They won the premiership in the seconds as well, adding more merriment to the occasion!

13

The Demon Era and "Bluey" Shelton

The Demon Era, Demon Champions; Alexandra FC, Watchem/Corack FC, Lalbert FC, Alexandra FC, Birchip FC, Cudgewa FC, Melbourne FC, Collingwood FC, Essendon FC; Ron Barassi Jnr, Norm Smith, "Mulga" Shelton, the Chittys, Rob Fox, Eddie Jackson, the Andersons, Brian Carroll and MMFL stars.

In 1958, when former Melbourne premiership captain, Noel McMahon, headed to Rochester, the Demons were around the middle of a period when they played seven Grand Finals in a row. They were runners-up to Footscray in 1954 but won the flag in 1955, 1956 and 1957. However they lost to Collingwood in 1958 before winning two more flags in 1959 and 1960. Ron Barassi, John Beckwith, Big Bob Johnson, Laurie Mithen, Brian Dixon and "Tassie" Johnson were key players in that era – the list could go on. Probably, the most famous of them all was Ron Barassi.

Ronald Dale Barassi was born at Castlemaine in 1936 and spent his early years living in Guildford with his grandfather Carlo because his widowed mother had to remain in Melbourne to work and obtain money for the family. Carlo Barassi, like many who came to the diggings, failed to find gold and turned to agriculture to make a living.

Young Barassi was a promising footballer who was determined to follow in his father's footsteps and play with Melbourne; but in those days this would not have been possible because of the zoning rules. Each of the 12 clubs in the VFL at that time had a zone in Victoria from which they could recruit players and young Ron didn't live in Melbourne's zone.

As the Melbourne Football Club had kept a careful eye on young Ron since his father's death they lobbied for a rule change that would allow him to play for the Demons. It was at the Melbourne Football Club's instigation that the father-son rule was brought in. This rule has rightly allowed many young men to have the opportunity to emulate, or even exceed, the deeds of their father, at what is normally their family's favoured club, irrespective of the zone in which the potential VFL player lived.

As Ron Snr had played 58 games with the club, Ron Jnr was signed by Melbourne when he was playing with Preston Scouts in 1952. When his mother moved to Tasmania, young Ron moved into a bungalow in the home of Melbourne coach, **Norm Smith**. Barassi always acknowledges the role that Smith, a natural leader and role model for young men, played in his development as a man and as a footballer. And what a champion young Barassi was to become!

Ron Barassi Jnr is one of the all-time best-known VFL/AFL footballers. Not only was he a champion player and captain, playing in six premierships for Melbourne, being captain in two of those, but he was also an outstanding coach. He surprised the football world by moving to Carlton in 1965 where he coached that team to two flags. In 1973 he took on the challenge of coaching North Melbourne and had success with that club taking them to their first flag in 1975, to be repeated in 1977. After a less successful stint at his original club he retired in 1985 only to be asked, in 1993, to take on the task of coaching the Swans who were struggling after their move to Sydney. He was able to lift that club out of the doldrums by the time he retired in 1995.

If the Demons, under the leadership of Smith and with Barassi at his peak, had won the premiership in 1958 as well, they would have had six flags in a row, a record unlikely to be ever beaten. Prior to 1958 and up to the present day Collingwood's record of four flags from 1927 to 1930 stands supreme.

In 1958, assisted by wet weather and led by acting captain, Murray

Weideman, and ruckman, Barry "Hooker" Harrison, the Magpies played extremely tough football and reversed a 45 point defeat in the second semi-final to defeat the Demons by three goals, thus keeping their premiership record intact. Had Noel McMahon played another season, perhaps the result would have been different. McMahon was one of the most vigorous defenders in the League, well known for his strong dashes out of defence. He had flattened Bobby Rose with one such dash in the 1957 Grand Final. The wet conditions in 1958 would have suited him. McMahon might have put the lid on some of the Collingwood aggression and allowed the Demons' game to flow more freely.

Snippet

Ex-Geelong player and Fremantle coach Damian Drum worked as an Assistant Coach to Ron Barassi when Barassi took over the coaching role at Sydney. Once I heard Damian address the guests at a dinner where he was the key note speaker. Among other remarks that he made during his speech, he spoke extremely highly of Ron Barassi, claiming that he was a great Australian. He praised Barassi's integrity and his honesty and claimed that he possessed a rare quality found in people. He pointed out that Barassi wanted to hear what people had to say about an issue and would argue strongly for or against a point of view but once the discussion was over Barassi would bear no animosity against his verbal combatant. Things would continue as if the debate had not occurred. As this was the case, people felt free to point out their concerns to Barassi.

Barassi could separate the person from the argument – a great quality in a leader; others can't do this so easily.

"Mulga" Shelton at Lalbert – 1959

The 1959 season was much better for Lalbert. Younger players including John Curthoys, Ken and Gordon Allen, as well as Dermott and Gary Power, were improving immensely. Furthermore Barry Kelly, a star centre half-back and sprinter from St Pat's Ballarat, who had played for

Lalbert only in school holidays in 1958, was home for good. And David Meehan was learning to make better use of his height in the ruck. But to top it all, a new coach had been signed up – John "Mulga" Shelton.

Mulga came originally from Koo-wee-rup in East Gippsland and had played six games for Fitzroy. He earned his nickname because of his hardness at the ball. Not an eloquent speaker and no strategist he inspired his team by his example, being an excellent mark and an accurate kick, and always looking for an opportunity to shepherd for one of his team-mates. With regard to Mulga's coaching it also must be said that in the days when "you only handball if you are in trouble", "you keep to your position", "you never kick across goals", and "you go back and take your kick if you take a mark", Mulga did encourage a "play on" style more so than most coaches of that era and this accounted, to some extent, for Lalbert's success.

Disappointment

The season began well and after nine rounds, when each team had played each other once, Lalbert was on top having only one loss, against Lake Boga, by a point.

Although Lalbert drew with both Nyah and Lake Boga in the second half of the season they were well on top of the ladder when they came to play Quambatook in the fifth last round of the "home and away" games. Lalbert won well. The Dick Makeham trophy for Lalbert went to rover Pat Power. My friend, Jenko, won the trophy for Quambatook. It was written of him in the *Quambatook Times*, "He gives all he has got, and gets plenty dealt to him. He never complains, but gets up off the turf and goes in all the harder."

On the Sunday following the Quambatook match, after a game of golf at Lalbert in the afternoon, I was hit with severe abdominal pain. Phonse drove me to see the nearest doctor at Wycheproof, who diagnosed my problem as appendicitis, necessitating an immediate operation at the Wycheproof Hospital.

The operation was a success but I was left with a 12 centimetre scar. I was told by the doctor that I had "six weeks off work and there is no possibility that you could play football for the rest of the season". I spent a week in the Wycheproof hospital, during which time my mum, Muriel, stayed with the Meehans who took her to visit me every day.

I returned home to Melbourne to recuperate. Lalbert ended the season on top of the ladder but went out "in straight sets", losing narrowly to both Nyah and Lake Boga. In all, Lalbert had three losses and played two draws for the season. The total of their losing margins for the three losses was 14 points – a disappointing season for Lalbert and for me.

Snippet

The drawn game between Lalbert and Lake Boga in the second round of the draw shows how keen the competition was between these teams in 1959. Each team scored only six goals for the match, with Lalbert kicking five of theirs in the first half. Lalbert led by two points at the last change and kicked only six behinds in the last quarter. Boga kicked eight behinds to close the gap. Only four goals were kicked after half-time. The best players for Lalbert were J Gilmore, A. Alexander, K.Allen and P. Power, while Boga were best served by L. Mitchell, N. Woods, N. Masters and G Carmichael.

I had travelled from Melbourne to watch the preliminary final between Lalbert and Lake Boga at Swan Hill and was asked by the club secretary to pick out Lalbert's best player. Without any doubt in my mind, I chose Coach Shelton as he battled his heart out all day trying to lift his team and, as always, doing some very useful things himself.

A couple of years later, after I had left Lalbert permanently, I returned there to catch up with friends. To my surprise I was told in the Lalbert pub that it was then common knowledge that Shelton had "sold out" in the preliminary final in 1959. He had been paid "to play dead" in the match.

I told my informants that if Mulga had "played dead" then he had certainly fooled me as I had voted him to be Lalbert's best player. I also pointed out that he must have fooled a number of others too as, at the end of the 1959 season, I had been appointed by the club to be on a sub-committee to discuss his re-appointment for 1960. The club, falling on harder times, wanted to keep him on but at slightly a reduced rate. It is hard to control football rumours in country towns (and elsewhere), particularly when money is involved.

Mulga Shelton had a better offer elsewhere and couldn't be convinced to stay. He left the club at the end of the 1959 season. Eventually he played with Dandenong in the VFA.

Lake Boga was beaten in the 1959 Grand Final by Tyntynder who were led by ruckman **Mal Richardson**, an inspiring player and coach.

Despite their quick exit from the final series, Lalbert had some success for the season, as can be seen from the cutting from the *Swan Hill Guardian*. Lalbert centre-man **John Curthoys**, won the Mid-Murray League's Best and Fairest Medal, on a count-back from Nyahwest's Graeme McCartney, who had played with Richmond in the previous year. Mulga Shelton was ninth with eleven votes. Brian Said, from Tyntynder, who also polled well, was an ex-Oakleigh player who had moved to Swan Hill in his employment.

Jim Slattery, who replaced Jack O'Connor at the Meatian School and played for Lalbert, came second in the voting for the seconds' competition. Slattery was a fast and courageous centerline player who could kick equally well with either foot. It surprised me that he wasn't chosen more often to

Major points scored in the voting were:

FIRSTS
John Curthoys (Lalbert) 2, 3, 2, 3, 3, 2, 3, 1, 19; count-back from Graeme McCartney (Nyahwest) 19.

M. Richardson (Tyntynder) 18; R. Clarke (Nyah) 16; P. Phelan (Nyah) 16; N. O'Bree (Swan Hill) 13; I. Dixon (Woorinen) 13; B. Said (Tyntynder) 12; J. Shelton (Lalbert) 11; K. Reid (Lalbert) 10; L. Robinson (Quambatook) 10; G. Carmichael (Lake Boga) 10.

SECONDS
N. Beasy (Woorinen) 2, 3, 3, 2, 3, 13; J. Slattery (Lalbert) 1, 1, 3, 3, 2, 3—13.

play with the firsts. Maybe he was too often distracted by Dot Power at the Lalbert garage. Jim from a large Catholic family over Rochester way, had a sister Monica who became a Brigidine nun. As we have seen, Jack O'Connor played in a premiership team for Rochester. As destiny would have it, Jim Slattery, from Rochester, married Dot Power. Both did well by their changes of location.

Finals – city and bush

Every cloud has a silver lining. I lived back in Melbourne for six weeks while I recovered from my appendix operation. This gave me the opportunity to watch more football, including a semi-final in the VFA, the already-mentioned preliminary final in which Lalbert played, a couple of finals in other country leagues where I had teacher friends playing and also the VFL Grand Final.

One of the matches that I saw after returning home was the first semi-final in the VFA between Oakleigh and Coburg. After being "also-rans" for a few years after their successes in the early 1950s, the Oaks had a resurgence towards the end of the decade. The recruitment from Chelsea of John Coughlan, a natural leader, helped this.

Although Oakleigh had beaten Coburg by 40 points in the last round, Coburg was too good in the semi-final winning by 27 points. The Oaks would have to wait a little longer for their next flag.

In another week of my extended sick leave I journeyed to the north-east of the state to see Alexandra play Broadford in the preliminary final of the Waranga North-East Football League (WNEFL). Jim McKenna, the friend from teachers' college, was teaching at Alexandra and playing for that team. In 1957, Jim had played with Cudgewa, in the Upper Murray League, when he was teaching at Lucyvale, a small rural school out of Corryong. Jim was a quick and handy full-forward or half-forward flanker, who was capable of kicking goals from a good distance.

Bob Chitty and his Brothers

Cudgewa, the team for which Jim McKenna played in 1958, had a famous football export in Bob Chitty, the Carlton captain in the 1945 "bloodbath" premiership. His deeds as a hard man at Carlton are suitably recorded but it is not well known that he was twice Carlton's Best and Fairest. Bob was one of 12 children from a keen football family. One of them, Peter, who had played two games of VFL football for St Kilda before the War, was captured in Singapore by the Japanese and put in the Changi POW camp. After the War, the former Sergeant Peter Chitty was awarded the British Empire Medal (BEM) for his "unselfish conduct and courage" while working on the Burma railway as a POW.

None of the Chitty brothers were playing when Jim McKenna was at Cudgewa but some still followed the club. Jim was having a successful season and doing well in an important match. He took a good mark, near the boundary, a couple of metres in front of his opposing full back who continued on his path and flattened Jim. Players came from everywhere and with some spectators jumping the fence, a real mêlée broke out. Jim, a bit groggy, was about to get up when he heard a voice, from someone bending over him, "Don't get up. The buggers'll kill you. I'll keep guard." Which he did. The speaker was a spectator; one of the Chitty brothers – tough opponents but loyal friends.

An Alexandra Final

After taking up a teaching position at Alexandra in 1958, Jim McKenna quickly found a place on the forward flank for Alexandra.

Jim was pleased that he had Rob Fox playing alongside him at centre half-forward for Alexandra. Fox had played 52 games in that position for Essendon from 1955 to 1957, kicking 34 goals. Not comfortable with city life he returned home to Yaark, near Alexandra, after playing in the Bombers' losing Grand Final side in 1957.

Fortune was kind to Jim in another way as well. Eddie Jackson was playing in front of him in the centre. Eddie Jackson, a member of the 1948 Melbourne Premiership team, was an indigenous footballer who was noted for his great ball handling skills and accurate disposal. In his mid-thirties in 1959, he was still playing good football.

In 1958, Avenel, another team in the WNEFL, enjoyed the services of **Ian "Bluey" Shelton** who would also do well at Essendon. Centre half-back Shelton had some interesting tussles with Fox in 1958 and on occasions Jim McKenna benefited from crumbing their contests. Shelton was second in the WNEFL Best and Fairest Award, being runner-up to Peter Brodie of Euroa. Peter Tossol, who had played for St Bede's College when I was at De La Salle, came third, with Eddie Jackson coming fifth.

Although his career was marred by accident and injury Ian Shelton was very successful at Essendon where he played from 1959 to 1965. One of the toughest backmen of his time, Bluey was centre half-back in the Bombers 1962 flag-winning team and in their runner-up team of 1959. He won the Best First Year Player award in 1959 and twice represented Victoria in interstate matches.

In 1959 Alexandra finished third behind Seymour and Broadford and defeated Avenel in the first semi-final. As Seymour defeated Broadford in the second semi-final, Alexandra had to play Broadford in the preliminary final, the game which I saw. In a hard-slogging contest, Broadford won by 11 points. Fortunately, from my perspective, both of Alexandra's ex-VFL players, Fox and Jackson, did well with Fox kicking four goals and Jackson two. Seymour defeated Broadford in the Grand Final.

Snippet

The Bombers were lucky to get the services of Bluey Shelton. His grandfather, Dick Shelton, as a seven-year-old, nearly drowned when, on his way to school, he fell into the swollen Hughes' Creek at Avenel. A 10-year-old lad, who was passing by, jumped in, pulled young Dick out and took him, wet and shivering, to the nearby Royal Mail Hotel which was owned by the boy's parents. Overwhelmed by the bravery of the young rescuer, they later presented him with a 2.21 metre long green silk sash with a gold bullion fringe on each end.

Fifteen years later, the rescuer was captured at a "shoot out" at the Glenrowan Hotel. He was wearing the sash underneath his armour. That sash, given to the young rescuer whose name was Ned Kelly, is on display at the Benalla Museum.

A Hard Luck Final

Watchem-Corack, Paddy Rohan's team in the North Central League, also made the finals in 1959. Birchip, Watchem-Corack ("The Combine"), St Arnaud and Donald were the top four, with Wedderburn, Wycheproof, Narraport, Charlton and Boort finishing in that order out of the four.

Donald defeated St Arnaud in the first semi-final and Watchem-Corack lowered their colours to Birchip. Euan Gardiner, the Watchem-Corack rover kicked five goals and was best on ground.

The losing team's fullback **Graeme Anderson** had a special mention in the *Charlton Tribune* as he "was fighting against terrific odds with deadly full forward Cook to combat. In the first term Anderson was the hardest worked man on the field and, despite the odds, saved many a good try by Birchip."

The Combine defeated Donald in the preliminary final and had to line up, in the following week, against Birchip, once again at Charlton where the second semi-final had also been played.

According to the *Charlton Tribune* at the time, the decision to play the game at Charlton again caused much consternation among other clubs, particularly Birchip, Watchem-Corack, St Arnaud and Donald, who were teams in the original "line competition". A section of the Ouyen/Mildura train line formed the basis of the league which was first formed in the St Arnaud/Birchip area; just as a part of the Robinvale line was the basis of the competition in which Lalbert once played. To have a footy final, particularly the Grand Final, meant bringing money into the lucky town.

And every town wanted its turn. This continues to be the case today.

Paddy Rohan, who had played for the Combine in both finals, came home to Oakleigh for a week's break after his team had won the preliminary final. He made sure he had a quiet time and kept fit by training with Oakleigh CYMS.

I decided to journey in convoy with Paddy on the Friday before the game and stay overnight with Bob and Rhonda Taylor where Paddy lived. Unfortunately Paddy's car broke down, but with the assistance of a mechanic at Learmonth, who put in hours of work, we arrived at Bob and Rhonda's place at about 1:30 am. Needless to say, Paddy did not perform at his best the next day and Birchip won the flag

The best player for Watchem-Corack was **Brian Carroll** who played as a follower. Gardiner and Anderson also did well. Euan Gardiner had come to the Combine from Essendon seconds and was a very good rover at a time when the Bombers had excellent rovers in Jack Clarke and John Birt. It was impossible for him to break into the Essendon side in the Clarke/Birt era.

The *Charlton Chronicle* also mentioned that Jim Brennan had "played good football throughout the final series". Brennan was a legendary player in the North Central League, being a strong full-forward who was an enormous kick. I saw him play one of his few games at full-forward with Richmond in 1952 but he was too short to hold down the key position.

The Watchem-Corack full-back, **Graeme Anderson**, also played in the VFL. He was recruited by Carlton in 1961 and played 79 games for the Blues mainly in defence. Perhaps the highlight of his career was the replay preliminary final in 1962, when he took two crucial marks against Geelong, in front of a crowd of 99,000 people. Graeme Anderson's father, **Frank Anderson**, had a more distinguished career at Carlton than his son. Coming from Brunswick in the VFA as a full forward he had some success in that position before moving to defence where he played at both full back and centre half-back. He was a beautiful kick, winning a kicking competition against American soldiers, stationed in Melbourne during World War II, using both the Australian and American balls. A vigourous player, he was reported eight times, but suspended only twice, being given four weeks on both occasions. In 1959 he was the "no-nonsense" publican at the Watchem hotel.

Snippet

Follower and half-back flanker, Brian Carroll, was another Watchem-Corack member of that Grand Final side who later played VFL football, having 10 games with Fitzroy in 1963. A bank officer, who worked in a number of different towns, Brian had an excellent career in country football.

A VFL Grand Final

Phonse Meehan, although very interested in footy, had never seen a VFL Grand Final so he made the effort to accompany me to the 1959 one. The match was between the Demons, still at their peak, and Essendon. After an even first half, Big Bob Johnson kicked two goals in quick succession towards the end of the third quarter and Essendon lost momentum, falling away in the last quarter to lose by six goals. Ron Barassi and Alan Rowarth kicked four goals apiece for the Demons while "Bluey" Adams and Johnson each kicked three. Barassi, wingman Ian McLean and Big Bob were best for Melbourne with backmen Shearman and Epis and rover John Birt the Bombers' best.

Thanks to Ned Kelly, Ian Bluey Shelton (from Avenel), was centre half-back for Essendon.

My guest, Phonse, enjoyed the game and was particularly impressed by the colourfulness of the spectacle and the pervasive excitement of the atmosphere at the ground.

Snippet

In the late '50s, Paddy Rohan, Jim McKenna, Ray Clarke, a friend from Oakleigh, and I holidayed at Lorne during the Christmas school holidays. Not many people travelled to distant places like the Gold Coast and Port Douglas in those days. Often VFL players would be seen at Lorne, frequenting the Lorne Hotel or the Pacific Hotel which was run by ex-Collingwood champion Ron Todd. One year Big Bob Johnson and another Oakleigh mate, Les Bibby, stayed a few days at the same guest house as my mates and I. One morning, over breakfast, I asked Big Bob what he thought was necessary for a player to be a League footballer. Big Bob replied, "He must be a good footballer."

"Of course," I commented, "but what specific assets, like pace, marking and kicking ability are the most essential?"

Big Bob responded, "Norm Smith says it's 99 per cent guts and you can split the rest up any way you like."

Norm Smith, the coach of the great Melbourne sides of that era, certainly ensured that his players took that belief to heart.

Final Season with Lalbert

I played only six games with Lalbert in 1960 because I was transferred to Gardiner Central, in Melbourne, for the second term of that year. Coached by Ern Collihole, who had played 17 games with South Melbourne, Lalbert made the finals but were once again unable to win the flag. I had the thrill of kicking a goal with my last kick for Lalbert.

Both David Meehan and Barry Kelly had blossomed as footballers. David, with vigorous Jack Gilmore beside him in the first ruck, came second in the newspaper award for the League's best player. David Meehan and Barry Kelly signed with North Melbourne. Meehan did pre-season training at North in 1961, played five games with the seconds and one with the firsts. He then returned home as he was much happier playing with Lalbert. Barry Kelly did likewise after 14 games in the firsts.

It was most satisfying to play footy with my team mates at Lalbert and I experienced playing against some excellent players in opposition teams, including the McCartney brothers at Nyah, the Old brothers from Tolleybuc, centre-man Gordon Carmichael and rover Bill Ewart from Lake Boga as well as Robin Poole (Swan Hill), Jim Little (Tooleybuc) and Peter Dow (Tyntynder). The latter three later played with North Melbourne.

Another outstanding Mid-Murray League footballer was the previously mentioned Mal Richardson of Tyntynder who began his football career with a team in the Mountain District League. Like Glen Bow, Richardson is an example of an outstanding footballer and leader who, by changing clubs, brought success to another club at a time when it (and the town) was running low on luck. Over the years, there would be many such footballers, across various Victorian country leagues; people who are well remembered long after they have moved on, and are often deservedly called "legends".

A Great Experience

In the 60 games that I played in the Mallee there was only one game where it was too wet to kick drop kicks. Before television in the country, the local football team was the heart and soul of the town and the district. It was talked about in the street, in the pub, after church on Sundays, at clearance sales, and, in my instance, with parents, before and after school. On 3SH, Swan Hill, there were three radio programs that were devoted to the local footy; one on Friday evening when teams were announced and an ex-local champion gave a preview of each game; another on Saturday evening when results were given with a listing of best players, the goal kickers and comments about each game; and thirdly on Sunday morning when the previous day's results were again given and discussed.

Each week the game played on the Swan Hill oval was broadcast. This happened on about ten occasions for me when I was playing in the MMFL. This pleased my parents.

Then there were the newspapers, *The Swan Hill Guardian* and *The Quambatook Times*. These also contained the selected teams, game previews as well as kick-by-kick match descriptions.

There was great motivation to do well, particularly if you were an out-of-towner who was keeping a local boy out of the side. Besides that, there were good crowds and in most instances reasonable change rooms. Lalbert's rooms were among the best in the competition.

Many young rural school teachers of that era would have similar feelings to me about their country football experiences.

As mentioned, I was transferred to Gardiner Central School in Melbourne, to commence in Term 2 in 1960. I had taught at State School Number 4296, Cokum Reserve, for three years and one term. The number of pupils grew, in those baby boomer years, from 11 to 21 but I continued to be the sole teacher. The school, now well closed, served the community for over fifty years. I lived with the Meehans, "my second family", all of the time I was there. There were no six-monthly changeovers.

Phonse Meehan passed away in 1998. I readily and proudly accepted the invitation to join the four sons and a son-in-law to carry his coffin at the funeral.

14
De La "Old Colls" and "Black Jack" Coughlan

De La Salle Old Collegians, First Premiership, a wet Grand Final, Old Colls' stars, Melbourne University High School Old Boys, Geelong Amateurs, an Oakleigh flag, a Tassy game to remember; South Melbourne FC, Western Bulldogs FC, Oakleigh FC, Sandringham FC, Wynyard FC, North Hobart FC; the Murphys, Bill Faul, Jim Hawkins, Ron Todd, and John Devine.

M id-May 1960 saw me as the teacher of 43 Grade 3 children at Gardiner Central School in Melbourne and back living at home. I enjoyed being part of a larger staff and it was there that I met my future wife, Marj.

Of the many good pupils that attended the school in my time at Gardiner, Jeffrey Rosenfeld (at left) was one of the best, later becoming well known as a neurosurgeon treating both media personality Molly Meldrum who had a serious fall from a ladder and the legendary footballer, Jim Stynes.

Professor Rosenfeld told the *Herald Sun* after an operation that he carried out in 2011 that Stynes continued to surprise medical staff. "I don't know the exact number of operations I have carried out on him now, I have lost count," he said, "Jim is an amazing stayer who just bounces back and a lot of people just don't bounce back like he does."

Australia-wide people were saddened on Tuesday, 21 March 2012, when it was announced that **Jim Stynes** had passed away. A State Funeral was held for him on the following Tuesday at St Paul's Cathedral, Melbourne. Jim Stynes will long be remembered as a great footballer and more importantly as a wonderful Australian. Many fine tributes were written about Jim after his passing and the eulogies spoken at his huge funeral were very moving.

> **Snippet**
>
> Although never a football player himself Professor Rosenfeld had another link with football. In his childhood he became a member of St John Ambulance when the local divisional representatives came to Gardiner Central School to seek new members. In that capacity he attended many football matches. He eventually became Commissioner of St John Ambulance in Victoria and continues to support that organisation.

De La Old Old Collegians Football Club

When I returned to Melbourne I was keen to continue my football career. As Ray Clarke, my mate from school and teachers' college days, was playing for De La Salle Old Collegians ("Old Colls") in the Amateurs. I joined him at that club.

Jim Hawkins, a school leader and good sportsman when I was in the junior forms at De La Salle College, was largely responsible for the founding of the Old Colls club. On leaving school he played with Richmond Under 19s and seconds for a couple of years before he was recruited to St Kevin's in the VAFA. While playing there in 1954, he formed the opinion that if he rounded up a few friends from De La whom he knew were good footballers and recruited other old boys who were playing elsewhere as well as some good footballers from those who were leaving school in 1954, a team could be put together that would do well in the lower grades of the VAFA competition at least.

Some of the players that he had in mind included Maurice Murphy,

John Gilfedder, Colin Browne and Bill Watts among his school contemporaries and school leavers Max Brown, Bernie Teague, Greg Reardon and Tom Duggan. He put his plan to the Old Colls' Committee and obtained their support to field a team. After further recruiting and the appointment of Jim Smith as coach, the first De La Old Collegians team ran onto the ground at Heyington at the commencement of the 1955 season in the E Grade VAFA competition.

No doubt other of the many Old Collegians teams that compete in the VAFA began in a similar fashion.

The team had success in its first year, but it didn't come easily. At that time the first two teams at the end of the season were promoted to the next grade while the lowest two in the grade above dropped back. De La finished third in 1955. As was often the case in the early years of competition football, the minor premiers had the right to challenge if it failed to win the flag. De La defeated Trinity in the preliminary final, thus earning promotion, but they then had to defeat the top team, Old Geelong Grammarians, twice – firstly in the Grand Final and then in the Challenge Match – to win the flag. The team successfully did this, proving that they had well and truly won the right to be promoted to D-Grade.

The brilliant **Maurie Murphy** won the Club Best and Fairest award in the club's inaugural season.

Jim Hawkins was captain of the team. Jim told me years later that in 1955 De La often had only 20 players from which to select a team and yet over the next 50 years it was to become a power in the VAFA competition, fielding six teams each Saturday in 2012. No doubt Jim could feel justly proud of his early efforts to get the club started.

De La Salle Old Colls' First Premiership Team, 1955

Back Row: J. Smith (Coach), J. Coughlan (Trainer), B. McCusker (Sec), C. Browne, W. Atkin, M. Murphy, W. Watts, M. Linard, J. Gilfedder, A. Moss, L. Spriggs, P. King, L. Watts (Trainer), L. Cosgriff (President)
Centre Row: K. Harrington, A. O'Callaghan, J. Hawkins (Capt), W. Hollier (Vice Capt), C. Cantwell, D. Faulkner
Front Row: P. McCormack, T. Duggan, M. Brown, J. Varcoe, G. Reardon

(With permission from Jan Ashford, wife and sole beneficiary of Michael Ashford, the author of the book 'Pride and Premierships', from which the photo is taken)

Into A-Grade

In May 1960, when I joined the Old Colls, they were a strong team and on the way up, having risen to B-Grade in the VAFA competition in relatively few years.

The coach, Ken Purcell, was experienced, enthusiastic and highly respected. The players knew each other well and played as a team. Furthermore, the club had recruited intelligently and included among its players some very competent footballers such as rover Peter Giles, forward John Tindley, wingmen Peter Hanneberry and Park Shiel as well as follower Bill "Toby" Pearson. Bernie Teague and Bill Watts continued to do well.

To make A-Grade in the following year, we had to reach the Grand Final, as the promotion/relegation system in the VAFA at that time continued to operate as it did in 1955.

Although our form was a little up and down we were on track to make the finals as the year progressed, and this we did.

After finishing second and losing the second semi-final to University High School Old Boys (UHSOB), De La had a great victory in the preliminary final defeating Kew at Victoria Park, thus, for the first time, winning a place in A-Grade for the following year.

The win was a great team effort and there were great celebrations after the victory. De La Old Colls had made it to A-Grade, irrespective of the result of the Grand Final the next week. Unfortunately for me, I had missed both of the finals with a bad dose of influenza.

The victorious team against Kew was left unchanged for the Grand Final. I was able to train in the week before the match and was selected as one of the reserves. This resulted in me sitting on the bench, with good friend John Samon, on a wet and windy Grand Final Saturday, at the South Melbourne Technical School oval and watching De La do battle with UHSOB. Although De La had their chances, we were behind for much of the game and despite a rally in the last quarter, we were beaten by 27 points.

The UHSOB full forward on that day was **Graham Beissel**. While Beissel was a brilliant full-forward in the Amateurs, he proved his class and versatility by playing in the centre for Essendon when the Bombers beat Carlton by more than five goals to take out the 1962 Grand Final.

Better players for the De La team in 1960 were captain Vin Pilkington; ruckman Bill Watts; rover Peter Giles; defender Bernie Teague, who had improved his kicking, and ruck-rover, Toby Pearson. The latter three represented the VAFA in interstate football.

The De La Old Boys team for its first game in A-Grade was as follows:

Backs: B. Teague, V. Pilkington, J. Kelly;
Half-backs: G. Compton, P. Wright, J. Firman;
Centres: P. Hanneberry, J. Samon, P. Sheil;
Half-forwards: B. Conroy, P. Griffin, C, Glover;
Forwards: J. Alford, J. Gilfedder, R. O'Toole;
Followers: W. Watts, P. Heany, B. Blight;
Reserves: D. Glynn, B. Broderick

Bernie Teague was captain of this first De La side in A-Grade with Bill Watts as vice-captain. Together with John Gilfedder and Peter McCormack, these two hold the distinction of being the only players to represent De La in all five grades on their trip to the top level. John Samon, who sat on the bench beside me at that 1960 Grand Final, was in the centre for De La's first game in A-Grade.

That game was the first in the seniors for half-forward flanker, Colin Glover. He remembers the game well and described his experience of it to me as follows:

> It was against Uni Blacks and I was removed from the ground at three-quarter time, not having had one disposal. We won that game by under six points when Graeme Compton kicked a huge torpedo punt goal from a long, long way out.
>
> My disappointment at performing so poorly was significantly eased when my opponent that day, Tony Anderson, lined up for Melbourne VFL next week! Tony Anderson went on to play 75 games for the Demons, playing in their 1964 VFL premiership team and representing Victoria in that year.

Colin Glover became a De La legend, playing 255 games with the club (184 with the seniors and 71 with the reserves). He coached the reserves for three years. Colin was Club President for three years and Secretary from 1993 until 2008. In 2012 he was the Senior Team Manager, a position he had held since the Club's A-Grade premiership in 1991. Few people have given as much to any club as Colin Glover has given to De la Old Colls.

A Geelong Amateurs Star

I remember well the 1960 trip to play Geelong Amateurs at the Queens' Park oval at Geelong. Like most of the De La team I spent the afternoon trying to catch Number 6 of Geelong. The player's name was **Ian Redpath**.

13 August, 1960	THE AMATEUR FOOTBALLER	Page Thirteen

"B" SECTION
GEELONG
(Light Blue & Green)

1. CRILLY, D.	10. MAUNSELL, J.	20. BENT, G.
2. RODJERS, J.	11. VAUTIER, J.	21. BURCH, I
2. RODGERS, J.	12. LAMB, J.	22. COOPER, B.
3. O'SULLIVAN, J.	13. TURNER, E.	23. ROWE, S.
4. GUTHRIE, W.	14. OSBURN, R.	24. SUMNER, I.
5. ANDERSON, P.	15. LUSCOMBE, R.	25. TANIS, N.
6. REDPATH, I.	16. LAMB, N. J.	26. WHITE, F.
7. MAY, R.	17. KEYS, R.	27. MURRAY, D
8. BAUER, P.	18. GUNN, B.	28. HATTON, L.
9. PITMAN, G.	19. ALLEN, P.	30. ILLINGWORTH, R.

DE LA SALLE OLD COLLEGIANS
(Blue and Gold, Gold Monogram)

1. GILES, P. E.	15. KELLY, J. M.	29. TEAGUE, R. J.
2. SEXTON, B. A.	16. COMPTON, G. F.	30. SLATTERY, B. R.
3. REED, K.	17. HANNEBERRY, P. E.	31. CAHIR, L. W.
4. RAYNOR, B. R.	18. PILKINGTON, V. T. (capt.)	32. DUGGAN, T. G.
5. TEAGUE, B. G. (v.-capt.)	19. HEFFERNAN, T.	33. O'HALLORAN, B. J.
6. TOOGOOD, W. J.	20. WRIGHT, W. P.	34. GLYNN, D. J.
7. TINDLEY, J. W.	21. O'TOOLE, R. I.	35. ANDERSON, P. E.
8. McCORMACK, P G	22. DILLON, J. F. X.	36. SEXTON, D. A.
9. FAUL, Robt.	23. WATTS, W. S.	37. QUINT, J.
10. SHIEL, J. P	24. CONWAY, P. J.	
11. PEARSON, W. A.	25. CLARKE, J. R. J.	38. BROWN, B. W.
12. NESBITT, B. A.	26. PEACOCK, T. P.	39. McCROHAN, B. E.
13. FAUL, Ron	27. GRIFFIN, P. H.	40. O'BRIEN, K. E.
14. SAMON, J.	28. HAWKINS, J. F.	

A brilliant footballer, Redpath was to prove De La's nemesis on more than one occasion. He kicked four goals in the team that defeated De La at the Queen's Park oval in that 1960 match in which I played. Three years later De La played Geelong in a semi-final. The account of that game in Michael Ashford's book, *Pride and Premierships – a History of De La Salle Old Collegians Football – 1955 to 1980*, includes the following:

Perhaps De La might have come out better if there had been a cricket match on at Geelong that day. A chap named Ian Redpath might have donned pads and gloves, instead of boots. He gave De La the run around in a great display that led Geelong to a crushing victory. "Bluey" Donovan was given the task of chasing Redpath – and so there has been one lone voice at Test matches over the past fifteen years abusing Redpath for any reason; Bluey has never forgotten him.

Ian Redpath played in 66 Test matches for Australia, scoring 4,737 runs at an average of 43.45 including eight test centuries. An opening batsman he sometimes looked uncomfortable against fast bowlers but he had a very good record against both the terrifying West Indies' speedsters of his day and England's very aggressive John Snow. He was an outstanding close-to-the wicket fieldsman taking 83 catches in Test matches.

Snippet

The names Robert and Ron Faul also appear on the De La list. Robert captained the De La Salle College First XVIII in 1955 and Ron became a legend at the De La Old Colls as a player and clubman. Their father was **Bill Faul** who was imported from West Australia to play for South Melbourne in 1932. He came second in the Brownlow Medal in that year and won the Swans' Best and Fairest award. One of South's "Foreign Legion" (players from other states), he played in the Swans premiership team in 1933. After 117 games he became playing coach of Prahran and later took Moorabbin, as non-playing coach, to a premiership in the VFA. He also coached Northcote. One of the VFA's longest serving coaches, he was coach of VFA teams for a total of fifteen years. He returned to coach the Swans in 1960-61.

The Murphys

Maurice Murphy was a talented centreman in De La Salle Old Coll's movement through the grades in the club's early years although he was no longer playing with the club when I was there. In 1965, his younger brother John began playing with the club. As it was put by Michael Ashford in his history of the club:

> This year saw the first appearance of Barry Martin, who was to make regular appearances along with John Murphy, when both were in town on holidays from the Columban Missionary (Seminary) in Bobbin Head (NSW). Although spending all of the year in Rugby dominated New South Wales, these two men were automatic selections whenever they hit town as both were brilliant, courageous footballers.

Obviously John Murphy was a very good footballer. Further evidence of his ability is also found in Ashford's club history. He writes that

> Peter Strickland (a stalwart club administrator) had taken, each year, to naming his best ever De La side. Having witnessed with great intensity most of the 400 games De La played over fifteen years, he was in a good position to name a team. At the Fathers' and Sons' Annual Dinner in 1970, where Hawthorn coach John Kennedy was guest speaker, "Stricko" named his team. Maurice Murphy was in the centre and John Murphy was centre half-forward.

John Murphy, after giving his order and the community many years of service, left the priesthood. He later married an ex-Brigidine nun, Monica, the sister of Jim Slattery with whom I played footy at Lalbert. They had a son, named **Robert Murphy,** who inherited football genes from both sides of the family. With pace, courage, skill and the ability to use both sides of his body, Robert was to become well known in AFL circles as a brilliant utility player for the Western Bulldogs. In 2011, on the day of Robert's 200th game with the Bulldogs, leading football writer Mike Sheahan, of the *Herald Sun*, penned the following about Murphy:

> He's been my favourite at the Whitten Oval for years. Probably from the moment I saw Robert Flower in him – a rakish, fragile-looking young bloke with No. 2 on his back, the complete set of natural skills, the grace of an ice-skater – I've loved watching him

play. It's 200 games for Murphy tonight against Adelaide at Etihad Stadium and I'm keenly looking forward to him playing a big one.

Murphy didn't let Sheahan down. The next day in the same paper, under the headlines "Murph magic guides revival", writer Mark Robinson commented that Robert Murphy "has played in more important games, no doubt, but very few would have left him as proud as he was last night. Murphy celebrated his 200th game with a best-on-ground performance and a significant victory over Adelaide." No doubt the Murphy clan was equally proud of him.

The Oaks Again
After De La Old Colls lost the Grand Final in 1960, there was one consolation for me. It was that Oakleigh won the VFA premiership. They had recruited well to recover from their mid-'50s slump to be a power again by the end of the decade. Alby Pannam, who played against Alan Hird in the 1950 VFL second's Grand Final, was appointed coach of the Oaks in 1959. They advanced quickly up the ladder to finish third and, as we have seen, they were beaten by Coburg in the first semi-final. Pannam's coaching and a successful recruiting program over a couple of years brought this about.

By 1960 Oakleigh's list included the already-mentioned John Coughlan who was captain, ruckman Vic Naismith, interstate rover Ray Alsopp, defender Gordon Peake and forward Jack D'Arcy from Richmond, as well as Bill Jones, a rover who had played in the Magpies' losing Grand Final side in 1956. Milne McCooke, a burly centre half-forward who had played 13 games with the Saints, was vice-captain.

After beating Oakleigh in the second semi-final, Sandringham was favourite for the 1960 Grand Final. Their star full-forward was clergyman Denis Oakley, the brother of former St Kilda winger and VLF administrator, Ross Oakley.

Dad, Ramon and I joined a large crowd at St Kilda for the game.

Apart from the resting rover, Bill Jones, all of the other forwards were tall men able to play in key positions. Pannam had a strategy of rotating these forwards around the six forward positions. The Sandringham backmen were uncertain as to which player they should be minding. With only sixteen men in each side, as was the case in the VFA in those days, there was also plenty of room for the Oaks to use handball, much of which was instigated by Coughlan. This was particularly so in the second quarter when Oakleigh, kicking with the wind, raced to a 35 point lead at half-time. The match was then never in doubt. Oakley was held goalless by full back Buckley who, in the very mobile Oakleigh side, was able to sneak up forward and kick a goal himself.

Snippet

From 1896, when eight wealthy VFL clubs broke away from the VFA, the first formal body set up to run Australian Rules, there was great competition between the two bodies. The VFA, in particular, experimented with the rules and regulations to try to attract a greater following.

Over the years, at various stages they tried an "order off" rule, a free kick for out of bounds, two substitutes for injured players and medical attendants at the ground. They introduced a throw pass which was to make the game faster and more attractive. This was in place after World War II. Some of these changes became permanent, some were also picked up by the VFL and some were subsequently abandoned.

In the '40s, they relaxed permit regulations, allowing players to transfer from the VFL to the VFA without a permit from their VFL club. Champion Collingwood full forward **Ron Todd** made use of this change when he was paid a huge sum of money by a bookmaker supporter of Williamstown, to transfer to that club in the VFA in 1945. John Wren offered to more than match the bookmaker's offer for Todd to stay at Collingwood but the Magpies stopped that move. Perhaps they didn't wish to see a system of offer and counter-offer set up to retain players who could freely move between the VFL and VFA without permits. Still in his prime, Todd kicked 188 goals for Williamstown in that year.

Another VFA change was to bring in the sixteen players per team rule, with the wings being removed. Two reserves, instead of one, were also allowed. This rule was in place at the time of the 1960 Grand Final between Oakleigh and Sandringham. However if the VFA wished to compete in the ANFC carnivals they had to revert to the VFL rules. This they did.

A further ploy by the VFA was to invite clubs from the outer suburbs to join the Association as it was in these suburbs that population growth was occurring after World War ll. Clubs such as Dandenong, Sunshine, Frankston and Waverley joined. In time the VFA, with its many clubs, some very strong and some quite weak, set up two divisions with a promotion/relegation system as in the VAFA. This was in place in the '60s.

After the 1960 flag the Oaks once again slipped until they were relegated to B division in 1966. Among the reasons for this slide from prominence was the loss of John Coughlan in 1963 to take up a playing coach position for Wynyard, a coastal town in Tasmania, in the North-West Football Union competition.

More about John Coughlan

Marc Fiddian in his book, *Devils at Play – A history of the Oakleigh Football Club* writes of Coughlan:

> ... in 1957 Oakleigh needed a captain as it was under a non-playing coach. Coughlan was given the job and held it for a record six years. His leadership was aggressive and sometimes inspiring to lesser mortals. From 1957 until he left Oakleigh after season 1962, Coughlan was an automatic choice in representative VFA sides. Third in the 1957 Liston Trophy, Coughlan was probably the biggest single force behind Oakleigh's 1960 premiership.

Fiddian goes on to quote former leading field umpire Jim McMaster who said that Coughlan "was an umpire's nightmare because he was so unpredictable. John was hard to control, but was good for the VFA as he brought people to the games" ... McMaster added that "Coughlan used to make him feel welcome before a game and introduce him to any new players, but other umpires shuddered when they heard they had an Oakleigh game."

A mobile big man, John Coughlan was a good mark, a wonderful kick and a very quick thinker on the football field. He was also a fitness fanatic. A great leader, he had the ability to inspire his teammates and upset opposition players and supporters with his confidence and ability. Furthermore he had a knack for attracting publicity.

To continue the Coughlan story, we must fast-forward to 1980. I was then working in Warrnambool and playing cricket with CBC/South Warrnambool Cricket Club in the local competition. Also in the team was an academic, Dr Peter Hay. Over a beer after a game with Pete, the conversation moved from cricket to football and he found out that I was from Oakleigh. And I found out that Pete grew up in Wynyard in Tasmania. The talk then quickly moved on to John Coughlan with me telling Pete of his deeds at Oakleigh and Pete in turn telling his story of John Coughlan, Pete's football hero as a teenager, growing up in Wynyard.

One of Pete's tales was of when Coughlan spoke at the Club's Under 17 trophy night, the year before he took over the coaching job. Pete was a player in the team. "To be a good footballer, you have to be big and you have to be ugly." Coughlan began. He paused and carefully surveyed the room, full of young players. He then went on, "Well you blokes are certainly ugly enough."

Dr Peter Hay's career subsequently took him back to Tasmania where he became Reader in Geography and Environmental Studies at the University of Tasmania, Hobart. In 1998, it was said of him in *The Australian* newspaper that he is Tasmania's pre-eminent public intellectual.

A man of wide interests he writes across a range of topics and included in his book, *Vandiemonian Essays*, is an article entitled "Half Time with Stout John" which tells of his memories of "Stout John Coughlan" and in particular, Hay's recollections of Coughlan's pre-match and half-time addresses to the Wynyard players. Hay then goes on to write about the famous (in Tasmania, at least) 1967 Tasmanian State Premiership Final.

Dr Peter Hay referred to Coughlan as "Stout John" rather than as "Black Jack" as did the media. No doubt Pete had in mind both Coughlan's build and also the use of the word "stout" to imply steady, reliable, loyal and trustworthy. Hay claims that Coughlan revolutionised football on the North-West Coast on and off the field, "he introduced the play-on game. Crowds flocked to see him play, and consummate showman that he was, he knew how to play the crowd as well as a game of footy".

Pete, also a published poet, then proceeds to use his skills to describe his memories (perhaps romanticised over time) of Coughlan's pre-match addresses

> which commenced at three-quarter time in the twos – they were thus 35 to 40 minute affairs. Half-time speeches were necessarily shorter, but they followed a similar pattern. Low key and chatty at first. The marvellous redolence of Penetrene. Old town identities, the community's physical and mental flotsam, hanging on every word. Wide-eyed, worshipful kids. Coughlan working around his team, finding cause for congratulations here, for a mild rebuke there. Invariably a sob story extraneous to the game itself, but serving to tie what was happening in the change rooms to the expectations of a wider community, beyond the sacred doors. Blood quickening. The rational mind becoming dull, the visceral senses taking over. The master orator building it up, building it up, turning the emotions up, still up, to emerge in a frenzied crescendo, a pure soaring impassioned energy fit to change the world.

Although he attended the game, Hay didn't hear Coughlan's speeches before or during the 1967 State Final. He wished he had.

At that time, in Tasmania, there were three football associations and, at the end of the season, the premiers from each would be engaged in a series of matches to determine who would play off in the State Final, with the winner being able to claim that it was the best Tasmanian team for the season. In 1967 Wynyard, from the North-West Football Union, and North Hobart, from the Tasmanian Football League, played the State Final at Burnie's home ground, West Park, on the last Saturday in September.

Coughlan led the Wynyard team while the playing coach of North Hobart was **John Devine**, the former tough Geelong defender who had played in the Geelong 1963 premiership team. When Devine came to North Hobart, he had to coach from the boundary for six weeks as he was serving out a suspension incurred in the VFL. Nevertheless he took his team from last in the previous year to finish fourth in 1967, from which position they won the flag.

As Peter Hay put it, the legendary rival coaches in the 1967 State Final were "two of the most rugged coves ever to pull on the boots in Tassie".

There was a feeling of excitement and expectation among the large crowd as the game started. North, kicking with the wind, was first out of the blocks, leading by over three goals at the first change. Their lead could have been more only for inaccuracy in front of goal. The second quarter was all Wynyard's, scoring eight goals six to North's two goals three, giving Wynyard a twenty point advantage at the long break. Again making good use of the scoring end, North fought back to lead by fourteen points at the final break. With great determination, Wynyard managed to level the score 19 minutes into the last quarter. Eleven minutes later, Wynyard lead by the narrowest of margins. Devine, who had kicked five goals as a ruck-rover, was awarded a free kick for holding the man on North's half-forward line.

The clock was ticking. North full forward, David Collins, led and marked, within very easy kicking distance, as the siren sounded. The umpire paid the mark, but all hell broke loose as the Wynyard supporters swarmed onto the oval. They surrounded Collins who was unable to take his kick despite the efforts of the North players and the police to clear the crowd. Amidst this commotion some Wynyard supporters really made sure that Collins would not kick a goal, even if he had the opportunity to do so. They removed the goal posts and took them from the oval. With no goal for Collins to shoot at, the match was abandoned. The game was later officially declared "No game".

Writer and journalist for *The Age* newspaper, Martin Flanagan, has suggested that his good friend Peter Hay may have been involved in the removal of the goalposts. Hay is non-committal about the question. In his youth, Hay was passionate in his support of Wynyard and it is my view that if he didn't play a role in the incident, he would be very disappointed, dare I say, ashamed that he wasn't involved.

Devine was regarded as best on ground. Coughlan, who claimed that the mark had been taken after the siren, declared with Churchillian eloquence that there should be a re-match and that Wynyard would take on North anywhere, "on the beach if we have to". North refused the offer believing that a re-match would sanction mob rule.

In 2007, the AFL commissioned artist Jamie Cooper to produce the painting, *The Game That Made Australia,* to celebrate the 150th anniversary of the "birth" of our Australian game. Amongst the many memorable moments from the game depicted in the painting is one of the scoreboard at the West Park oval showing the final scores in the 1967 Tasmanian State Final. In front of the scoreboard are a couple of Wynyard supporters slinking off with a goal post. Coughlan and Devine, as playing coaches of the opposing teams involved, will go down in history. The painting hangs at the Docklands' headquarters of the AFL.

Ironically, a few years later saw both Devine and Coughlan on the same side. They were both Labor members of the Tasmanian House of Assembly.

15
VFA Sundays and Frank Davis

VFA Sundays, Tough Finals, VFA stars, Oakleigh YCW, Three flags; Dandenong FC, Port Melbourne FC, Mazenod Old Collegians FC; "Big Bob" Johnson, "Frosty" Miller, Fred Cook, Phil Cleary, Paul Callery, Jeff Moran, Ross Smith and Heath Black.

My dad Mick Reed, in his seventies, had become a good friend of Frank Walsh, a well respected football writer for *The Sporting Globe*. Together they went to many Sunday VFA games, and both VFA and VFL Saturday matches after I retired from playing in 1966.

VFA football was at its peak in terms of publicity and performance in the '60s and '70s.

The commencement of Sunday matches in 1960 and the televising of VFA matches by Channel 0 (now 10) created great interest in the game. Furthermore, there were many personalities who played the game with such flair and with such ability that they drew crowds to watch them either in the flesh or on the TV. Included in this group were John Coughlan (Oakleigh), **Jim "Frosty" Miller** (Dandenong), **Fred Cook** (Yarraville, Port Melbourne, Moorabbin), Bob Johnson (Oakleigh) and later **Phil Cleary** (Coburg). Miller and Cook were colourful full forwards, while Cleary was noted for his ruggedness. Miller kicked 885 goals at nearly five goals per game for Dandenong while Cook kicked 1364 goals in his 305 game VFA career.

Cleary played 205 games for Coburg and coached the club between 1984 and 1992, leading them to premierships in 1988-89. He coached the VFA representative side five times. He later became well known as a television broadcaster as well as a member of Federal Parliament winning the seat for the Wills electorate on the resignation of Bob Hawke in 1992.

Port and Dandy

Dad and Frank Walsh were among the 17,000 spectators at the Port Melbourne versus Dandenong Grand Final at the Punt Rd oval in 1967. It was an extremely rugged match with the Port Melbourne captain, Brian Buckley, threatening to lead his team off the oval in the second quarter for what he saw as poor and biased umpiring. To that point Dandenong had received 26 free kicks to Port's eleven. However the game did continue and Dandenong won by 25 points.

The Dandenong playing coach, Alan Morrow, who had played in the St Kilda premiership team in the previous year, was Dandenong's best player.

Dad and his mate Frank Walsh, who were disappointed by the "goings on" at that match, would have been more disappointed had they attended the "replay" Grand Final between the two teams in 1976. Before a crowd of over 32,000 at the Junction Oval, the Port Melbourne team had its revenge, but it wasn't without bloodshed. Five minutes into the second quarter, full forward, Fred Cook, was flattened after kicking a goal, resulting in brawls breaking out all over the field.

Those involved included trainers and runners as well as players. When the game settled down Port was able to win relatively easily by 57 points. Fred Cook kicked five goals six behinds for the match to bring his season's total to 124.

Nine people were reported, including a Port Melbourne trainer and a Dandenong runner. A total of 14 weeks of suspensions were handed out to the players while the trainer was given 12 months and the runner six weeks.

Oakleigh CYMS/YCW

Formed back in 1932, the Oakleigh CYMS Football Club later disbanded, because of the outbreak of World War II. Little is recorded about the team in its early years but it was known that it didn't win a premiership before the War.

The club re-formed again in 1956, playing in the Open Age CYMS competition at the Police Paddock with its old changing shed. When the Oakleigh Districts vacated the Rec the CYMS took it over of a Saturday with the under age YCW sides using it of a Sunday. Subsequently two clubs merged, the CYMS competition folded and an Open Age section was introduced in the YCW competition. This meant that the teams from Sacred Heart parish in Oakleigh were part of a single club that played in YCW competitions and used the Rec as their home ground. The coach of the senior team was George Allen, an experienced footballer.

Below is a poem which featured in the Oakleigh *CYMS News* on the week of a final. It was written by Frank O'Shea, who was a member of the inaugural CYMS team in 1932 and the dad of Bill O'Shea, one of the players in 1956.

Before the Match

It was Saturday afternoon at the Police Paddock, the Oakleigh CY ground.
In the old tin pavilion, you could not hear a sound
For the coach Old Man Allen had climbed up on a seat
And with one hand on his tummy, he gazed thoughtfully at his feet.

The players stood in silence to hear what he might say,
To receive their final instructions before they went out to play;
Old 'Kega' sat in a corner, on his dial a silly grin
Beside him stood the tall boys – Frank Tighe and Peter Quinn.

Now, the coach he rubbed his tummy, as if he had a pain
And, Kirk was heard to murmur, "Was it tears or was it rain?"
But the old man lifted up his head and stood firm upon his feet,
"Now, listen to me lads," he said, "this team we've got to beat."

The lads listened intently to what the good coach said,
How the rucks should palm the ball and how the forwards should be fed.
"When you backmen clear the goal, drive it out there on that wing,
Don't double back across the goal, think of the trouble that could bring."

"When you're going for the ball, don't go in at a trot,
But grit your teeth and go in hard and give it all you've got."
Now you just take The Bomber, he knows what to do,
He doesn't try to dodge the packs, but chops his way, straight through."

"Some of you can't kick the ball, and some can't mark for nuts,"
And some of … Oh I wish you had half young Honan's guts.
For I can forgive a trier if he happens to make a blue,
But I can't forgive a quitter, who chucks it half way through."

"You fellows in the forward line, have just got to pull your weight,
And when you get the ball, make sure you kick it straight,
The last time that I played, don't think I want to skite,
Got five kicks, but kicked five goals. Now fellows, am I right?"

"That match down at St Kilda, could have been our first defeat,
The St Kilda boys stayed with us, and ran us off our feet,
Our back line was well beaten, we were wide open at the seams,
One man it was that saved us, His Reverence Father Eames!"

"Yes Father is always with us when we are trying to save those goals,
But are we always with His Reverence when he's striving to save our souls?

"There's a lot more I'd like to say but I haven't got the time,
For the President will sure go crook, if we cop another fine.
Now, you should all know what to do, each man should know his job,
So get out there upon the ground and do this blinking mob."

Back at the Rec

In 1961, I returned to play at the Rec with my old mates at Oakleigh in the B-Grade South section of the Open Age YCW competition. We had a good year and reached the Grand Final. The players were very nervous about the game both for the team and for themselves. The team was on top of the ladder throughout the year but we were very conscious of the fact that a football team from the Sacred Heart parish hadn't won a premiership, although it fielded its first team nearly thirty years before. It had certainly got close, reaching the finals in a couple of the seasons immediately prior to 1961 and losing a Grand Final to Mentone CYMS as a result of atrocious kicking.

A number of good players from those years, including ruckman Peter Quinn, followers John Comerford and Bill O'Shea, defenders John White, Jack Thompson, Greg Honan, Ted Healy and vice-captain Barry

Carr, were still playing well. Newcomers Ron Megna, Paddy Rohan from Watchem-Corack, Brian Bonar and Eddie Walsh gave added depth to the side. The latter two players came from the Oakleigh VFA club.

Experienced centre-line player Jack Gubbins was again the captain while Mr Frank O'Shea, Bill's dad, was the team's well respected and football-wise coach. He was ahead of his times by encouraging the team, when attacking from the flanks, to centre the ball to a spot 30 yards (about 27 metres) in front of the goals rather than kicking the ball into the goal square. Full forward Ron Megna was adept at finding space there and kicked many goals from marking in that area.

Grand Finals

There was a feeling of tension in the shed as we changed, but Mr O'Shea gave us confidence before we went out, telling us that we were an experienced team and that we all knew how to play. All we had to do was to keep doing what we had been doing throughout the year.

There was a strong southerly blowing. We were playing Elwood who had finished third but had won their semi-final and the preliminary final quite comfortably. We won the toss and kicked with the wind. Everything went right for us in the first quarter and we kicked eight goals while Elwood failed to score a goal against the wind. Holding Elwood to only a couple of goals in the second quarter, we had the match virtually won at half time. We completed the job in the second half.

The whole team played well and we were all very happy to be part of the first ever premiership team from Sacred Heart.

The team's success continued as it won two additional flags over the next four years. The return of Jim McKenna and Kevin Jenkins from the bush, with their country football experience, certainly helped.

The 1961 season was a memorable one for Oakleigh YCW. As well as winning the Open Age premiership, the club won the Under 19 and the Under 17 flags. Big Bob Johnson coached the Under 19s. A particularly courageous side, the leading players in the team were Mick McMahon, Peter Woods, Brian Browne, Kevin Norris, Mick Skehan and Kevin Farrell.

By this time, Big Bob had played in five premiership teams for Melbourne and was one of the best known VFL players, not only in Melbourne, but, as an interstate and Carnival footballer, also in those parts of Australia where Aussie Rules was played.

Frank Davis was vice-captain of the victorious Under 17s. Captain Dick Weston and on-baller Peter Wiseman were both later to play VFA football.

Three years later, in 1964, Frank Davis played for Melbourne in its premiership team. Demon coach, Norm Smith, recognised Frank's ability to play close and tackle hard and picked him to play on Des Tuddenham, the Collingwood champion, in the 1964 Grand Final. Tuddenham had played a wonderful second semi-final, kicking seven goals in the Magpies' defeat of St Kilda.

Although Tuddenham kicked three goals in the Grand Final he was not the influential player that he had been the fortnight before. The match was a classic game with Melbourne back pocket player (and interstate cricketer), Neil Crompton, moving up the ground to kick the winning goal shortly before the final siren.

Highly respected at the Demons, Frank Davis was club captain from 1970 to 1972, winning their Best and Fairest award in his first season as leader. An underrated player, he represented Victoria at interstate football during his career. Davis played 168 games for Melbourne.

Frank Davis went to school at Salesian College, Chadstone. Each year a special match is played between Mazenod College, Mulgrave, and Salesian College, Chadstone, for the **Johnson/Davis Cup**. Matt Johnson, who played for Footscray, was the first ex-Mazenod College boy to play VFL football while Frank Davis was the first ex-Salesian College boy to do so. Sam ("Francis Samuel") Reed was captain of the

Oakleigh YCW Under 19 Premiers 1961

(With permission from Oakleigh Amateur Football Club)

Back Row: P. Sturrock, J. Launder, P. Woods (Vice Captain), F. Craven, R. Johnson (Coach), K Norris, G. Edwards, B. Brown

Centre Row: Fr Sheehy (Chaplain), K. Collins, J. Salmon, R. Epstein, A. Sherman, K. Ryan, A. Brown

Front Row: N. Wearne, M. McMahon, (Captain), D. McVilly, M. Skehan, J. Campbell, T. Greely, K. Farrell

first Mazenod team to win the Johnson/Davis Cup. The coach of the team was Springvale champion Damian Carroll. Sam Reed is the son of George Reed III, the grandson of George Reed Snr.

Back-to-Back Flags

After their success in 1961, the Oakleigh YCW Open Age team moved up to the A-Grade South section and won the flag again in 1962, beating

Oakleigh YCW Under 17 Premiers 1961

(With permission from Oakleigh Amateur Football Club)

Back Row: G. Browne (Trainer), T. Dorizzi, J. Forscutt, L. Walker, C. Dobson, J. Power, T. Killen, W. Aron, D. Tait (Manager)

Centre Row: P. Wiseman, J. Skehan, M. Murphy, G. Wormington, R. Weston (Captain), R. Weston Snr (Coach), F. Davis (Vice-Captain), M. Izod

Front Row: C. Barlow, J. Collins, N. Jones, P. Egan, R. Gawne, K. Norman

Mascot: A. Reeves

East Camberwell YCW on a windswept oval at Albert Park, just across the road from the lake. In a low scoring game we were three goals up at three-quarter time and Oakleigh's strategy was to keep the ball in the "dead pocket" for as long as possible.

Peter Quinn rucked superbly, palming the ball to Oakleigh players who turned towards the boundary and kicked it along the boundary, not worrying if the ball went out of bounds. There was no "time on" in that competition, nor was there a penalty for kicking the ball out of bounds on the full.

My then-fiancé Marj Graham brought her dad and two brothers, Brian and Bill, to watch the game. Standing at the fence in the last quarter, Brian, unaware of Oakleigh's tactics, quickly chased after the ball to retrieve it when it went out of bounds near him. To his surprise, he received a torrent of abuse and advice from nearby Oakleigh supporters. "Don't pick it up!" "Let the boundary umpire get it." "Kick it on further." "Kick it across the road." "Let it go into the lake."

Brian kept his hands in his pockets the next time the ball came near him.

Oakleigh held off East Camberwell to win by a couple of goals.

My parents were again enthusiastic supporters of our team. Mick was so keen that he was the only non-player, or non-official, to be invited to be in the 1962 Premiership team photo.

After an average season in 1963 and a poor season in 1964 the Oakleigh Boys did well again in 1965, winning the flag by beating Hampton in the Grand Final. At the end of season Presentation Night for the Oakleigh YCW club, Kevin Jenkins was awarded the Open Age Best and Fairest.

Receiving the trophy for Best and Fairest in the Under 15 team that night was **Paul Callery**, who went on to have a very successful and varied football career. Like Big Bob and Frank Davis he went to Melbourne, playing with their Under 19s from 1967 to 1969 and was their leading goalkicker in those three years. He was Best and Fairest for the team in 1968 and also won the Morrish Medal in that year. Moving to the Melbourne Reserves, Paul won the Club Best and Fairest in 1970 and the Gardiner Medal for the VFL Reserves competition in that year also.

Commencing his senior career with the Demons in 1970, Paul Callery played 181 games of VFL football for Melbourne, St Kilda and South Melbourne. The smallest player in the VFL in his era, Paul was very popular with supporters. He was Melbourne's leading goal kicker in 1971 with 44, finished second in the club's Best and Fairest award and polled seven votes in the Brownlow Medal that year.

Oakleigh YCW Open Age Team, Premiers 1962

(With permission from Oakleigh Amateur Football Club)

Back Row: G. Browne, J. Launder, T. Healy, J. Comerford, R. Epstein, W. Beckwith

Centre Row: Mr J. Ryan, B. McCarthy, J. McKenna, B. O'Shea, P. Quinn, B. Carr, K. Rohan G. Honan, Mick Reed

Front Row: K. Reed, K. Jenkins, J. Gubbins (Captain), Mr O' Shea (Coach), J. White, L. Bibby, R. Clarke

On retiring from VFL football, Paul played for Dandenong in the VFA in 1981 and, returning to his roots, was playing coach with the Oakleigh VFA team from 1982 to 1984. He has also been a fitness advisor at Richmond, skills coach at Collingwood, a runner for St Kilda and in 2012 was a football commentator on radio, with a special interest in game statistics.

In 1977, Paul took up a lecturing position at Christ College Chadstone., which was a Catholic teachers' college and the forerunner of the Australian Catholic University.

When Paul took up the position at Christ College he joined **Jeff Moran** on the Physical Education staff. Jeff is one of the 20 ex-St Kilda players who had the privilege of playing in the Saints 1966 premiership side. He was on the wing in that team and kicked a goal in the low scoring game.

Moran also played in the St Kilda's losing 1971 Grand Final side against Hawthorn, before a crowd of over 118,000, of which I was one, at the 'G. The game is memorable for number of reasons.

Firstly it was a very tough encounter with hard men, John Kennedy the coach of the Hawks, and Allan Jeans at the helm for the Saints. Champion goal kicker Peter Hudson was flattened early in the game by the Saints' Kevin "Cowboy" Neale. The "payback" occurred later with Hawks' rover Leigh Matthews taking care of the opposition's Stuart Trott.

Secondly, it was a game when the Hawks had a great comeback. Twenty points down at the last change, Kennedy moved Peter Hudson to centre half-forward and flanker Bob Keddie to full forward. Keddie, a good player all day, was brilliant with his last quarter goals bringing his tally to four gaols for the game. The Hawks kicked seven goals to the Saints' three in the final term to win by seven points

Finally, the game was a never-to-be-forgotten match because Peter Hudson missed an easy shot for goal in the last quarter. Had he kicked the goal he would have broken Bob Pratt's still standing record of 150 goals in a season.

On retiring from the Saints, Jeff Moran continued his career with Dandenong in the VFA. He had played 155 games with St Kilda.

Snippet

Jeff Moran was living in Shepparton in 2011 when his former coach at St Kilda, Allan Jeans, passed away. Interviewed on the ABC there, like Dermot Brereton (and many others), Jeff had good things to say about Allan Jeans. He also saw Jeans as a terrific role model. "He was just one of the most inspiring people I have met in terms of, not only his coaching ability, but in his role as a mentor for young blokes like myself." Moran was only 18 when he went to St Kilda and he said that Jeans was second only to his parents in helping him to form his life values.

Footy boots for Timor Leste

Paul Callery has continued to his employment at the Australian Cath-olic University (ACU). He went on to obtain a Doctor of Philosophy (PhD) qualification and in 2012 was a senior lecturer in the School of Exercise Science. He has a special interest in helping the Timorese people. In 2012 he took a group of students to Timor Leste (Timor East). They were accompanied by excess luggage comprising 600 pairs of footy boots intended for use by children, aged from seven to fifteen. The boots were donated by a number of Catholic primary and secondary schools in Melbourne. The photo above (by Clothilde Bell from *Catholic Education Today*) shows Paul and Stephen Elder, the executive director of the Catholic Education Office, surrounded by boots before heading for Timor Leste.

The boots are part of the *Future in Youth* project run by the University to help disengaged youth in Baucau, Timor Leste's second largest city. The trip was very successful, with Paul commenting that the only problem was that they had just 600 pairs of boots when they could have used 6000. The project was established by Dr Callery and **Dr Ross Smith**, also a footballer-turned-academic.

Dr Smith, well known as the ex-St Kilda rover who twice won the Club's Best and Fairest award, was rover in the Saints' 1966 premiership side and won the Brownlow Medal in the following year. Smith took a long time to hit his straps as a champion, earning only six votes in the six seasons previous to his Brownlow Medal win with 24 votes. He captained Victoria in the 1972 Carnival and was a successful coach of Subiaco in Western Australia. Smith was named as the first rover in the Saints' Team of the Century.

Between them, Callery and Smith played nearly 400 games of senior football and both were able to engage in professional careers while doing so, continuing their studies to the highest level after retiring from playing footy.

The "Nodders"

As mentioned earlier, Sam Reed (right), the great grandson of George and Annie Reed, was captain of the first Mazenod team to defeat Salesian College and win the Johnson/Davis Cup. A very promising young footballer, Sam played for two years with the Oakleigh Chargers after which he was recruited by Mazenod Old Collegians (the "Nodders") in the VAFA where he has had considerable success playing over 150 games with the club. His older brother Patrick donned the Nodder guernsey a similar number of times. Parents, George and Liz, have been strong supporters of the club. In 2013 George was timekeeper when the club was in C-Grade.

On being runners-up at that level the Nodders will be back in B-Grade in 2014. In 2013, Sam, a previous Best and Fairest winner, was third to Tim Bourbon, with Ben Phipps being runner-up.

Earlier Stars for the Nodders

The Mazenod Old Collegians Football Club (MOCFC) team began in 1978 in the Eastern Churches Competition and moved to VAFA F-Grade in 1989. With immediate success they reached A-Grade after eight years, winning five senior flags on the way up. Over the years many excellent players have represented the club. Some of the outstanding players have been:

> Tim Chilcott, who played over 300 games for the Club, was in six senior premiership teams. He captained the team from 1990-94.
>
> Jerome Dunne, captain for a number of years, was instrumental in the club's success and moving into A-Grade.
>
> Daniel Ryan, a centre half-back of the Glenn Jacovich mould, was capable of controlling an opponent and making decisive attacking moves into the forward line.
>
> The Murray Brothers (Mark, David and Chris) between them played almost 400 games for the club. They have been staunch supporters of the club adding their expertise at all levels.
>
> Matthew Arnot made his senior AFL debut for Richmond in 2013. A Mazenod Under 19 and senior player, Matthew became the latest of a number of ex-MOCFC players to reach AFL senior level, the best known of whom would be West Coast Eagles premiership player, Ashley Hansen and Western Bulldogs' captain, Matthew Boyd.

Heath Black

In 2013 the senior team was fortunate to have Heath Black, an ex-Mazenod student, join his two half brothers Jace Kelly and Shawn Black to play with the Nodders. Like all of the team, Heath the former St Kilda and Fremantle player was devastated by the Nodders' narrow defeat in the Grand Final. He had never played in a flag-winning team.

Heath notched up nearly 200 games in a successful AFL career which was marred by personal problems. Being recently diagnosed with depression and adult ADHD, Heath has written a book, entitled *Black*, in which he tells his story to help others with similar problems.

He is very busy facilitating and giving programs to groups all over Australia with a number of major employers including Rio Tinto and various education systems making use of him. He also works with the Western Australian Suicide Prevention strategy.

When asked who he thought was the best footballer that he had played with he nominated St Kilda's Robert Harvey, claiming that Harvey "had the ability to run at high intensity, recover quickly and to do it all again". He also praised Harvey's humility.

From Heath's perspective, Fremantle's Chris Connelly was the best coach that he had played under. He appreciated the trust that Connelly had in him in allowing him to play the role of a sweeping half-back flanker where he could initiate attacks. Heath also enjoyed being part of the leadership group under Connelly.

FIDA

The Mazenod Old Collegians Football Club has been heavily involved in the Football Integration Development Association (FIDA) for a number of seasons with senior players being involved in the coaching and match management through Mazenod Panthers Football Club. The main purpose of FIDA is to initiate access for people with an intellectual disability to the game of Australian Rules football. Attendees of special schools are qualified to play, and are especially welcome to come along and enjoy a game of footy with the mighty Panthers.

16
The Vietnam War and Glen James

The Vietnam War, the War and football, Lalbert success, Lalbert stars, Tiger flags, the "Oaks" and "Big Bob", Oakleigh stars, Waverley Park; Lalbert FC, Richmond FC, Oakleigh FC, Geelong FC, Collingwood FC, Glenelg FC, Maffra FC; Tom Hafey, Graham Cornes, Wayne Closter, Graham Burgin, Graham Robbins, Brian Ford and Bourkes.

One Sunday in the early '70s, our family visited Mum and Dad for lunch at their home in Oakleigh. As was often the case I took a couple of our children to the swings that were in one corner of the Rec.

An under-age YCW football match had just been completed and a couple of dads were having a kick with some of the younger lads. I heard one of the men, about fifty metres out from goal, call out, "I'll put this through from here." It was Jack Gilmore, my teammate from Lalbert. Jack had a son playing for Bentleigh YCW against an Oakleigh team that Sunday. Speaking to him, I found that Jack had left the farm in Lalbert and, after running a hotel in Charlton, was then living in Bentleigh and working as an estate agent. We later met at a hotel in Springvale and had a good chat, talking of Lalbert Football Club and the success that the Club had enjoyed since each of us had left it.

Lalbert played in five Grand Finals between 1962 and 1966, winning the flag in 1962 and 1964. Many of the names in teams of those years had been in Lalbert teams when Jack and I had played there, including Powers, Meehans, Nalders, O'Mearas and Allans. In the 1966 Grand Final team there were seven Powers, four Meehans and three Allans. Barry Kelly and John Curthoys were still in the side.

In addition to the locals, two great assets who came to the club during the 1960s were Mal Richardson and John Howden. Richardson had coached Tyntynder to the premiership in 1959. He was a great ruckman in country footy, tall and raw-boned; the type of player who could inspire a team. Howden was the local school teacher who had played good football elsewhere as he moved around the bush in his profession. He was a ruck-rover and, together with Richardson and rover Owen Power, they were a formidable combination at centre bounces.

I was pleased about the Lalbert flags in the '60s but I was probably equally as satisfied by the premierships won by the Tigers and the Oaks in 1967. Despite the fact that the Oaks' win was in Division Two, they were on the way back.

A Lalbert Team from the '60s

Back Row: M. Power, M. Fox, G. Power, L.Power, K. Meehan, B. Kelly

Third Row: O. Power, V. O'Meara, C. Power, D. Free, G. Power, D. Meehan, R. Allen, D. Power, R. Nalder, R McFarlane

Second Row: C. Nalder, Doug Brown, M. Richardson, B. Jobling, T. Sheppard, M. McGregor, G. Openlander, K. Allen

Front Row: P. Power, J. Curthoys, Mascot Roberts, M. Power, W. O'Meara

Tiger Flag

The Tigers broke their long drought since 1943 by defeating Geelong in the 1967 Grand Final. The win was the start of a new era for the Tigers. They had abandoned their Punt Road oval to play at the MCG which was better suited to their style of play. Also, they had appointed as coach a young **Tom Hafey** who had a great coaching record in Shepparton in the previous year. They played an attacking, long kicking game as did their Grand Final opponents, Geelong. Paddy Rohan, Jim McKenna and I were among the 109,396 people who attended the game.

Richmond won but may have been a bit lucky to do so. The final scores saw the Tigers victorious by nine points in a high scoring game but an incident in the last quarter of the match indicates that the result could have gone the other way.

Tiger full back Fred Swift took a mark on the goal line in the dying minutes of the game. The issue was whether Fred marked the ball in front of the line or whether it was through for a goal when he marked it. As luck would have it, I was in a perfect position in the stand to view the incident and there is no doubt that the goal umpire made the correct decision. Then again I may have been a little biased.

All in all, the entire 1967 AFL Grand Final, like its counterpart in Tasmania was a memorable game.

A final comment on this match is that if Geelong had not cleared John Devine, who was still in his prime, to coach North Hobart in 1967, then the results of two historic Grand Finals, one in Tasmania and one in Victoria, may have been different.

A Tiger Era

After the Tigers won the flag in 1967 they remained at or near the top of the ladder for the next seven years winning three more premierships and being runners-up once over that period. They then picked up another premiership in 1980. A glance at the Tiger Honour Board of captains, coaches, best and fairest winners and leading goal kickers shows that the success was due to the number of highly talented players who represented the Club over those years including the following: Fred Swift, Roger Dean, Royce Hart, Francis Bourke, Ian Stewart, Geoff Raines, Rex Hunt, Neil Balme, not to mention Dick Clay and big occasion player Billy Barrot. Tommy Hafey coached the team for the four premierships.

Graham Burgin (at right), a Mt Waverley resident and a dual premiership Tiger defender from that era, told me that Tommy Hafey was the right man in the right place at that time. Len Smith, the coach before him had encouraged his team to move the ball quickly while Tommy went one step further and encouraged the players to play on at all costs. Burgin said that Hafey liked his players to take risks and back their judgement even if such an  approach had failed at the first attempt. Try again and it might come off.

According to Graham Burgin, Hafey believed in kicking long and "using the corridor" as we would say today. He called it "straight down the guts". The recruitment of tall players, even for flanks and wings, helped the Tigers to out-mark their opponents.

A stickler for fitness, Hafey led by example, putting himself through the same challenges as the players. He also invited running coach Percy Cerutty to come to the club and talk to the players about fitness. Cerutty made his Portsea training camp available to the club and the players did plenty of running up and down the sandhills there, helping them to keep going right to the end. In the 1969 Grand Final Richmond, four points down at three quarter-time, kicked 4 goals 7 behinds in the final term to Carlton's two behinds.

Above all, Hafey had success as a coach because in contrast to previous coaches, Len Smith and Jack Titus, he was closer to the players' ages, had their respect and trusted them to do what was asked of them.

Snippet

Graham Burgin was a dashing half-back flanker, recruited to Richmond from Vermont when he was still eligible to play with the under 19 side. After not feeling at home when initially invited to train with Hawthorn and then Collingwood, he was made welcome at Richmond when the club paid his train fare to get to training on his first night, and gave him a towel and a football after his second run with them. He signed with Richmond shortly after.

His career was marred by injury as he missed most of the 1969 season only to return to the team in the second last round and then play centre half-back on Robert Walls in the Grand Final keeping Walls goalless. He was on the half-back flank in the 1967 premiership win over Geelong.

In the 1990s Burgin was Team Manager for nearly seven years. Graham told me that apart from Royce Hart in practice matches, speedy left-footer John Sharrock was an opponent whom he found difficult to play against. When asked to name his first pick if he had to select a team from the footballers with whom he played for or against, he went unhesitatingly for triple Brownlow Medallist, Ian Stewart, who was highly skilled at all facets of the game and could play anywhere.

The Bourke Family

Further success came to the Tigers in 1980, under the coaching of Tony Jewell. The team was augmented by the goal kicking prowess of Michael Roach while Kevin Bartlett (the Norm Smith Medallist with seven goals in the Grand Final) and **Francis Bourke** were still there to be major contributors.

While the latter player's record is well known and documented on a plaque in the main street of his home town, Nathalia, as is the fact that **David Bourke**, the son of Francis had 85 games for the Tigers, the skill of the family's patriarch, Frank, is often not recognised.

In 1946, after finishing runners-up in 1944 and fifth in 1945, the Tigers began the season well, winning four of their first six games. **Frank Bourke**, a full-forward who had played one game with the Tigers in 1943 before he joined up to serve in World War II, returned to play with them in that year. Frank was on top of the League goal kicking list after nine games, ten goals ahead of Sam Loxton of St Kilda with the great Fred Fanning of Melbourne coming third. Frank had been selected to play for Victoria but tragedy struck in the next game when he badly injured his knee. Although Frank played a few games in 1947, this injury virtually ended his VFL career as his knee was never the same again.

With Frank's career cut short after 16 games and Francis playing 300 games, David's 85 games brought the family's total (family photo above) for the club to over 400 games – a significant performance. Only three families (Pannam/Richards at Collingwood, Rankin/O'Donnell at Geelong, and Tuck/Ablett at Hawthorn) have bettered this with a single club).

Frank Bourke passed away on 27 December 2011, just a few weeks short of his 90th birthday. Funeral services were held at Holy Family Catholic Church, Mount Waverley, and at St Mary's Catholic Church, Nathalia. He was laid to rest at Nathalia.

The Mount Waverley service was well attended and eulogists remembered Frank as a fine man and a loving husband, father, grandfather and great-grandfather. His friendliness and wit were also noted. A lover of many sports, Frank used to jokingly claim that he could have played Test cricket, just as Sam Loxton did, after he retired from playing footy. Frank used to say that it was his captain's fault that he didn't emulate Loxton – "My captain always sent me in, in the middle of a hat-trick!"

A number of ex-Richmond footballers attended Frank's funeral, including Emmett Dunne and John Nix. Dunne, who has had a very successful career in the police force, has served as a member of the AFL Tribunal.

Snippet

Below is Francis Bourke's football record as detailed on one side of the Francis Bourke plaque in the main street at Nathalia:

Games: 300

Goals: 71

Best and Fairest: 1970, Runner-Up; '72, '74, '75, '76 Captain: 1976-1977

Premierships: (5) 1967, 1969, 1973, 1974, 1980

Senior Coach: 1982, 1983

Richmond Life Member: 1976

Richmond Team of the Century: (wing)

Richmond "Immortal": 2005

AFL Team of the Century (Selected 1996): (wing)

AFL Hall of Fame (Inducted 2002)

AFL Life Member (Elected 1982)

Jack and Joan Hamilton

In 1968 I was offered a position as a lecturer at Frankston Teachers' College. The charming Joan Hamilton was on the staff there and I had the pleasure of meeting Joan's husband, Jack Hamilton, at a couple of staff socials. Jack, known for his sense of humour, was at that time the VFL's Chief Commissioner, a very responsible job. When asked who might replace him in the position when he retired, Jack, who had a way with words replied, "A man who jumps out of telephone boxes and has a big 'S' on his chest."

Vietnam War and Football

At that time the Vietnam War was being fought. There is no doubt that many promising footballers had their careers interrupted or stopped because of their conscription and consequent service in that War. One was **Wayne Closter**, who played in the centre for the losing Geelong side in the 1967 Grand Final against Richmond, and was called up for National Service, subsequently serving in Vietnam. On his return he missed most of seasons 1969 and 1970 because of a skin complaint contracted in Vietnam. Despite his break from football Closter played 191 games and kicked 72 goals for the Cats. A beautiful mover, he used both feet so well that it was difficult to tell which was his natural foot.

Another footballer who played only five games of VFL football but is particularly well known to Aussie Rules lovers had his football career interrupted by being drafted into the defence forces and sent to serve in Vietnam. His name is **Graham Cornes**. His five games for North Melbourne in 1979, when he was past his prime, was a minor break in a stellar career in the SANFL. Cornes was in his second season with Glenelg when he was drafted to serve with the 7th Battalion of the Royal Australian Regiment in Vietnam.

On his return home he continued his career playing with Glenelg. This helped him settle back into the community, far better than many of his fellow veterans who suffered badly from post-traumatic stress after the War.

In all, Graham Cornes played 317 games with the club including stints as captain and coach. He was twice picked as an All-Australian player and twice as the coach of that team. Another claim to fame is that, as coach of the South Australian side in State of Origin games, his team beat the Victorians six times in a row. No doubt he relished each victory over Victoria as he once said that "it surprises a lot of people inside Victoria that football can be played outside Victoria in a fashion that will bring success at a top class level". Cornes was appointed coach of the inaugural Adelaide team in the AFL.

Graham Cornes had the ability to take freakish high marks. One of his marks is included in Jamie Cooper's painting *The Game That Made Australia*.

Already recognised in the Glenelg and SANFL Halls of Fame, Graham Cornes was inducted into the AFL Hall of Fame in 2012.

Despite his personal success in the sport he claims that his proudest moment in football was when his two sons, Chad and Kane, were members of the Port Adelaide's AFL flag-winning side in 2004.

In 2012, enjoying a successful career as a drive-time sports program host on radio, Cornes is active in veterans' affairs, including being Patron of the Vietnam Veterans' Motorcycle Club. He has been awarded an OAM (Medal of the Order of Australia) for his services to the community.

Snippet

Just as Graham Cornes had his senior football career interrupted by the Vietnam War, others would have missed out on their chance to play top level football because of the War or the National Service call-up associated with the War. One such player was John Callery, the brother of Dr Paul. Like Paul he played his early football with Oakleigh YCW then moved on to play with the Melbourne Under 19 side where he won the Club Best and Fairest award. He was called up for National Service and, although he played some footy with Labrador in Queensland while he was in training, his time out of football, at a crucial time of his football career, meant that he didn't "make the big time". On returning to civilian life, John played with Berwick where he made a great contribution to the club, notching up a record number of games for their senior team.

Glen James

Another football identity who was called up in the draft and spent one year in Vietnam is Glen James. The son of an Indigenous Australian of the Yorta Yorta people, Glen James was 10th of 14 children. He grew up in Shepparton and as a young man enjoyed playing football. However, after breaking his jaw while playing he decided to be an umpire.

James subsequently became a very successful umpire, being the first Indigenous Australian to umpire at the highest level. In all, he umpired 166 VFL/AFL matches including the 1982 and 1984 Grand Finals.

The 1982 Grand Final would have been a challenging game to umpire. Richmond, finishing on top of the ladder, was favourite to defeat the Blues in the Grand Final. But it didn't happen that way.

Highlights of the match were the return to the game of the Blues' Ken Hunter after being knocked out by a fair bump from Jim Jess, the rare skills of Peter Bosustow and Wayne Johnston (the "Dominator") of Carlton and the attraction of a well-built female streaker to Carlton's Bruce Doull. Carlton's captain, Mike Fitzpatrick, was a great on-field leader and the Blues won by three goals.

Glen James' fellow Indigenous Australian, Maurice Rioli, played a classic game in the centre for the Tigers and won the Norm Smith Medal for best on ground. James' umpiring of this difficult match was such that he was given the Grand Final between the Hawks and the Bombers in 1984. The Bombers, with Bill Duckworth starring, were successful in that encounter.

Highly respected, Glen James was President of the VFL Umpires' Association in 1985 and was selected as umpire in the Indigenous Team of the Century.

Graham Robbins

After working at Frankston Teachers' College, I was able to transfer to a position of lecturer at Toorak Teachers' College (TTC). There I was lucky enough to be able to coach the College football team which played in a mid-week competition comprising teams from the half a dozen or so teachers' colleges around Melbourne.

TTC began the season slowly but the coaching team, which included assistant coaches Reg Chapple and Hayden Power, was able to inject some spirit into the boys and they began to play well. The outstanding player in the Toorak side was Graeme Robbins who was on the list at Richmond.

The Melbourne Teachers' College (MTC) team was coached by my friend, Jim McKenna, and traditionally they were very difficult to beat as they often had, among their students, older good footballers who were trained teachers returning to College to improve their qualifications in special areas of education. In that category for MTC was Bernie McCarthy, a tall, high marking centre half forward for North Melbourne. McCarthy, although a little inconsistent, was one of the best centre half-forwards in the game in his era, playing 148 VFL games for the "Shinboners", and kicking 80 goals.

As the season progressed, the improving TTC side had to beat MTC to make the finals. Largely because of the skill of Bernie McCarthy we were unable to do so. This meant that the remaining couple of games were "dead rubbers" as far as the finals were concerned. TTC were out of the race.

Graham Robbins had been playing excellent football in the Richmond seconds and been promoted to the senior side mid-season. He was doing well in the forward pocket as change rover with Kevin Bartlett.

On the day before our next match between the Toorak and Burwood Colleges I spoke to Robbins, "You'd better not play tomorrow, you might get injured. There's nothing hanging on it. We can't make the final. We will probably win anyway."

"No, I really want to play. I enjoy playing with the boys. We want to finish on a good note."

"It's up to you but I wouldn't recommend it. You could get injured, just when you are doing well with the Tigers."

"I'm willing to take the risk. I'm going to play."

Graham Robbins

On the next day, in the second quarter against Burwood, Graham Robbins fell under a pack and was badly injured. I took him to the Box Hill Hospital where Graham was told that he had a broken collarbone. It is not difficult to imagine his disappointment. And it was one of my saddest experiences in football when I took Graham home to his parents in Mount Waverley with the tragic news.

Billy Brown, who had been playing on the wing for the Tigers, took over the second roving position again and did well in that role. Although he starred with the reserves, Graham Robbins never became a regular with the Tigers. He had missed his chance. In all, he played 13 games, kicking 9 goals. During 1971 he transferred to Oakleigh in the VFA.

Also in the Toorak Teachers' College team was David Callanan, an Oakleigh lad who, with his brother, Jack Callanan, played footy and cricket with Oakleigh YCW. Their parents, Jack and Eileen Callanan, were great workers for the community.

The Callanan boys, members of a large family, had a good football pedigree in that their mum's father, David O'Donoghue, and his brother, Aloysius "Alan" O'Donoghue played VFL football. David was a defender for Collingwood, playing 53 games with the club from 1907 to 1911. Alan played initially for the Tigers but later had more success with South Melbourne. A ruckman and forward he starred in a 1914 semi-final and was a member of the losing Grand Final side a couple of weeks later. It was in that match that Bruce Sloss, who was later killed in action in World War I, was best on ground. Playing 46 games with the Swans, Alan was centre half-back in their premiership team in 1918 when they defeated the Magpies by five points. The Callanan brothers, David and Jack, while not VFL players like their grandfather and great uncle, were talented footballers with Oakleigh YCW.

Snippet

The best on ground in the 1918 Grand Final, in which Alan O'Donoghue played, was Vic Belcher, a ruckman who has the distinction of being the only South Melbourne player to play in two premierships with that club. As a young man who didn't drive a car he rode his bicycle from Brunswick, where he lived, to South's Lakeside Oval for training. He played a then-record 226 games with South before he moved to Fitzroy as coach. There he was successful with Fitzroy winning the 1922 flag. On retiring from active involvement with any club he became a VFL boundary umpire. Vic Belcher was named as back pocket in the Swans' Team of the Century. His brother, Allan played with Essendon and captained that club in their 1912 Grand Final defeat of South Melbourne. Vic Belcher was in the South side. It took just over 100 years until brothers again played against each other in a Grand Final. Stephen Hill (Fremantle) and Bradley Hill (Hawthorn) faced each other in the 2013 clash.

Volatile Oaks

With the loss of Coughlan and the retirement of others who were in the 1960 premiership team, Oakleigh slipped badly over the next few years until they reached a situation where they were once again relegated to second division in 1964. It was from there that they had to start rebuilding again. And the club was up to the task. With former champion Eric Beard as coach, the Oaks made it to the Grand Final in 1967. Playing Geelong West at Coburg, the Oaks had a win in a closely fought game to take out the flag. Brian Ford and Norm Luff were Oakleigh's best players.

Unfortunately, like Wayne Closter, both **Brian Ford** and "Swooper" Murnane, a recruit from Melbourne, missed some football because of the National Service draft but by the beginning of 1970 the Oaks were getting ready to fire. What's more they had brought off a great playing coach coup at the beginning of that season. Following two seasons with Hamilton Imperials in the Western Border League, the much travelled, highly successful **Big Bob Johnson** was signed to lead the Oaks in 1970. Big Bob, who had watched Smeaton, Baxter, and Hill at the Warrigal Road oval as a youngster, had returned home at the age of 34 to be at the helm in the club's revival.

And the recruiting continued. Over the next year or two, a lad who grew up in neighbouring Ashwood, Bill Barrot, from Richmond was snared along with another recruit, ruckman David Wenn who was also, in a sense, returning home. David Wenn was the son of former Oakleigh champion Max Wenn. Graham Robbins, from nearby Mt Waverley, then came to the fold from the Tigers in 1971.

Despite the expectations, 1970 was a disappointment in that Big Bob, after kicking two goals early in the first game for the season against Williamstown, broke his leg and was sidelined for the rest of the year.

Big Bob surprised everyone by returning to the game in 1971 and continued to build the team. Leading from the front he kicked 91 goals in that year.

The next season, 1972, was again "the year of the Oaks". Finishing on top of the ladder, a feature of their game was their accurate kicking for goal, again led by Johnson. In a match against Port Melbourne, Johnson kicked 11 goals straight out of a team total of 26 goals, 4 behinds.

Swooper Murnane and Graham Robbins were also known for their great accuracy in front of goal.

The Oaks defeated Dandenong in the second semi-final and played them again in the Grand Final. Dad, Ramon and I were among the large crowd that attended the game at St Kilda.

Although the scores were level at half way through the third term in the Grand Final, Oakleigh steamed away by kicking 12 goals to six in the remainder of the game. Swooper, with seven straight goals, Ford, Barrot, Wenn, rovers Robbins and Taylor, plus Big Bob (with five goals) were the best of an even team.

In 1972, Brian Ford was second in the J. J. Liston Trophy. Johnson came equal fifth in the Association goal kicking with 69 goals, while Robbins, who won the Club Best and Fairest award, kicked 68 goals.

With the retirement of Big Bob Johnson and the loss of other senior players, the Oaks were runners-up in 1973 and 1974. The years under Johnson rivalled any of Oakleigh's other great eras in terms of local support, if not in success, as only a single flag was produced. But the team that won the 1972 premiership must rate as one of Oakleigh's best. It was also their last First Division premiership, with their only later flag being the 1988 Second Division premiership.

Retiring from playing with Oakleigh at the end of 1972, Big Bob Johnson's career had been outstanding. He played in five premierships for Melbourne, where he played 140 games for 267 goals. He captained and coached East Fremantle to four successive Grand Finals for one flag, winning the WANFL goal kicking in 1966 with 89 goals. He kicked 105 in 1965, but didn't win the WANFL award in that year. He represented both Victoria and Western Australia in Carnival football. He was named in the Melbourne Team of the Century.

Old Bob Johnson played 113 games with the Demons and kicked 302 goals. A combined effort of 253 games for 569 goals and six premierships was a great family contribution to the Club.

Family Success

While breaking his collarbone playing with Toorak Teachers' College may have cut short the VFL career of **Graham Robbins**, he still had a long and successful career in football.

On leaving Oakleigh Robbins captained South Adelaide in the SANFL and represented South Australia in a match against Western Australia. He later played and coached in the Gippsland area where, at one stage, he worked as a development officer for the VFL. He played with Sale and was named in the Sale Team of the Decade for the 1980s. He also had a long involvement with the Maffra Tigers being playing coach there in 1983 and 1984, assistant coach in the early 2000s and at the age of 59 taking on the role of non-playing coach there in 2009.

Two of Robbins' sons, Ben and Craig, returned home to play under their dad. Ben had played 92 games of AFL football and younger son, Craig, was an experienced player with Old Collegians in the VAFA. Would the Tigers, and the Robbins family, have a season to remember?

Perhaps they would. Making the Grand Final, Maffra had to play the Latrobe Valley's long-time pacesetter, Traralgon, at the Morwell ground.

Three points ahead at the first change, the Tigers were three goals down at half-time, only to fight back and be just three points down at the last change. They kicked nine behinds in a row in the last quarter and were still three points behind at the final siren.

But the game wasn't over. Just prior to the siren, burly forward Nick Horsford marked strongly some 40 metres out from goal. He could take his kick. The crowd was anxious as it waited to see what Nick would do. Was he a reliable kick? Would nerves get the better of him? The crowd was hushed as Nick moved in to kick. But when he calmly put the ball between the big sticks, the Maffra crowd erupted and pandemonium broke out as joyous supporters shouted and hugged each other. The Tigers had won the flag.

Craig Robbins won the Stan Aitken Medal for Best on Ground in the Grand Final. Other excellent players for Maffra were D. Adams, B. Durrant, and J. Butcher. Nick Horsford kicked two goals as did B. Rathnow. Single goal scorers were J. Butcher, D. Stubb and Ben Robbins. Maffra and the Robbins family had a day, and a season, to remember.

The Tigers, again under Graham Robbins, made it back-to-back premierships in 2010.

Like Glen Bow, Mal Richardson, Keith Warburton and Ron Paez, Glen Robbins was one of those footballers who could lift a team and a town when they moved in to lead the local footy team.

Graham Robbins' nephew, David Robbins, won two J. J. Liston awards for Best and Fairest in the VFL playing with both Springvale and Port Melbourne.

VFL/AFL Park

In 1959, the VFL made a decision to build its own stadium to improve its bargaining position in negotiations with the MCC about finals to be played at the MCG, with the long term view of playing the Grand Final at its own new stadium. With this in mind, the VFL purchased land near the corner of Jells and Wellington Roads in Mulgrave.

Delighted with the plan, I became a VFL Park Member as soon as possible. The Park was handy to home and I looked forward to having a seat at VFL finals.

With our young children I attended many games and enjoyed outstanding performances by the likes of Barry Cable, Peter Hudson and Alex Jesaulenko at the Park in the early years of its usage.

When being developed, VFL Park had a lot of money spent on its drainage system. One Sunday morning, a member of the football panel on the TV program *World of Sport*, in discussing the previous day's games, commented that the playing surface of VFL Park was a disgrace. He pointed out that a fortune had been spent on the ground and yet it was in dreadful condition while at the same time the players were doing drop kicks at lesser grounds at Footscray and Geelong. Of course the panel member didn't know that Waverley Park was in a far wetter rainfall belt than Footscray and Geelong.

I have often since wondered whether the VFL had studied Melbourne's rainfall patterns before building a stadium (which became known as "Arctic Park") at Mulgrave – on top of cold, wet and windy Wheelers Hill. I suspect that VFL administrators, concerned with the demographics of the location, gave no thought to the local weather conditions.

Moving on

In 1974, I took up a position at Christ College, Chadstone, right beside the Chadstone Shopping Centre. Not long after I started there we had our fifth child, another son Brendan, whose birth was followed a few weeks later by the sudden death of my Mum, Muriel, a loving and caring mother and grandmother who supported her family in every way.

Mick, then 75, kept on living in the family home in George Street and continued to take a great interest in life, in general, and football, in particular. However, after Richmond sacked Jack Dyer as coach, he began to lose his enthusiasm for the Tigers and his allegiance moved slowly across to Hawthorn, particularly when Leigh Matthews came on the scene. He admired Matthews immensely because he "never took his eye off the ball". Being a lover of the underdog, he also thought that the Hawks "were given a poor go from the media".

Mick Reed had to wait until 1975 before he had another Reed to support on the football field. Our third child, Tim, started playing Under 10 football for St Leonard's Glen Waverley in that year. His granddad enjoyed watching him in action.

After three years at Christ College and tiring of the increasing busyness of city life, Marj and I were eager give our children the experience of living in the country and I took a lecturing position at Warrnambool Institute of Advanced Education. It was in Warrnambool that our family's football interests further developed.

17
'Bool Days and Wayne Schwass

A sporting town, Junior footy, the Hampden Football League, a tough Grand Final, A two-game coach; Warrnambool FC, South Warrnambool FC, South Melbourne FC, St Kilda FC, Hawthorn FC, Colac/ Coragulac FC, Collingwood FC, Richmond FC; Des Rowe, Peter Cook, Roy Cazaly, "Tiger" Bence, Colin Watson, Paul Couch, "Goose" Maguire, Adrian Gleeson, Brendan Keilar, the Browns, the Howards, Shaun Ryan and the Wearmouths.

It was a very hot day in January 1977 when Marj and I, with our then five children, arrived in our Holden Kingswood wagon at Warrnambool, a coastal town of around 18,000 people, 260 kilometres south-west of Melbourne.

To my satisfaction there was evidence of sport everywhere. The house that we rented was on a corner, and a hundred metres along the side street was the Warrnambool High School behind which were a number of sporting facilities including sports ovals and bowling and croquet greens. The Reid Oval, the "Number One" football and cricket ground in the town, was part of this complex.

And then there was the beach and the lovely surf of Lady Bay, with its challenging sections for older youths as well as its more gentle areas for young ones. Not far from the beach, nestled in the sand dunes, and protected from the ocean breezes, were seemingly dozens of grass tennis courts.

Not only were there sporting venues, there were also sports people in evidence around the town. Well-known ex-Geelong champion wingman,

Leo Turner, had his electrician business prominent in Fairy Street, while the truck of plumber, Len Mann, premiership ruckman for Melbourne, was often seen around the streets, as was fitness fanatic, ex-South Melbourne defender Don Grossman, doing his daily walk.

In the early '80s Colin Eales was a member of the administrative staff at WIAE.

Colin was on the half-forward flank for Geelong in the famous 1967 VLF Grand Final, playing well and kicking a goal. He had a particularly good final term managing to get three kicks at goal in the very tight game. Fortunately for the Tigers, all of his chances missed. He was recruited from Penshurst, north of Warrnambool, and played 56 games with the Cats, kicking 56 goals.

Student Counsellor, Ian Slockwitch ("Slock"), a champion schoolboy footballer at St Pat's Ballarat, who played a couple of games with Richmond in the '60s before knee injuries ended his VFL career, joined the WIAE staff a year or so after I did. Slock had won the inaugural Brother Bill O'Malley trophy for Best and Fairest for St Pat's Ballarat. The Trophy was named after Brother Bill as he successfully coached St Pat's for many years during which time they were undefeated in their inter-school competition.

Slock has a photo, with him in it, of the 1961 Richmond team. The coach of the side was **Des Rowe**, a member of the Tiger Team of the Century. Also in the photo are Roger Dean, Billy Barrot, Mike Patterson, Paddy Guinane, a former Richmond YCW player, Fred Swift, and Alan ("Bull") Richardson (the father of later legend Matthew Richardson) all of whom would be champions in Tom Hafey's later premiership teams.

Basil Moloney, like Slock, from St Pat's Ballarat, was another in the photo.

Snippet

Basil Moloney featured in a notable incident during his 21 game career. Playing against Geelong, Moloney got into a scrap with Geelong centreman Alistair Lord and Lord was reported by a boundary umpire for the incident. Lord's identical twin brother, Stewart, who was also involved, claimed before the Tribunal that he was the guilty party and that the umpire had reported the wrong player. The case was thrown out. Alistair won the Brownlow Medal that year. Stewart Lord's evidence probably saved his brother from losing the Brownlow, as reported players who are found guilty cannot win the Medal.

The Sharks

In short there was a good sporting feeling to Warrnambool and to my workplace when we arrived there. And to top it all a football team, the Institute Sharks, was formed in 1976 and entered the local Warrnambool and District Football League. Although too old to play at that time I supported the team. Later my family and I became more involved.

Links with Warrnambool Football Club

As part of my role at WIAE I co-ordinated the in-school teaching practice of students who were studying to be primary teachers. A co-worker with me was Nance Cook, an ex-teacher who had come to Warrnambool in 1959 with her husband, **David ("Peter") Cook**. Peter had been appointed coach of Warrnambool Football Club (the "Blues") in the Hampden Football League. A follower/forward, Cook had played 14 games with Melbourne, over the period 1956 to 1958, before a road accident injury cut short his VFL career.

In 1959 Cook was snatched from the Port Fairy Club, who had offered him a one-year contract. At the last minute, Warrnambool upped the ante by signing him for two years. However Peter Cook was to stay with the club for much longer than that. He coached for four years, with his team winning flags in three of these (1959, 1960 and 1962). Resigning as coach because of business commitments, he continued as a player and was again a member of a premiership team in 1963.

Coached in 1963 by Glen Bow, who had played for Quambatook when I was with Lalbert, Warrnambool had at that stage won five flags in seven years. Glen Bow, a much travelled footballer, was recruited by Warrnambool from Perth who had demanded a transfer fee for Bow's clearance. The Blues, with premiership success behind them at the time, had sufficient money in their coffers to afford him.

Warrnambool defeated Colac in the second semi-final in that year. A report on that game in the Warrnambool Football Club history, *Birth of the Blues,* indicated that "Glen Bow and ex-skipper Peter Cook showed the Blues how to win by dominating the air and the ruck all day." Peter Cook was again among the Blues' best players in their subsequent victory over Colac in the Grand Final. Another good player in that match was rover Bill McConnell. An excellent tennis player as well, McConnell won the Maskell Cup for Best and Fairest in the Hampden League in 1962. He later came to work at WIAE as an accountant.

The Warrnambool side was also greatly helped in that highly successful era by forward Stan Noakes who won the club goal-kicking award from 1959 through to 1963 amassing 406 goals over those five seasons including 100 in 1961. Noakes had come from Merbien and, although 6 feet 4 inches tall, he was as mobile as a rover. Also a spectacular mark, it is said that he would have kicked even more goals had he been a more accurate kick.

Following Stan Noakes as a goal kicker, on-baller Ian Hughes was the Blues' leading goal sneak for four out of the next five seasons. In the early '60s he had a couple of seasons with North Melbourne, playing in the Seconds, before he came to Warrnambool. Ian Hughes came to work as a science teacher at the Warrnambool Technical College and subsequently took up a position in the Applied Science Faculty at WIAE.

Tragically, both Stan Noakes and Ian Hughes developed multiple sclerosis and died as young men.

Cricket at CBC – South Warrnambool

In 1978, our second year there, I played cricket with the CBC-South Warrnambool Cricket team in the Warrnambool and District Cricket Association. The club had two senior teams and also an Under 16 team (the "Colts") that played in the local competition on Saturday mornings.

Glenn and John Maguire played with the club. John ("Goose") was to make a name for himself in the district as a star centre-half back in some very successful teams for South Warrnambool. His son, Matt Maguire, also proved to be a strong defender. He has played well over 150 games of AFL football, initially with St Kilda and then with the Brisbane Lions, where he joined another player with Warrnambool connections, Jonathan Brown.

Brendan Keilar

A very prominent cricketer with the CBC-South Warrnambool Colts team in season 1978-79 was **Brendan Keilar** (at right). He was a very capable all-rounder, topping the Under 16 team's batting averages with an average of 26 and being the recipient of his team's Club Championship award. He was also an excellent footballer, as was his father Harry, who was a premiership player for Warrnambool in the Hampden League and  was a co-author of *The Birth of the Blues*, the history of the Warrnambool Football Club.

A year ahead of our eldest son, Michael, at CBC College, Brendan Keilar was described by the Principal of CBC Warrnambool as "... an outstanding student ... a person of determination, high principle and above average academic success ... He has taken part in all school activities, as an outstanding athlete, footballer and cricketer and sports captain."

Brendan became headline news Australia-wide on 18 June 2007 when he and Paul De Waard, a 22-year-old backpacker from the Netherlands, went to assist Kaera Douglas, a young woman who was being assaulted in a Melbourne Central Business District street. Brendan was shot dead by the assailant while Paul was seriously injured.

Brendan left behind his wife and three young children. In his professional life Brendan had been fulfilling the earlier promise that he had shown at Warrnambool. At the time of his heroic act, he was a successful property solicitor after attaining Law and Commerce degrees from the University of Melbourne.

Continuing his sporting career Brendan played cricket with Balwyn Cricket Club and football with University Blacks in the VAFA.

The 87th Annual Report of the Balwyn Cricket Club, in honoring Brendan, says of him:

VALE – Brendan Keilar (1963-2007)

Brendan was fatally wounded in a city shooting while going to the aid of others. His actions touched those in the wider community, and for those that attended the funeral it will not be a day easily forgotten.

Brendan was a fine all-rounder who played 135 games with Balwyn from 1987-88 through to 2000-01 scoring 2112 runs and taking 176 wickets.

Brendan was a popular and outgoing member of the club who also served as the ESCA delegate for a number of years and was also a frequent participant in past player functions and activities. A number of club members were particularly close to "BK" and there is a special bond for those that were members of the dreamers in the late 1980s.

Brendan was clearly valued as a cricketer and well respected as a person at the club.

While playing football with University Blacks, Brendan won the prestigious Cordner Medal for Club Best and Fairest. According to his former team-mate Justin Gray, Brendan was "a ferocious and skilful rover". Justin also said that Brendan's action was "exactly the sort of thing that you would expect Brendan to do".

To honour Brendan's memory, the University Blacks have instituted the Brendan Keilar Medal, an award given to the Club's best player for the season as voted by the players.

After Brendan's funeral, Premier Steve Bracks announced that there would be a permanent memorial in the City to honour Brendan's action. Premier Bracks said that Brendan "did the instinctive thing that many people around Australia would do". He added that the point of the memorial is to keep such selfless acts of bravery in the forefront of public consciousness.

Brendan was awarded the Royal Humane Society of Australasia's Posthumous Medal for Bravery and also received the Bravery Medal from the Australian Government. (Both were awarded in ceremonies at Government House, one in 2008 and the other in 2009).

Mr De Waard received a Silver Medal for Bravery.

It is difficult to imagine exactly how family members would react to such a happening. They would be torn between grief at the loss of the person and pride over his heroic act. The Keilar family released the following statement after the receipt of the Royal Humane Society Australasia's award. The statement read:

> We are immensely proud of Brendan, and to have his courage and selflessness recognised in this manner means so much to us. Many people were affected by the tragic events of 18 June 2007, and for some the pain and anguish continues. To all of those, especially Paul de Waard and Kaera Douglas, we wish you all the strength you need as you continue on the road to recovery.

As announced by Premier Bracks, a plaque to honour the bravery of Brendan Keilar and fellow hero Paul de Waard, was later inserted in the footpath at the corner of Flinders Lane and William Street, Melbourne.

Junior Football

When we arrived in Warrnambool there were three levels of football. There was junior football, which comprised school and inter-school football as well as under-age competitions which were run by a local organisation. There was also the Warrnambool District Football League (WDFL) which ran an older under-age competition as well as senior and reserve grades open-age competition. Teams in this competition were based in or nearby Warrnambool. The strongest competition in the region was the Hampden Football League (HFL) which included the major towns along the Princes Highway between Colac and Port Fairy as well as Coragulac and Mortlake. Two teams, South Warrnambool and Warrnambool, were based in Warrnambool.

School Footy

Tim, our second son, was keen on footy and had begun his football career in Glen Waverley. On moving to Warrnambool he continued to play under-age football. Moving through the age levels Tim played Under 12, Under 13, Under 14 and then two years at the Under 16 level mainly with the CBC team. Tim was attending CBC College at that time. The Under 16 team won the premiership in Tim's first year.

The captain of the team in Tim's first year with the Under 16s was Shane Timms, the son of former Esssendon player Ken Timms, a versatile footballer who played forward pocket and ruck-rover in the Bombers' 1962 premiership side although he had success in both attack and defence. Representing Victoria twice, he played 134 games for Essendon and kicked 112 goals before he left the club to coach Colac and later South Warrnambool.

Being in Year 11 at that time Tim Reed was also a regular player in the CBC College First XVIII. In the College team that year was classmate **Adrian Gleeson** from Koroit. Adrian was an outstanding schoolboy long distance runner who showed great potential as a junior footballer. He lived up to expectations when he was recruited by Carlton in 1986 where he had eleven seasons with the Blues, playing 176 games and kicking 174 goals. He was described in *The Encyclopedia of AFL Footballers* as "a skilful burrowing rover with good goal sense … gritty and determined." Gleeson, a Victorian representative, was a very handy player around stoppages and was a member of Carlton's 1987 premiership team as well as their losing Grand Final team in 1993.

Words of Wisdom

Damian Howard, a member of the under-age teams in which our son Tim played, was a talented and courageous young footballer and son of Leo and Teresa Howard. Leo was a very successful footballer playing with Warrnambool when that club joined the HFL in 1933. He was a member of premiership teams in 1935, 1937 and 1939.

Damien's siblings include entertainers Shane and Marcia Howard. Shane Howard is a well known singer, song writer and music producer who has won an Australian Recording Industry Association (ARIA) award. In the 1980s, he was the lead singer in the band *Goanna*. Their song *Solid Rock* inspired many to look more deeply at issues relating to indigenous people. Shane's involvement in this field led him to be invited to take a leading role in the pre-game celebrations before the 2012 Dreamtime Game between Essendon and Richmond at the 'G. He has also performed as part of the pre-match entertainment at an AFL Grand Final.

Another son, Brendan, like his dad, had premiership success being in flag-winning teams with Warrnambool in 1986 and 1988. In the latter year Brendan came third in the Maskell Medal for Best and Fairest in the HFL. Damian Howard played in the successful Warrnambool team in 1987, while Brendan was overseas. So Howard boys played in three consecutive premiership teams for Warrnambool. All three successful teams were coached by ex-St Kilda player, Grant Thomas. Older brother, Eric, also played for Warrnambool and was awarded a Half-Blue for football at Melbourne University, where he played for Newman College.

I remember well an incident that involved their dad, **Leo Howard**.

A CBC Under 14 football team was playing in the Grand Final. Three fathers gathered around the boundary before the game started. I was one of them. Each of us had a son playing and in each case the son was the oldest football-playing son in the family.

The dads began talking about the game and about what each of them had told their sons before they left home. Eager for CBC to win, it turned out that they had all said much the same thing.

The importance of the match had been stressed as had the fact that many footballers never get a chance to play in a Grand Final. That it would be a tough game was pointed out and that grand finals are different. That the boys would have to give of their all, and may have to suffer a bit in doing so, was other advice. That they must tackle hard, and make sure that the opposition felt it, was also mentioned.

Leo Howard joined the group. Damian was in the team too.

Someone asked Leo, "What did you say to Damian, this morning?"

His reply was along the following lines:

> I was up before Damian, cleaned his boots and put a block of chocolate under his pillow. When he thanked me for the chocolate, I thanked him for the pleasure he had given me, watching him play this year. I then wished him good luck and told him to enjoy the game.

Leo had been there before and knew what was important. In fact he had seen two of his sons, Stephen and Shane, play in a flag-winning CBC

Under 17 team some years before. Leo recognised that winning is good, but for a dad to have the opportunity to see his son running around the football ground and having fun, is far better. Shane Howard went on to play with the Dennington Under 18 team. For Shane, that season "confirmed that I was better suited to music".

WDFL Under 17 Premiers 1970 – Christian Brothers College

Back Row: J. Mugavin, G. Wormald, P. Kearney, G. Pye, Stephen Howard, M.Gleeson

Middle Row: J. Lenehan, R. King, K. Gleeson, J. Willis, I. Anderson, C. Grace, M. Van Run, Shane Howard, B. Bowman, R. Hall, T. Fitzgerald, K. Kavanagh

Front Row: G. Sheehan, A. Gray, N. Carter (Captain), J. Hammond (Coach), G. Coffey, G. Lynch, P. Anderson, J. Carmody

Snippet

The 1988 Grand Final in the HFL was a particularly exciting one for the Howard family. Not only did Brendan play for Warrnambool but Marcia Howard was chosen to sing the National Anthem prior to the commencement of the game, arriving in a helicopter to do so.

Senior Football

The Hampden Football League (HFL) was formed in 1930 when four clubs – Terang, Camperdown, Mortlake and Cobden – broke away from the Western District Football League (WDFL) which had been formed in 1925. The breakaway clubs did so because they didn't want to travel to play at Hamilton, a WDFL club, as the dairy farmers from these clubs struggled to milk their cows at the right time if they made the long trip to Hamilton. In 1933, Warrnambool and South Warrnambool also broke away from the WDFL and joined the Hampden League. Colac and Port Fairy were admitted in 1949, followed by Koroit and Coragulac in 1961.

Meanwhile the WDFL was adding clubs such as Portland and Casterton from the west and in 1964 it merged with the South-East and Border Football League to form the Western Border Football League which is still in existence and comprises nine clubs. There have been a number of changes to the HFL since 1961. In 2011 the HFL comprised the following clubs: Warrnambool, Terang-Mortlake, South Warrnambool, Cobden, Koroit, North Warrnambool, Port Fairy, and Camperdown.

In 2013 Portland and Hamilton rejoined the Hampden League. The brief history of the above leagues shows that, as circumstances change, clubs merge or move to different leagues to maintain their viability. And at times leagues also have to merge in order for football to survive in a particular region.

Don Grossman

Around this time I continued my involvement in football by umpiring in the Reserves grade of the WDFL.

The WDFL official, who was the recipient of the umpires' reports, and also their paymaster, was Don Grossman who, as we have noted, was one of the many players reported in the 1945 "Bloodbath" Grand Final.

On leaving South Melbourne, Grossman took up the position of playing coach of Warrnambool where his team reached the Grand Final twice in the six years he was there. Warrnambool was beaten by Colac on both occasions. In 1951, he won the Maskell Cup for Best and Fairest in the HFL. He then coached South Warrnambool, winning the flag in 1954, his first season at the club. Grossman later coached a number of teams in the WDFL, playing well over 100 games in that competition. He became a football legend in Warrnambool.

An ex-WDFL footballer and friend of mine, Mick O'Shea, told me, on hearing that Grossman collected the match reports, that it was appropriate that Grossman was involved with umpires. He added: "Don played in the Warrnambool and District League until he was well into his forties, coaching a number of different teams in that league," and that "Grossman, like Ted Whitten, had 'umpired' many matches that he played in."

A Very Successful Umpire

Another young man who umpired in the WDFL when the Reed family was living in Warrnambool was **Shaun Ryan** who began his umpiring career in 1992. After two years of umpiring in Warrnambool Ryan then moved on to the Geelong and District Football League before he began with the VFL in 1997. He umpired his first AFL game in round one, 2003. In a brilliant career he umpired five AFL Grand Finals including the 2010 replay between Collingwood and St Kilda. His last was the 2011 Grand final between the Cats and the Magpies, as he surprisingly announced his retirement late in 2011. Sherele Moody of *The Warrnambool Standard* reported the event on 12 October 2011 and noted that in making the announcement Ryan said that "he

Shaun Ryan (With permission of Emmanuel College)

was looking forward to devoting time to his family and continuing his legal career".

South Warrnambool Under 18s

In 1984, our son Tim played with the South Warrnambool HFL Under 18 team, coached by Leigh McCluskey in the HFL.

McCluskey, a talented mid-fielder with the South Warrnambool senior side, proved to be a positive and successful coach. He subsequently coached the South Warrnambool senior team, North Warrnambool in the HFL and was Assistant Coach (to Damian Christensen) at Geelong Falcons.

Three members of the team played VFL football, the most notable of whom was **Wayne Schwass**. After a season with the seniors at South Warrnambool, Schwass went to North Melbourne where he won the Morrish Medal for Best and Fairest in the VFL Under 19 competition in 1987. A stylish left footer, he was capable of long runs from the wing, followed by lengthy kicks into the forward line. He won North's Best and Fairest twice and played in the club's premiership team in 1996.

Traded to Sydney for Shannon Grant in 1997, he won that club's Best and Fairest award and All Australian selection in 1999. One of the few players to win Best and Fairest trophies at two clubs, he represented Victoria three times and played a total of 281 games kicking 186 goals. Schwass was one of those players who could be moved up forward or down the backline when needed, often rejuvenating his team when the move had been made.

Wayne Carey, the great North Melbourne player, was inducted into the AFL Hall of Fame in 2010. He said in a subsequent interview with the *Herald Sun* (4 June 2010), that "the best I played with was Wayne Schwass, followed closely by Anthony Stevens". A high accolade indeed!

Snippet

In 1985 North Melbourne initiated and played in the first of the Friday night televised VFL matches which have since become a popular feature of the game. During the '90s, games featuring the 'Roos were a highlight of the week for many VFL/AFL fans. Marj and I, living back in Melbourne at the time, looked forward to the end of each week – Friday night, fish and chips for dinner, a glass of red, an open fire and North on the telly, with such crowd-pleasing players as Carey, Longmire, Stevens, Archer and, of course, Schwass. North has played in more night games than any other club.

Stephen "Shorty" Anderson, a diminutive rover, was recruited to Collingwood and won the Gardiner Medal for Best and Fairest in the VFL Reserves in 1991. He played four games with the seniors and kicked two goals. Not big enough to hold his place at Collingwood, Anderson returned to South Warrnambool to become a legend with the club and in the Hampden League.

The remaining player from the Under 18 team to play VFL football was Richie Umbers whose dad, Geoff, had a couple of games with Geelong in the '50s. Richie played four games with Brisbane in 1990. He later returned to Warrnambool to be a very good ruckman with South Warrnambool.

Others in the team, particularly, Dominic Quinlan and Chris Lee became successful footballers for South Warrnambool.

Of course Schwass was not the only VFL/AFL champion to come from South Warrnambool. In earlier days, Kevin "Cowboy" Neale, who kicked five goals in the history-making 1966 Grand Final win for St Kilda, was a very versatile ex-South Warrnambool player.

Another, more contemporary, ex-South Warrnambool player to do well at VFL/AFL level is Leon Cameron, who had successful careers at both Footscray and Richmond. A beautiful mover and adept with either foot, Cameron won Footscray's Best and Fairest award in 1993. He played 172 games with the Bulldogs, kicking 68 goals, and 84 games with the

South Warrnambool Under 18 Premiership Team, 1984

Back Row: R. Fitzgerald, D. Quinlan, C. Lee, M. Owen, T. Reed, D. Fotheringham

Middle Row: S. O'Neill, D. Sloane, B. Sheppard, B. McNamara, S. Brooks, C. Holmes, R. Umbers, P. Lee, R. Owen, L. Sloane (Property Steward)

Front Row: A. Creece, J. Eccles, W. Schwass, S. Anderson, L. McCluskey (Coach), R. McIver (Vice-Captain), B. Williams, S. Rayner (Manager), M. O'Neill (Trainer) Absent: Shane Timms (Captain)

Seated in Front: Team mascot and John DeGrandi, the team's boundary umpire

Tigers for 40 goals. Leon was appointed as Assistant Coach at Greater Western Sydney for season 2013 and Head Coach from 2014.

In more recent times Jordan Lewis came from South Warrnambool to be a premiership star with the Hawks.

Cazaly, Watson and Bence

Colin Watson a St Kilda player in the 1920s also came from South Warrnambool. Spotted by **Roy Cazaly**, when still a schoolboy, he was brought to the city by Cazaly to play initially with Port Melbourne but later with the Saints.

A solidly built centreline player who was fast, courageous and an accurate kick, Watson won the Brownlow Medal in 1925. In those days the umpire awarded only one vote to the best player in each game. In his winning year Watson played in 15 games and won nine best-on-ground votes. Watson was lured back to the country as a coach while still in his prime and was playing coach of Stawell and also South Warrnambool before returning to the Saints after seven years' absence. He continued to star at the VFL level winning interstate representation on his return.

Roy Cazaly, who recruited Watson to St Kilda could lay claim to being Australia's most famous footballer. The song *Up There Cazaly*, written and recorded by Mike Brady, is regarded as the Aussie Rules anthem by many who believe that, along with the National Anthem, it should be sung before every AFL Grand Final.

While living in Warrnambool, I heard that Cazaly had coached South Warrnambool and that he had recruited Colin Watson from there. However nowhere in stories about Cazaly could I find evidence of this. A search through 1919 editions of *The Warrnambool Standard* clarified the situation. In 1919, a team named South Warrnambool & Railways played in the Warrnambool District League. This team was probably an amalgamation of two former clubs, South Warrnambool and Railways. Often in the paper the name "South Warrnambool" was used and "Railways" was omitted. Also in the competition were Allansford, Warrnambool Rovers (often called simply Rovers), Dennington, Koroit and Port Fairy.

The towns from which the teams came were all along the Melbourne to Port Fairy railway line and sometimes special trains were run to accommodate the football crowd. It appears that in 1919 it was agreed to play four rounds of matches prior to the finals. This meant that each team played each other four times resulting in a 20 game season for each club. With this number of matches to be played the season continued well into November. St Kilda, for whom Cazaly played in the

VFL, didn't make the finals. His season was finished rather early. South Warrnambool had an up and down season and were struggling to stay in the top four.

A report in *The Warrnambool Standard* on 27 October 1919 about the match between South Warrnambool (and Railways) and Dennington indicated that:

> South Warrnambool was represented by a strong combination and had the services of Roy Cazaly of the St Kilda League team. He made considerable improvement in the South team as coach, while his marking, kicking and ground work stamp him as one of the finest players who have played the game in Warrnambool for some years.

South Warrnambool & Railways finished fourth and played Koroit, the minor premiers, on the next Saturday. A report of the match in *The Warrnambool Standard* of Tuesday 4 November 1919 tells of Koroit's victory and the end of the season for South Warrnambool. Cazaly was easily best on ground, while future Brownlow Medallist, **Colin Watson** (still a schoolboy), was in South's best players. It was after these two games that Cazaly brought Watson to Melbourne. No doubt money changed hands to persuade Cazaly to be playing coach of South Warrnambool for two games.

The best player for Koroit was Bence. **Roy Bence** was recruited from Koroit to South Melbourne in 1922, after Cazaly had moved to South. One wonders if Cazaly had a role in this recruitment. Bence then went to St Kilda in 1925, when Cazaly was at Minyip, and became a very successful rover there, playing 144 games and kicking 83 goals. Nicknamed "Tiger", Bence fearlessly attacked the ball and was handy around goals.

Couch Courage

Just as the children of George and Annie Reed left home in Costerfield when they reached adulthood, so too did our Michael, Liz and Tim.

In 1985, when Tim Reed moved to Melbourne, Wayne Schwass remained in Warrnambool and played with South Warrnambool seniors in the Hampden League. They had a strong team bolstered by a couple of professional footballers who played footy in Darwin over the summer months and travelled south to play in the winter. They also had a particularly tough playing coach in Kevin McVilly who was well known in Hampden League circles. The local Derby between Warrnambool and South Warrnambool always attracted much publicity in the town. A young Paul Couch was rover for Warrnambool.

Youngest son Brendan and I went along to watch the game.

"It's a pity that Tim went to Melbourne. He could have been playing for South today," we commented as we walked to the Reid Oval, believing that it would be good to see Tim play in the Hampden League.

I changed my mind not long into the game. South hit Warrnambool with everything and Warrnambool was not backward in "returning the compliments". It was one of the toughest games of footy that I had ever seen. A particular target was the Warrnambool rover, the young left-footed Paul Couch, who had his nose broken early in the game. Undeterred, Couch continued to give everything for his team and in an outstanding performance was a key player in his team's victory, kicking five goals himself.

Couch continued to show the same skill and courage when he moved to Geelong in the following year.

Paul's father, Bill, a legendary Warrnambool player, was also noted for his courage and continued to play strong football after he lost three fingers in a gunshot accident.

One of Paul's brothers, also Bill, was a very good footballer for Warrnambool. Both Bill Snr and Bill Jnr were selected in the Warrnambool Football Club's Team of the Century.

A Hampden League Grand Final

Another Hampden League game that stands out in my memory was the 1985 Grand Final between South Warrnambool and Colac-Coragulac (the "Tigers" or the "Combine").

In 1984, former Fitzroy, Essendon and Coburg player, **Brian Brown**, was appointed coach of the Combine. Brown was a handy back pocket player who played 52 games with Fitzroy and a couple with the Bombers. Brown's 52 games with Fitzroy proved to be a significant number as 50 games were needed to allow his son, **Jonathan Brown**, to be drafted to Brisbane, the former Fitzroy side.

Brian Brown's early career was marred by injuries which caused him to miss the 1980 season completely. South Warrnambool had a talented and tough side in 1985 while the Combine had a relatively young side, although former St Kilda utility forward, Stephen Theodore, was in great form. Theodore played 134 games for the Saints and kicked 111 goals. The match was played at the Reid oval in Warrnambool in front of a then record crowd.

The game was an extremely tough encounter with many players losing blood throughout the game and two players from each side being reported. According to the *Warrnambool Standard*, dated 23 September 1985, "four senior Colac-Coragulac players have broken bones in their faces and several South Warrnambool players suffered facial injuries."

The paper went on to say that those players reported "can count themselves to be unlucky as they should be fronting the Tribunal along with about 15 others whose punches escaped the umpires' notice".

Colac-Corragulac won a high scoring game 22.14.146 to 14.6.90. Brian Brown was in the best for the Combine. **John "Goose" Maguire** (father of Matt Maguire) was named in the paper as best for South Warrnambool. On the Monday following the Grand Final, the reporter from the *Warrnambool Standard* wrote of the after-match happenings in the Combine's rooms:

Brian Brown, victorious coach of Colac-Coragulac, stood proudly in the rooms and surveyed his teammates. It was an uproarious scene; just a curious mixture of jubilation, relief and weariness that only a grand final creates.

The reporter then contrasted this with the before-match mood in the Combine's rooms:

> Two hours before, Brown was striding forcefully among his charges, preparing them for battle with his own special brand of motivation.
>
> The Tigers lay on the floor in a circle, clasping the hands of the teammate either side and feeling the surge of determination as Brown bellowed, "There will be times during the match," he said "when you will place your bodies at risk for the most trivial tap-on. You will back-up, not allow your mates to do all the work, never shirk an issue and you must run all day."

After the game Brown went on to say, "We haven't got a lot of stars, but I knew if everyone made a commitment we would win. I asked the blokes before the game for commitment and they really responded."

He then added that they "expected fireworks and they handled it well," before commenting that "the pattern of the finals had been that the side going in for the ball, particularly early, would get the support of the umpires if there was any rough stuff." He could be justly proud of his young team's effort and his own positive coaching.

Brian Brown coached the Combine for one more season and then continued as a player in 1987. He won the Maskell Medal for Best and Fairest in the Hampden League in that year. He later coached Koroit, playing mainly at centre half-back there. In 2011, I met Martin Williams who had played on the back flank alongside Brown in that team. He told me that "Brian Brown was by far the most courageous player I ever played with – stop at nothing to get the ball and handball it out to you. And you had to be there to get it!"

Like father, like son; Jonathan Brown is known, in recent times, as one of the most courageous (and talented) players in the AFL.

The Re-match Grand Final

South Warrnambool met Colac-Coragulac next in a Grand Final in 1990 at the Reid Oval in Warrnambool. The match was an important one for South Warrnambool. They had played well in the three seasons prior to 1990 but the ultimate prize had eluded them. Their coach at the time was Noel Mugavin, a Port Fairy lad who had played 41 games for 22 goals with Fitzroy, as well as a couple with the Tigers. Although he came to South as a playing coach he had retired by 1990 and the club was keen to win a flag for him.

This time the victory went to South who, inspired by forward Darren Bolden's five goals in the first quarter, were never headed and won by over 100 points. Bolden left the field at quarter-time with an injury.

Best Players for South were Michael and Nigel Kol, Tony Russell. Phil Bradmore, Andrew Hardiman and Rob Lee. I was pleased with the performances of the latter three, all whom were teacher education students at WIAE.

The Brown/Mugavin/Picken family

Although, in 1990, South Warrnambool revenged their 1985 defeat by Colac-Coragulac, the premiership honours remained in the family as Brian Brown married Noel Mugavin's sister.

Another Mugavin daughter married Collingwood champion, Billy Picken. From Macarthur in the Western District, Billy came to Collingwood as a forward with highly skilled high marking ability, but his kicking let him down and he was moved to centre half-back. Playing over two hundred games with the Magpies, he won the Copeland Trophy for Collingwood Best and Fairest in 1983.

By 2011 Billy Picken's son, Liam Picken, had made a name for himself as a very effective tagger for the Western Bulldogs. He came to the Bulldogs after being Best and Fairest for the Williamstown Seagulls, in the VFL, in 2008. In his first match for the Bulldogs, in 2009, he played a very effective game against North Melbourne, keeping Brent Harvey, the Kangaroo champion, goalless. To the end of the 2013 season Liam Picken had played 107 games for the Bulldogs. There is no doubt that the Mugavin/Brown/Picken family has made a great contribution to Aussie Rules football.

Both Brian Brown and Noel Mugavin were employed as teachers at Emmanuel College, Warrnambool, formed from the amalgamation of the former Christian Brothers' and St Anne's Colleges.

Grant Thomas

In the years between Colac-Coragulac's premiership in 1985 and the South Warrnambool flag in 1990, Warrnambool held sway in the Hampden League with four premierships in a row. There is little doubt that the appointment of Grant Thomas, as playing coach of Warrnambool in 1986, was an insightful move by the club. Thomas, a late developer, had played just over 80 games of VFL footy when he came to Warrnambool, but he had been around VFL clubs for eight years and when he finally settled down as a regular with St Kilda, he was a fine centre half-back.

As a playing coach, he had the ability to get the best out of the players, particularly the youngsters in his team and, as a versatile footballer, he was able to play in any key position or in the ruck as required. On the few occasions that I saw Thomas in action, he showed that he had the capacity to alter the course of a game in a way that not many players have been able to. I rate him as one of the best country footballers that I have seen. Thomas was held in such esteem at the club that he was named as centre half-forward and coach in the Warrnambool Team of the Century.

Thomas was appointed coach of St Kilda in 2002. Whether or not he was a success as an AFL coach is hard to say. He certainly managed to get his team to reach the finals but he was unable to win a flag with them. And it must be remembered that in the years in which he was coach, Brisbane, Port Adelaide, Sydney and West Coast had teams which were very difficult to beat. If AFL coaches are to be judged solely on premierships there are very few successful coaches – only 12 in the last 21 years.

Inspiration!

Bren and I have memories of another HFL game that we saw. It must have been in 1982 or 1983 and the match was between Warrnambool and Port Fairy. We were interested in going to the game because **Ronnie Wearmouth** was the playing coach of that team. Ronnie, the son of a 100 game Footscray wingman Dick Wearmouth (at right) originally came from Noorat in the Western District. Ronnie was a cheeky live-wire rover on the field and a character off it. He is remembered by footy fans for his flowing hair and speedy dashes, heading goalward around the wing. Wearmouth played 186 games for the Magpies and kicked 127 goals.

The game was all Warrnambool for the first three quarters and they were leading by around seven goals at three-quarter-time. I suggested to young Bren that we should go out to the Port Fairy huddle at three-quarter-time to listen to how an ex-180 plus game VFL star motivated his players when they were looking defeat in the face.

We positioned ourselves within earshot of the coach whose inspiring words were along the following lines:

> Righto you blokes! We are going (expletive deleted) awful. We have to do (expletive deleted) better. We can win this (expletive deleted) game. We are going to win this (expletive deleted) game! And I'll tell you what. If we don't win this (expletive deleted) game, it will be the (expletive deleted) sandhills at Port Fairy for all of you at seven

(expletive deleted) o' (expletive deleted) clock, tomorrow (expletive deleted) morning. And you won't (expletive deleted) like it!

The ball was bounced to start the final quarter and a skuffle, then a mini-melee, broke out. The umpire grabbed the ball and, to get play going again, turned his back on the disturbance and bounced the ball. Wearmouth was first to see what was happening. He was onto the ball and took off. With hair flying, he took several bounces and goaled. This was the start of a torrent of goals for Port. They won the match. There was no (expletive deleted) running on the (expletive deleted) sand hills on the next (expletive deleted) morning.

Wearmouth later said of his own coaching, in the *2011 AFL Grand Final Record*, "I got too hyped up. The style of coaching was totally wrong – coaching hot Gospel style. I didn't handle things well and when I think about the number of blokes I abused over time, it makes me cringe."

In 2011 Wearmouth was a long haul truck driver, based in Townsville.

18

The Sharks and Gary Ablett Snr

The Institute/Deakin University "Sharks", the Shuffle, Shark stars, Academic Help, the "Minnows", the Hawks; Northcote FC, Hawthorn FC, Geelong FC; Bob Johnson Snr, Sir Douglas Nicholls, the McCorkells, Phil Bradmore, John Sherwood, Dermot Brereton, "Dipper" DiPierdomenico, Jason Dunstall and Leigh Matthews.

In 1986, three of our children were living in Melbourne. Michael was studying Arts at Monash University; Liz was studying Medicine at the University of Melbourne while Tim was living in Carlton and working as a courier.

Tim decided to try himself out at Northcote in the VFA. He played one game in the under 19s, one game in the reserves and, although a bit light in weight for the competition, finished the season with the seniors. I was pleased that Tim was wearing the same colours that **Bob Johnson Snr** and **Sir Douglas Nicholls** had once worn – a team that had won four VFA flags in the six years from 1929 to 1934 (with the Oaks winning the premiership in the other two years).

When playing with Northcote, Tim was in the senior team that played against Oakleigh at the Warrigal Road ground – the oval where many years before, on many occasions, Mick Reed along with his boys, had barracked for Oakleigh.

Mick was 88 and still living in Oakleigh when Tim was playing for Northcote. Mick walked the two kilometres from his home to the Oakleigh ground to watch the game and he wasn't sure which team to barrack for as he had barracked for Oakleigh for so long and yet he wanted Tim to do well with Northcote.

It turned out that the Oakleigh team was much stronger. Tim had to battle hard all day and Northcote was well beaten. On his long walk home again, Mick certainly felt proud to have seen his grandson playing senior VFA football on the Warrigal Road Oval. But he would have felt happier if Tim had been playing for the Oaks.

The Sharks

In 1987, Tim returned to Warrnambool to do a Bachelor of Business degree at WIAE. As he had been away from the town for a couple of years he had no strong tie to any local club. He chose to play with the Warrnambool Institute Sharks in the Warrnambool District Football League (WDFL) as a couple of mates from school were with that team. He enjoyed his time there immensely and in fact married one of the Sharks' supporters.

The Sharks team was formed in 1976, and it is sad to say that apart from a couple of years when they reached the Grand Final they have never been a force in the WDFL.

A number of factors have contributed to this, the first being that many local lads who came to the Institute as students already had club allegiances with teams in the WDFL or in the HFL. One student, who was studying Education when I arrived there, was **Leigh McCorkell** who was an outstanding player for Warrnambool in the HFL. Tallish and well built, without being overly heavy, Leigh was a great all-round footballer for Warrnambool, winning the club Best and Fairest award as well as rising to the position of captain and later coach of the club. He was also chosen as back-pocket in the Warrnambool Team of the Century. With such a career ahead of him at the very financial Warrnambool club, there was no way that he (and others like him) would strip with the Sharks.

A similar problem arose with students who came to WIAE from outside of the town. Being good footballers, some students saw their future at the stronger and more financial clubs in the Hampden League. A number of such footballers spring to mind, all Education students, but doubtless there were others in different courses. **Phil Bradmore** was one of these. Coming from North Shore in Sydney he played 15 games with Footscray in the late '70s and early '80s. He transferred to West Perth playing 139 games there and winning the Club Best and Fairest award, the Breckler Medal, in 1985. He also represented WA in interstate football. Arriving at Warrnambool in 1989, he was snapped up by South Warrnambool, winning the Maskell Medal for Best and Fairest in the HFL in that year. As we have seen, Bradmore was a member of the South Warrnambool premiership team in 1990 with fellow students Andrew Hardiman and Rob Lee, good big men who chose to play with South Warrnambool rather that with the Sharks.

Hardiman came from Mount Gambier and had played in a premiership team with North Gambier in 1987. A key position forward or backman, he had also been a member of the losing South Warrnambool sides in 1988 and 1989. In his student years at WIAE there was always talk of him playing with the Sharks but it never eventuated.

A local lad, ruckman Robbie Lee, played with under-age CBC teams before going to South Warrnambool, as did his brother Peter whose career was marred by injury.

Snippet

The **McCorkell** family is well known for their football exploits. Leigh's father, **Ron McCorkell**, won the Warrnambool Football Club's Best and Fairest award in 1954 while his uncle, Brian, also played for the Club. Leigh's brother, **Peter McCorkell**, was another Club Best and Fairest winner. Six of Ron's grandsons played with the Blues including Justin who also coached the senior team.

The "Shark Shuffle"

The Sharks had a very interesting ritual when they won a game. All players in the team were required to perform the "Shark Shuffle" before they came off the oval. This meant that they had to slide to the ground, as if performing a rugby try, and with one arm out in front of them and the other arm on their back with their hand upright as a fin, they had to wriggle like a caught fish. The procedure looked even more effective if the ground was muddy. The ritual was captured on film on one occasion and played during a country footy segment on *The Footy Show*. There was also an article in *The Sun* about it.

The WIAE Sharks 1988

Back Row: C. Saywell, A. Dowd, J. Fitzgerald, G. Dowie, D. Clements, S. Stevens, M. King, A. Kidd

Middle Row: W. Atkinson (trainer) D. Wooles, T. Hearn, C. Ralston, F. Copes, "Big Red", A. Aulsebrook, L. Varga, M. Hillmacher, K. Radley, (unidentified)

Front Row: S. Atchison, T. Reed (Captain), N. Bourke, (Coach) S. Muscatello, C. Promnitz, M. Sully

Snippet

Prominent on the leading page of the Sharks website is a photo of the team performing the Shark Shuffle. A good size crowd is standing around enjoying the spectacle. The Sharks were doubly lucky on the day that the photo was taken as they must have had a victory and the ground wasn't wet.

For the WIAE students, Shark Shuffling became a craze with people shuffling in a wide variety of venues and mates taking photos of them. One student, to the amusement of his friends and the consternation of the academic staff, caused a stir at his graduation by doing the shuffle on the stage after he had received his graduation certificate. No action was taken against him.

Marj and I had to perform the Shark Shuffle ritual at the Club Presentation Night in the year when Tim won the Club Best and Fairest award. This was a condition of Tim receiving the trophy. After much coaxing we did so. It would have been true to say that we might have preferred to carry out the ritual on the muddy Shark Oval rather than on the floor of the now demolished Lady Bay Hotel where the function was held – too much evidence of inebriated players on the floor of the pub!

Shark Champions

Although the Sharks are yet to win a flag, over the years there have been many players who could have played in more successful teams both in the WDFL and in other higher level competitions. I saw a number of such players in my years of watching the Sharks in action. Perhaps the best way of recognising the better players with the Sharks over the years is to name the individuals who were selected to be in the "Sharks Champion Team" which was selected for the Club's 30th Anniversary celebrations in 2006, by which time the Sharks were referred to as the Deakin University Sharks. This happened as a result of the amalgamation between WIAE and Deakin University which took place in 1990. The merged institution formed the enlarged Deakin University.

The Sharks' Champion Team is as follows:

Backs: David Wooles, *Craig Ralston*, Chris McGrath
Half-backs: Matt Fisher, Jock O'Connor, *Jim Kyle*
Centres: Andrew Glover, Nick Alexayeff (Captain), Paul Tinker
Half-forwards: Ken Radley, Bob Bowman, *Rodney Ryan*
Forwards: Chris Lee (Coach), Chris Fleming, *Tim Reed*
Rucks: *Christian Saywell*, Chris Morrison, *Geoff Isles*
Interchange: Dane Newman, *Mark Azzopardi*, *Andrew Dowd*, *Gary Dowie*

Other great team men were also recognised including: **Runner:** Alan Aulsebrook; **Team Manager:** Eugene Grigg; **Goal Umpire:** John Sherwood; **Time Keeper:** Chris Jennings; **Trainer:** Colin Morris; **Gate Keeper:** Colin Wallace

During the years that I was living at Warrnambool, I frequently saw in action the twelve players whose names are in italics. They certainly gave me a lot of pleasure and deserved their selection. I also knew Ken Radley, Chris Lee and Geoff Isles as Teacher Education students. Radley was a well built left-footed flanker. Lee, a courageous forward/rover, had a successful career at South Warrnambool before he played with the Sharks, as did Jock O'Connor who was also a Hampden Football League representative player. O'Connor, a tough and athletic centre half-back, was an Art and Design student. Rover Geoff Isles had also played as an on-baller for Warrnambool in the HFL. Of course Marj and I were pleased to see that our Tim made the side. Eugene Grigg, named as Team Manager, had an outstanding career as a footballer in the Ballarat League, but had retired when he moved to Warrnambool. If it were possible to get all of the team, in their prime, onto the ground at the same time, they would be a strong combination.

Snippet

Alan Aulsebrook was chosen in the Sharks' Champion Team as a runner as this was a role he long carried out. But he was more than that for the Club. At various times he was a player, a coach, and a member of the Sharks' Committee. When the Club had its 30th Anniversary celebrations, he was Club president. It could be said that over most of those years, he was "always around the Club" making positive contributions.

The Sharks and the Academics

While the WIAE team was unable to recruit some of the better footballers among the students it was fortunate that some of the lecturing staff threw their weight behind the club. Teacher education lecturers, Ross Price and Rob Peake both had stints as coach with Rob Peake taking the team to the grand Final in 1990, only to be narrowly defeated by Russell's Creek before a large crowd at the Reid Oval. Inaccurate kicking early cost them the game. Rob's son, Matthew Peake, was later a star midfielder for North Ballarat. Phil Cleary, the TV commentator on VFA/VFL football often spoke highly of Matthew's ability. Matthew later had a lot of success playing in the Hepburn/Daylesford area. He was also a successful coach of South Warrnambool in the 2000s.

Other lecturers, who helped out with the Sharks, in my time there, were Keith James, Rod Coutts, Colin Ferguson, John Warhurst, Phil Hellier, Pete Hay, Clive Lindop and John Sherwood. While the first six named had Aussie Rules backgrounds, **John Sherwood** (right), who came from New South Wales, didn't. In light of this, John's work for the Sharks is highly commendable.

Seeing the club as a great community builder for the students, he had many administrative roles around the club and also filled in as a player when the seconds were short of numbers. He came to enjoy the game, trained hard and improved his skills. Eventually he got his chance and was picked to play in the seniors against Old Collegians. I attended the game and was dismayed when John fell awkwardly in an early contest. He was in great pain, stretchered off and taken by ambulance to the Warrnambool Base Hospital to be diagnosed with a broken leg. His football playing days in the senior side were short-lived (just part of one game) but he continued to be a great clubman for many years.

The "Shark Pond"

The Warrnambool campus of WIAE/Deakin University is called Sherwood Park because it was the name of the property when it was purchased from its previous owner.

The oval (The "Shark Pond") at Sherwood Park where the Sharks play their matches is named the Ian Hughes Oval after the former WIAE Science Lecturer, Ian Hughes, who was an outstanding footballer for Warrnambool and who died at a young age. A pavilion at the Ian Hughes Oval is called the **Dr John Sherwood Pavilion**, (below) in recognition of John's services to the Sharks footy club.

John Sherwood applied the same enthusiasm to his work as a scientist. His area of study was the physiochemical characteristics of natural waters and he worked on projects in Victoria, Tasmania and Papua New Guinea for the dairy industry, mining companies and environmental

agencies. His work has been recognised with many awards including a Lifetime Achievement Award from the Victorian Government. On WIAE's merger with Deakin University, John was made an Associate Professor.

The first captain of the Sharks was John Warhurst who had been playing coach of Flinders University in the South Australian Amateur League and had played two seasons with Norwood in the SANFL, playing a dozen games there as centre half-forward. John played a year with Warrnambool in the Hampden League in his first year at WIAE but joined the Sharks when they initially formed. He wrote in an email to me:

> ... it was a lot of fun without much success in the early days. I remember we had 40 turn out for our first practice and one of the problems was that we couldn't give everyone a game so they dropped away. I think it was a great development for WIAE in bringing students together and in helping to develop the WIAE identity. It also took me to a lot of smaller towns around the area.

He added he "remembered Jim Kyle, playing in the first year at least, and he was a good lanky ruckman". Kyle was the only lecturer selected in the Champion Team. A mobile tall man, he was picked on the half-back flank.

John Warhurst took up a position in Canberra in the middle of his second season with the Sharks. In 2012 John was an emeritus professor of Political Science at the Australian National University and a columnist with the *Canberra Times*.

The "Minnows"

In 1991 the WDFL had an Under 17 competition, in which our youngest son, Bren, played for the WIAE Sharks' team, nicknamed the "Minnows".

With great Shark football enthusiast, Allan Aulsebrook, I was pleased to be appointed as joint-coach of the team.

The boys really only wanted to play for fun. And this they did. They had few wins for the year but, as a number of the boys had not played a lot of football before joining the Sharks, this was not surprising. And every win was a mini-premiership.

Alan and I enjoyed our coaching roles and were delighted that each week just about everyone who was available "got a game" and yet at no stage in the year did we have to forfeit for lack of players.

The WIAE Sharks' Under 17 Team, 1991

(Photograph by Gary Francis)

Back Row: M. King, R. Sanderson, D. Quigley, L. Delaney, L. Slattery, M. Thompson.

Centre Row: K. Reed (Joint Coach), S. Garner, L. Kenny, C. Wright, J. O'Brien, M. Dawson, J. Hart, S. Timms, A. Auslebrook.(Joint Coach).

Front Row: S. Finn, J. Kelly, B. McKenzie, B. Ryan (Captain), B. Reed, S. Meade, D. McMahon.

Helmet wearing

In the late '80s, a number of Shark players had taken to wearing helmets during games as a result of a fatal accident to a well-known local lad in an HFL match.

The problem of the possibility of serious head injury from Aussie Rules has yet to be overcome as young people lose their lives or suffer serious consequences far too often from injuries incurred playing the game. In June 2012, Matthew Robbins, a former player who had a 146 game career with the Bulldogs, raised the question of the link between head high collisions that he had while playing and the depression from which he has since suffered. He commented in the *Herald Sun* that he's "not the only person to get depression that's come out of the AFL. You'd have to be naïve to think there isn't some sort of a link".

Perhaps all players should wear helmets. A number of highly successful footballers have done so in the past – Rod Ashman (Carlton), Nathan Burke (St Kilda), Shaun Hart (Brisbane Lions) and, earlier, Paul Callery (Melbourne and St Kilda) who was knocked unconscious nine times in his long career. Rod Ashman, a very successful rover in the 1970s and 1980s once explained why he wore a helmet saying, "Any contact around the face had me in trouble. These blows affected my vision and the only solution was to wear a helmet. I think the only times I did not wear a helmet in my final years was when it was too hot for comfort."

The issue of the seriousness of head injuries has also been raised by Brownlow Medallist Greg Williams, who claims that he has suffered memory loss which he blames on head injuries sustained when he was playing football.

Snippet

One day, probably in the late '50s or early '60s (the writer is vague about the exact date but clear about the incident) I was watching Carlton play Melbourne at the MCG. The ball was bouncing along the wing with Ron Barassi and John Nicholls running towards it, from opposite directions, about equidistant from the ball. I immediately thought to myself, "Someone is going to get hurt here. Neither of these will stop." And they didn't but on reaching the ball both momentarily took their eyes off the ball and gave each other a solid shoulder to shoulder bump. Both were a little unbalanced after the collision but, on recovery, Barassi was closest to the ball and gained possession. Neither was hurt. Today, it is likely that both players would have been "dragged" for not attacking the ball.

In 2012, in a discussion about the modern game with ex-Hawthorn star John O'Mahony, I mentioned this incident. He pointed out that Bob McCaskill, under whom John had played at Hawthorn, would have been happy with the approaches taken by Barassi and Nicholls. According to John, when talking about a situation when the ball was between two players, McCaskill would use the example of what happens when a bone is between two dogs. He said that the dogs would "go for each other" until one dog had frightened the other away, then the stronger dog had the bone to itself. McCaskill would say that approach was best on the footy field too. "If the ball is between you and an opponent, bump him out of the way first, and then the ball is yours." Food for thought?

The Era of the Hawks

In the seven seasons from 1983 to 1989, during which the Reeds were heavily involved with the Sharks, the Hawks played in every VFL Grand Final, winning four flags. They were premiers again, in the AFL, in 1991. Although Essendon was strong during those years, winning back-to-back flags in 1984-85, the years 1983 to 1991 could be termed the Era of the Hawks.

Coached by Allan Jeans for three premierships and Alan Joyce for two, the Hawks had some wonderful players during those years, including Michael Tuck who played in a record 11 Grand Finals for seven premierships over his career. Tuck also holds the record for the most number of VFL/AFL games played: 426 games with 320 goals between 1972 and 1991. His son, Shane, has been a solid player for Richmond in recent times. Other great Hawthorn players over that era include **Dermot Brereton, Robert DiPierdomenico, Jason Dunstall** and **Leigh Matthews**.

Snippet

One of the toughest players of his era, Dermot Brereton achieved success very young. He once said, "When I was a kid I wanted to be comfortable and I wanted to play in premierships. By the time I was 24 I had done all those things." He has made such a successful career in the media since retiring that by now he is probably more "comfortable" than he had hoped.

Jason Dunstall was a highly successful full forward while **DiPierdomenico** won a Brownlow Medal, much to his surprise. He said after his win, "I only came here (to the count at Melbourne's Southern Cross Hotel) for the free meal."

A tough, goalkicking rover for the Hawks, **Leigh Mathews** proved his worth as a champion over many years. After retiring as a player he improved his record by becoming a successful coach of the Magpies and subsequently the Brisbane Lions.

Other Eras

Over the history of the game there have been other periods of time where one club has been dominant enough to have a certain sequence of years called that team's "era".

In the first decade of the 20th century, Carlton had an era when they won three flags in a row under coach Jack Worrall.

Between the World Wars, Collingwood had a great era from 1927 to 1930 winning four flags in a row after being runners-up in 1926. Jock McHale, as coach, and the Collier and Coventry brothers were significant in those wins.

Melbourne, with coach Frank "Checker" Hughes, captain Alan La Fontaine and brilliant rover Percy Beams won three flags in a row from 1939 to 1941.

The Demons, under coach Norm Smith and star players Ron Barassi, Big Bob Johnson, Ian Ridley, Brian Dixon (and many more) continued their success in the '50s and '60s with five premierships in six years from 1955 to 1960.

No other team had an "era" of success until the Hawks during the '80s and in 1991, but many teams before this time had won back-to-back flags. Fitzroy did so in 1898-99 and 1904-05, Collingwood in 1902-03, 1935-36, Carlton in 1907-08, 1914-15 and 1981-82, Essendon in 1911-12, 1949-50 and 1984-85, Richmond in 1920-21 and 1973-74 and Geelong in 1951-52.

Although not winning back-to-back premierships, Geelong might claim to have been the best team in recent times as they won flags in 2007, 2009 and 2011 and made the Grand Final in 2008, thus playing in four Grand Finals in five seasons.

It would appear that over the period from 1897 until the 1980s the competition had been dominated, at the very beginning, by Fitzroy (whose team included indigenous player Joe Johnson) and then, at various times, by Carlton, Collingwood, Melbourne, Essendon, Richmond, Geelong and Hawthorn. By the mid-1980s both St Kilda and Footscray had been premiers only once, South Melbourne had not won a flag since 1933 and Fitzroy had not been successful for 36 years. And the clubs which had been less successful were struggling financially. Change was necessary if the game was to flourish. And, as we shall see in the next chapter, change was afoot.

Gary Ablett Snr – The Best?

Bren Reed had a break from football when he moved to Melbourne to study Education at the University of Melbourne. He preferred to watch

VFL matches and, although he barracked for the Tigers, he once again took every opportunity that he could to watch his hero, **Gary Ablett Snr**, play.

Just as the Hawks could be regarded as being the best football team over the past few decades, perhaps it could be said that Gary Ablett Snr is the best footballer of recent times. Although that era was rich in talented footballers, Ablett might get the nod because of his incredible skills and his ability to change the course of a match. Furthermore it says of him in *The Encyclopedia of VFL/AFL Footballers* that he "had the rare ability to attract people to the football just to see him play – a quality that defined his standing in the game". His fourteen goals against the Bombers in 1993 was the best single performance that I ever had the privilege to witness. Although perhaps not an unbiased comment on his father's ability, Gary Ablett Jnr observed recently for *The Age* (25 March 2013):

> In my opinion, my dad is the best player to ever play the game. Some of the things he could do, no-one else could do.

Brownlow Medallist, Brad Hardie, agreed with Gary Jnr when he wrote in the *Sydney Morning Herald* (2 April, 2013):

> Gary Ablett senior was the biggest freak I've ever seen. He played key forward despite not being overly tall. He was an outstanding midfielder when he wanted (needed) to be. He could have been a brilliant centre half-back if the occasion had demanded it.

Some might see goal-kicking machines Tony Lockett and Jason Dunstall, handball specialist Greg Williams, rugged and highly skilled Leigh Matthews or versatile and talented James Hird as worthy of being called the best player of the modern era, but for his breathtaking ability which I have witnessed, I would side with his son in putting Gary Ablett Snr in a class of his own. Perhaps the next best might be Gary Ablett Jnr, whose career is not yet over.

Back to Melbourne

As five of the six Reed children were living in Melbourne in 1992, and I was in a position to retire from full-time work, Marj and I, with our youngest child Natalie, then in Year 8, returned to Melbourne, to live in Mount Waverley, in 1993. I took a part-time teaching position at a Noble Park primary school.

19

The "Krushers" and the Carrolls

New Finals' Systems, A tragic Grand Final, The AFL, the "Krushers", the demise of the "Oaks", the loss of "the Rec"; the "Scorpions", the Box Hill Hawks; Des Baker, the Clokes, the Callanan/Fox family, Phil Maylin, Kain Taylor, Corey Young and Luke Power.

For the first few of decades after World War II there was a great general interest in the game and, particularly, the finals but a few clubs were having little success on the field and were beginning to struggle financially – signs of trouble ahead. The VFL needed to make a few changes to invigorate it as it moved through the 1970s.

Innovations

To give the game a lift, the VFL decided to introduce a new finals' system in 1972 with the top five teams playing in the finals. While one argument for doing so might be to give more teams a chance of winning the flag, the major effect of the move was to bring more funds into the VFL coffers. It might be said that the new system was devised to consolidate the final four, with the top team remaining on top (with a double chance) while second and third played for the second spot (and a double chance) with the loser settling in third position. Fourth and fifth teams played for fourth position with the loser dropping out. The finals then proceeded as under the Page/McIntyre system that had been in place for over 40 years.

The problem with the final five system was that while it gave the fifth team a chance at the finals, it made it almost impossible for the fourth or fifth teams to win the flag as they had to win four games in a row to do so. At the same time the top team had to win only two games in a row to be premiers. Only twice in the 19 years in which the system operated did the fifth team make the Grand Final. The Magpies did it in 1980 to suffer an 81 point loss to the Tigers in the Grand Final. Melbourne had a similar fate in 1988 going down by 96 points to the Hawks. Clearly both the Magpies and the Demons were exhausted when they reached the Grand Final after three tough games.

On the other hand the system was a great success financially with six finals being played instead of four. The extra finals drew around 130,000 additional paying customers each year – money that could be put to good use to help the struggling teams.

Another strategy to "renovate" the VFL was to move some of the weaker teams interstate. This occurred with South Melbourne transferring to Sydney, as the Sydney Swans, in 1982, and Fitzroy heading to Brisbane, as the Brisbane Bears, in 1987. The third remedial action was the addition of interstate clubs – West Coast Eagles in 1987, the Adelaide Crows in 1991 and the Fremantle Dockers in 1995. These changes brought about the demise of the VFL as such.

The top football league in Australia was no longer located in Victoria but spread across five states.

The Australian Football League (AFL) was then in its embryonic stage. The challenge for the AFL administrators is to nurture this new League until it settles down as did the VFL in the mid-20th century. In 2013, with the recent additions of the Gold Coast Suns and Greater Western Sydney, there were eighteen teams in the competition with the top eight playing in the finals. Again, with nine games being played, the finals are a great money spinner for the AFL, with teams finishing in positions five to eight having little chance of being premiers. They have to win four games in a row, at least three of which are against teams that finished higher than them on the final ladder – an extremely difficult task. However, the supporters of these teams do get an opportunity to see their team playing in the finals and have some bragging rights about their team so doing.

Where it goes from here is hard to say. Will more teams be added? Will the AFL be divided into two Conferences with the winner of each Conference playing off in the Grand Final? Who knows?

There is little doubt that the AFL still faces many challenges in its future. The huge differences between the skill levels of the top and lower teams, as well as the unfairness of the draw, where some teams play the weaker, newer teams more frequently than others, are not the least of these challenges. Perhaps the AFL will never have an era of stability. It may be in a state of continual evolution as it develops strategies enabling it to solve new problems as they emerge.

Old Teams, New Competitions

On retirement from my position at Deakin University, Warrnambool, in 1993, I made a career change when I took up a part-time teaching position at a Melbourne school and lived in Mount Waverley. Our son Tim, then married and living in Ashburton, played footy, initially for a couple of years with ANZ bank in the VAFA, where he was a team leader, and then with East Camberwell in the Southern Districts Football Association.

The East Camberwell club that Tim played for was formerly East Camberwell YCW, the old rivals of Oakleigh YCW. By this time the YCW competition, because of demographic changes and a declining interest in religion, had folded as had some of the weaker clubs. The stronger ones survived and moved on to play in other competitions. In fact, Oakleigh YCW dropped out of the YCW competition in 1972. They decided to join the Eastern Suburban Churches Football Association (ESCFA). This move enabled them to compete in a more local competition thus removing the problem of travelling across Melbourne to play their games. With this move the club was re-named Oakleigh Sacred Heart

Football Club. Having success in both C-Grade and B-Grade, the club rose to compete in the A-Grade competition in the late '80s. By that time, because of a lack of numbers, there was no junior team.

A Tragic Grand Final

Jack Callanan was the first President of the Oakleigh Sacred Club Football Club. Jack was the father of David and Jack Callanan Jnr both of whom had played footy at Oakleigh YCW in my last season of footy when I played in the reserves. Jack Snr had another four sons, Denis (dec), Martin, Stephen and Greg who also played for the club.

In 1974, with **Jack Callanan Snr** still president of the club, the reserves team, very capably led by **Jack Callanan Jnr** as playing coach, reached the Grand Final. Tragically, while watching the game, Jack Snr had a heart attack and passed away. Of course the game was abandoned, and support and sympathy were given to his sons who were playing.

An extremely well attended Requiem Mass was held at Sacred Heart Church in Oakleigh during the next week. Jack Snr's family, the football club and the parish as a whole were hard hit by Jack's death. He was remembered as a wonderful father and great worker for his community and his church. To honour Jack Callanan's memory the annual Best Clubman Award, **The Jack Callanan Memorial Trophy**, has been named after him.

As neither club felt it was appropriate to replay the Grand Final after the tragic event, both teams were declared Joint Premiers.

Jack Callanan Jnr has shown the same community spirit as his father. A teacher, he was deeply involved in the communities where he taught. His last teaching appointment was in Ballarat. There he took an interest in local footy and for many years he was the manager of the Springbank Footy team which played in the Central Highlands League.

Not to be outdone, Jack's spouse **Libby Callanan** has also made a great contribution to football. Libby along with the rest of her family are all Tigers fans. She is a "platinum" club member and has given more than ten years service to the Ballarat Tigers as secretary and bus organiser for regular trips to Melbourne to watch the Tigers in action. She was recently awarded with a certificate recognising her long and loyal service. Libby's three brothers, **Chris**, **Leon** and **Martin Cox,** all played at East Camberwell with Chris having a stint as senior coach.

Families like the **Callanan** and **Cox** families form part of the backbone of our great game.

The Oakleigh Krushers

The Emmanuel Krushers Football Club was formed from the Emmanuel Anglican church community in Oakleigh in 1962 and also competed in the ESCFA. **Des Baker** was a driving force behind the Emmanuel Football Club and in time it rose through the ranks from C Grade Premiers in 1963 to win the A Grade flag in 1981. However changing times saw it losing momentum as was the case with Oakleigh Sacred Heart Club. In 1992, both clubs welcomed the merging of the two and the birth of Oakleigh Amateur Football Club. Two rival clubs became one, joined the VAFA competition and took the "Oakleigh Krushers" as their nick-name. The Eastern Suburban Churches competition, like the YCW competition, also disbanded later.

Beginning in a lower grade in the VAFA the Oakleigh Krushers, with premierships en route, had risen to be in B Division by 2012. Unfortunately, the senior side had a poor year in 2012 and was relegated to C Division for 2013. After a slow start they finished the season on a promising note.

The Krushers' Under 18 team were premiers in 2012, beating Werribee by over 11 goals in the Grand Final. Best and Fairest for that team and also in the competition was **Aaron Cloke**, a nephew of former Richmond and Collingwood champion **David Cloke**. They repeated their effort in 2013 with Aaron Cloke kicking over 100 goals.

The club's home ground, The Scammell Reserve off North Road, Oakleigh, is entered from Jack McAlister Avenue, named after the former Oakleigh player and sporting identity. Scammell Reserve is the former home ground of the Emmanuel Club and its pavilion is named the **Des Baker Pavillion** after the great worker for that club.

Emmanuel Krushers 1963 Premiership Team

Back Row: D. Mann (Trainer), G. Dixon, A. Smith, R. Lewis, G. Brown, A. Buchanan, R. Levey, P. Rowlands, L. Mann, J. Harrison, D. Wilkinson (Trainer)

Centre Row: N. Norton, R. Fisher, C. Calvert, Jim Webber (Captain), D. Baker (Coach), J. Daniel (Vice-President), J. Slatter (Vice Captain), P. Kerley, P. Shepherd

Front Row: R. Morris, A. Molineux, C. Foley, B. Gardiner, J. Patterson, R. Jordan, P. Donnell

Hall of Famers

In 2012 the Oakleigh Amateurs held a Red, White & Blue Ball to celebrate the history of the club as it was 20 years since the Oakleigh Amateur Club was formed, 50 Years since the Emmanuel Krushers Club was formed, and 80 years since the Oakleigh CYMS/Oakleigh YCW/ Oakleigh Sacred Heart Club was formed.

To honour some of the great workers for the clubs over the years a Hall of Fame was introduced and ten men were initially inducted. The inductees had given great service as participants on the field and/or administrators in the parent clubs.

Des Baker, Kevin McQuillen, Peter Chapman, and Bob Benyon were inductees who had served the Emmanuel Club while Peter Quinn, Bill O'Shea, Jack Gubbins, Greg Cahill, Barry Alexander and Bruce Garner were from Oakleigh Sacred Heart or its earlier forms Oakleigh YCW and Oakleigh CYMS.

Brief details of the contributions made by each of the inductees are given below:

- After 120 games with Port Melbourne Des Baker retired from the top echelon and together with Audrey, his wife, gave his heart and soul to setting up the Emmanuel Football Club in the Eastern Suburban Churches Football Association (ESCFA) and seeing it become a power in that competition.
- Kevin McQuillan played 276 fearless games of the highest quality and was both the senior team captain and multiple Best and Fairest winner.
- Coming from Oakleigh VFA side, Bob Beynon played over 200 games with the Club and amassed over 800 career goals. He coached the Krushers to an A Grade flag in 1981 and was appointed as the ESCFA coach of representative teams.
- Peter Chapman has been over 45 years with the club, playing 283 games and being a dual reserves Premiership coach. He was one of the architects of the successful amalgamation of the clubs.
- Peter Quinn played with all three Oakleigh Catholic teams and in five premiership teams. He played over 400 games for the various clubs

and won a competition Best and Fairest award when he was in his forties.
- Bill O'Shea played with successful CYMS and YCW teams, including 2 premierships. He also coached a Sacred Heart team to a premiership. (Bill's dad, Frank O'Shea, coached the YCW team to three flags in the 1960s.)
- Jack Gubbins came to Oakleigh YCW as an experienced footballer and used his football brain to successfully captain the club to three premierships before he lent his knowledge to the reserves. Playing until well into his forties, he donned a guernsey over 400 times for the three Oakleigh clubs.
- Barry Alexander had four years with Oakleigh VFA side under Bob Johnson before injury forced a temporary retirement. He joined Oakleigh Sacred in 1977, amassing 135 senior games over seven years, playing in the 1984 Senior premiership side. Turning his talents to administration, he became Club President in 1985 and has since led the club in that role. He humbly attributes his success to the fact that he has "been blessed with dedicated and hard working committees throughout".
- Bruce Garner played his under-age football with Huntingdale High School and the VFA team Oakleigh, before he joined Carnegie. Coming to Oakleigh Sacred heart in the 1970s, he took over the back pocket position. In 1982, he debuted as reserves coach, a position he made his own. An Oakleigh Krushers committee-man over many years, he takes a great interest in the condition of the ground.
- Beginning with Oakleigh YCW as a 13-year-old, Greg Cahill played his first senior game in 1967 and was a member of the 1970 Premiership team, winning the Club Best and Fairest in that year. As an aggressive rover, he was runner-up in that award in the following year but missed the Grand Final through injury. Greg was part of a small group who lobbied hard to get Oakleigh YCW (Oakleigh Sacred Heart) into the

ESCFA and was a member of the newly named club's first Committee being Assistant Secretary and Treasurer. He was a member of the Club's senior premiership side in 1973, under the coaching of Mick Skehan, and of the reserves' successful 1975 team under Jack Callanan Jnr. He played his last game with the Club in 1980, completing a highly successful career as a player and an administrator.

Snippet

When asked details of his career with Oakleigh YCW/Sacred Heart, Greg Cahill included the following statement: "When you think about it, the playing and administration I was involved in has been a significant factor in my life in so many ways. I loved it."

I believe that Greg's statement touched upon something that is often overlooked. Footy clubs, even those competing in the lower echelons of the sport, like many other amateur organisations, provide excellent opportunities for people to have personal growth experiences which are not readily obtained in everyday life. These stand them in good stead in other endeavours for the rest of their lives.

Demography and the Rec

As we have seen, demographic changes to the suburbs of South Melbourne, Fitzroy and Oakleigh had grave effects on the football clubs in those areas. The Rec tells the story. At one point in the 1950s two clubs shared the ground before each had a ground of its own. In the 1960s, with the high birth rate after World War II, the Rec had to be subdivided into two Aussie Rules ovals to cater for the demand from the growing number of young people wanting to play the game. With demographic changes and the later amalgamation of the two church teams, only one oval was required and the Rec became available to be used for soccer by the Oakleigh Cannons, a team in the Premier League soccer competition. A new a pavilion, a grandstand (see above photo taken in 2012) and three soccer pitches have been placed there.

The Rec is still officially named the "Jack Edwards Reserve". Jack was a keen worker for sport around the Oakleigh district. I knew him when, as a young bloke, I played cricket in the ODCA for the East Oakleigh team which used the Rec. The Edwards family owned the Foresters Arms Hotel on the Princes Highway at Oakleigh. It was at this hotel that initial meetings of the fledgling Oakleigh Football Club took place in the 1890s. I'm not sure what Jack would think of "his" reserve being handed over to soccer. Life goes on.

This process didn't only happen in Oakleigh. In the suburbs and across the state, demographic changes impact heavily on the sport that is played in each locality.

No doubt soccer, other codes and other interests will challenge Australian football even further as our nation's major winter sport.

Springvale Football Club

The Physical Education teacher at my new Melbourne school was Jonathan ("Jono") Bence, a relative of tough ex-South Melbourne and St Kilda rover, Tiger Bence, who had played for Koroit against Roy Cazaly. Jono was not only keenly interested in footy but also actively involved.

Growing up in Springvale, Jono was a strong supporter and a fitness advisor of the Springvale Football Club ("the Scorpions") which was founded at the Springvale Hotel on the "bullock run" to Dandenong in 1903, just two years before the Costerfield Football Club. Springvale had success in a number of competitions before it joined the VFA, Division 2, in 1982.

Under the coaching of ex-Richmond and Demon player **Laurie Fowler**, the Scorpions won the flag in the VFA (2nd Division) in 1983, its second year in the competition, and moved up to 1st Division in 1984. Led by playing coach, **Phil Maylin** from Footscray, it won the First Division flag in 1987. It went on to become the outstanding team in the VFA (later the VFL) in the 1990s, winning four premierships in five years with back-to-back flags in 1995-96 and 1998-99.

Outstanding players in that era were **Denis Knight, Jason Caples, the Carroll brothers (Damian and John)** and **Kain Taylor** who won the Norm Goss Medal for Best and Fairest in the VFL in 1996.

Damian and John Carroll are the sons of Brian Carroll who played with my mate Paddy Rohan at Watchem/Corack and later with Fitzroy.

In the second decade of the 21st century, Springvale is now known as the Casey Scorpions and is part of the State-wide VFL competition. It was initially affiliated with St Kilda AFL Club but has been with Melbourne since 2011. The legal name for the club is still Springvale Football Club. Its home ground is Casey Fields at Cranbourne.

Jono Bence, runner (with permission from Jenny Owens)

Damian Carroll and the Box Hill Hawks

In 2011, Damian Carroll, who holds the Springvale club record of 233 games, was appointed coach of the Box Hill Hawks VFL club which is affiliated with Hawthorn in the

AFL. Jono Bence was on the fitness staff and also a runner for the club. Phil Cleary, the ex-Coburg champion and guru commentator of VFL football, has a high opinion of Damian Carroll as a man and as a coach. In *Inside Football*, on 13 June 2012, after the Box Hill Hawks had beaten Williamstown in the mist and drizzling rain that engulfed the Williamstown oval, Cleary had the following to say about the match:

> Three times during the last quarter Williamstown led by more than a goal and appeared destined for victory. In the end the sheer willpower of Box Hill drove them to victory.
>
> And no-one could deny the role coach Damian Carroll, a premiership champion with Springvale (Casey Scorpions) in the '90s, played in the six point triumph.
>
> There's something endearingly old world about Carroll ... while he is abreast of what the data says about a football match he is not one to underestimate the role character plays in driving a footballer to win a hard ball.
>
> Character was a badge of honour in the days when he powered his sinewy body to triumph at Springvale.

He went on to write how Carroll "implored his players to replicate the courage of captain Daniel Pratt, who'd been taken from the ground concussed in the third term ... No-one can ever be sure whether such player exhortations do inspire players. All we know is that despite Williamstown three times pushing the lead beyond a goal in the last quarter, the Hawks climbed from the damp Point Gellibrand surface to steal the game."

Cleary also noted the presence of **Brian Carroll** at the game supporting his son and his team:

> As has been the case since Carroll began his VFA career 20 years ago, father Brian was in the rooms at half-time Saturday lending moral support. A keen student of the game, Brian played 10 games with Fitzroy in 1963, won Brownlow votes and enjoyed premiership success elsewhere.

Cleary added that Brian "and his wife Mary were a fixture at Springvale games in the '90s (when Damian and John were starring there). Mary might no longer be with us, but her spirit lives on in her son."

A lovely tribute to the close football-loving Carroll family.

Another Flag

In 2013 the Box Hill Hawks won the VFL flag defeating Geelong, the favourite in the Grand Final. It was an interesting game, but the Hawks were never really challenged after half-time. It was a great win for all concerned and a great family event for the Carrolls.

A feature of the presentations was that hundreds of young and not so young children were allowed onto the Docklands oval to play kick-to-kick. With footballs going everywhere it was just like the "good old days" in the VFA.

The Demise of the Oaks

Whilst the Springvale Football Club continues to survive, the Oakleigh Football Club hasn't managed to do so. By 1994 it was obvious that it was going nowhere. Jono Bence and I went to the Warrigal Road oval to see the Oaks play Springvale that year. Oakleigh managed to keep within touch of Springy until three-quarter time when they were 21 points down, but in the final term Springvale scored nine of the last 10 goals. It was obvious that they were more skilled, stronger and better suited to the greasy conditions of that day. Brett Evans was a star for the victors, kicking seven goals.

Oakleigh's best player on that day was Oakleigh born and bred **Cory Young**, a courageous utility player who, in 1989-90, had six games with the Tigers before he went west and played one game with the West Coast Eagles. He had also been with Frankston before he returned home to Oakleigh.

Young appeared to have an attitude problem in his younger days which probably cost him a successful AFL career. However, by 1994 he had become an accomplished footballer. In that year he won the Oakleigh Best and Fairest award as well as the J. J. Liston trophy for Best and Fairest in the competition. This meant that an Oakleigh player, Eric Beard, won that trophy in the first year that it was awarded (after World War II) and an Oakleigh player again won it in the final year of the Oakleigh Football Club's existence.

It is heart wrenching when clubs and organisations fold, but the Oakleigh Football Club had served the community well when Oakleigh was a growing city, occupied largely by people of British origins. With post-war migration from the 1940s the demography of Oakleigh changed and its newer residents, largely from Italy and Greece, lacked any affinity for Aussie Rules. Soccer was their game. However, with premierships in the '50s and in 1971 it took some time for the effects of the changing population to come about.

The Oaks didn't field a team in 1995. The Warrigal Road oval became the home of the TAC Cup team, the Oakleigh Chargers, seen as a breeding ground for future VFL/AFL players, probably the most notable of whom is **Luke Power**, the triple premiership player for the Brisbane Lions, and former President of the AFL Players' Association. A courageous left-footed midfielder, Power played 282 games for the Lions. In 2012 he turned out for Greater Western Sydney. The Oakleigh Chargers won the Grand Final in the TAC Cup in 2012 defeating Gippsland by one point.

Snippet

Robert Oliver, a great grandson of George and Annie Reed, was manager of the Oakleigh Chargers in 2001-2. He had previously worked as a development officer for AFL Victoria for 13 years. In 2003 he moved to the USA where he coached the New York Magpies FC for five years, becoming a Life Member of that club.

20
Back to Lalbert and Tony Free

ANZAC Day games, Collingwood victories, "Back to Lalbert", tough times, Lake Learmonth, Tigers in town; Richmond FC, Geelong FC, Essendon FC, Carlton FC, Lalbert FC (Mallee Eagles FNC), Woorinen FC, St Kilda FC, Sydney Swans FC ; Matthew Francis, Kevin Sheedy, Paul Salmon, Gary Ablett Snr, James Hird, Gavin Wanganeen, Michael Long, Stephen Kernahan, Daniel Ward, Carl Ditterich, and Dale Lewis.

Matthew Francis, a direct descendant of Mamie Reed, is the great-great-grandson of George and Annie Reed. His parents, Ken and Lorraine Francis, had four children: Megan, Matthew, Anthony and Michael. Matthew and Anthony are twins.

> *There was joy among the Reed clan*
> *When the gossip got about –*
> *It had taken years to happen.*
> *"You beaut," we all did shout.*
> *One of George's progeny,*
> *Matt Francis was his name,*
> *He'd signed up with the Tigers,*
> *We think he'll get a game!*

George Reed kicked a footy around the goldfields at Guildford. **Matthew Francis** was to make it to the AFL and play on the 'G.

Matthew began his football career as a student at St Pat's College, Ballarat. On leaving school Matthew played with Ballan, where the family lived. It was while he was doing well there that he was signed by the Tigers.

According to *The Encyclopedia of AFL Footballers*, **Matthew** "was a ruckman or key defender who had a horror run with injuries at both Richmond and Collingwood. He played 19 games with Richmond, kicking 13 goals. Despite his injury riddled career the Magpies took him on in 1996. In his career with Collingwood he played 36 games for 10 goals."

In all Matthew played 55 VFL/AFL games and kicked 23 goals. A mobile but lightly built tall man, he would have had greater success had he not suffered from injuries. But his career was not without its high points.

ANZAC Day, 1996

Matthew Francis was in the Collingwood team that played Essendon in the ANZAC Day match in 1996. Essendon were away to a flying start in the first term scoring seven goals one to the Magpies' two goals four, but gradually the Collingwood boys narrowed the margin, kicking 15 goals to nine for the rest of the match. **Kevin Sheedy**, the Bombers coach, complained that the recovery was helped by poor umpiring which saw the free kick decisions going 38 to 16 in the Magpies' favour. Bruce Matthews saw it differently in the *Herald Sun* on the next day when he wrote the following:

> In the end the free kick inequality didn't cost Essendon the match. It was more their own ineptness in the mid-field duels. By the start of the last quarter it was only a matter of time before the Magpies hit the front. A Buckley goal after eight minutes put them ahead and the 'pies defended stoutly for another critical nine minutes until Matthew Francis found the target to finally crack open Essendon's resistance.

That goal in front of a crowd of over 80,000 at the MCG was probably the most significant kick of Matthew Francis' career.

James Hird was in the Bombers team that day and kicked four goals in their losing side. Rover Scott Russell won the AFL ANZAC Day Medal (for being best player in the Essendon – Collingwood match played on Anzac Day) in that year while ruckman Damian Monkhurst won it in the following year and forward Sav Rocca was successful in 1998. The three winners were Collingwood players. Matthew Francis played in all three matches and the Magpies were victors in each game. James Hird became an ANZAC Day specialist winning the Medal three times – in 2000, 2003 and 2004.

Matthew Francis later coached Redland in the Eastern Conference of the North East Australian Football League (NEAFL) in 2010. The NEAFL embraces teams from NSW, Queensland, the Northern Territory and the ACT. It has two Conferences, the Eastern and Northern, and includes within it the reserves teams of Brisbane Lions, Gold Coast Suns, Sydney Swans and Greater Western Sydney.

Spectators

Our return to Melbourne, with our home in Mt Waverley, meant that the Reed family was able to see more AFL games than they had been able to when living at Warrnambool.

A couple stand out.

Bren and I were present at the 1993 game between Essendon and Geelong when **Gary Ablett Snr** kicked 14 goals. One of his opponents on that day was a very young **James Hird** who on two occasions gamely managed to get in front of his opponent and, keeping his eye on the ball, beat Ablett for marks. Brendan was impressed with Hird's efforts. I told Bren that his grand-dad, Mick, had played with James Hird's great grandfather, George, at Costerfield. It was a *déjà vu* situation as, nearly fifty years earlier my dad Mick had told Ramon and me that he had played with George Hird, father of Alan Hird, who was then playing at the MCG.

Ablett later proved that being beaten to the ball was, for him, a rare event by taking more marks, including a skyscraper over a pack of players, and kicking more goals. Geelong lost the match, as **Paul Samon** was a very effective forward for the Bombers, kicking 12 goals.

1993 Grand Final

In 1993 I attended my first VFL/AFL Grand Final for over 20 years. That year Gary Ablett Snr, with 124 goals, won the John Coleman Medal as the top goal kicker during the season and **Gavin Wanganeen**, the indigenous Essendon utility player, won the Brownlow Medal. Essendon, known as the "Baby Bombers" had seven players in their Grand Final side who were under 21. Tim Watson, who had retired in 1992 came out of retirement to add a bit of experience to the side. There was a major surprise in the selection of the Essendon team when Derek Kickett, who had played in every game throughout the year, was dropped from the Grand Final side. However his replacement, Dean Wallis, proved to be more than equal to the task.

The Bombers played well to defeat Carlton rather easily but for me the real highlight of the match was the magnificent game played by **Michael Long** to win the Norm Smith Medal as best on ground. I can still see him in my mind's eye charging down the ground at tremendous pace, eluding or brushing past opponents and finishing his play with long and accurate kicks. On the other hand I also well remember Long standing stock-still on the wing, facing an opponent about a two metres away as if he was daring the Carlton player to come at him, both knowing that once the opponent made a move and committed himself Long would have the pace and ability to by-pass him and carry the ball forward. Long had 33 possessions with two goals in his masterly performance. Carlton centre half-forward **Stephen Kernahan** was also superb on that day with seven goals in a side that lost by over seven goals.

Back to Lalbert

Early in 2002 I received an invitation to attend a weekend reunion of the Lalbert Football Club to celebrate the 50 year anniversary of the 1952 Lalbert Premiership in the Mid-Murray League when it defeated Woorinen. Lake Boga, with the Finn brothers, had beaten Lalbert in the Grand Final in the previous year.

I was pleased to attend and stayed with a farmer friend, Jack Meehan, who had retired to a unit in Swan Hill. The first reunion event was on the Saturday afternoon when all were invited to watch Lalbert play Woorinen in the Central Murray League match at Lalbert. The match interested me for a number of reasons. Obviously it was an opportunity to catch up with former teammates such as Jack Gilmore, Jack O'Connor, Barry Kelly, Max McGregor, the Allan and Meehan brothers, as well a number of the Power clan. It was also good to renew acquaintances with many non-football-playing friends from the past.

The game itself was also of great interest as Woorinen had amongst its ranks two well-known football names and Lalbert had a former Tiger captain playing with them.

Carl Ditterich

The first name of interest in the Woorinen side was "Ditterich". Carl Ditterich's son, Caille, was playing for Woorinen.

From the beginning of his career in 1963 to his retirement in 1980, **Carl Ditterich** was an extremely prominent VFL footballer who burst onto the football scene as a blond, long-haired 17-year-old, being best on ground in his first VFL game in the first round of the 1963 season. He was never out of the limelight as a player, coach or personality for the 18 years that he was involved in VFL footy.

Of the modern-day players, he might best be likened to Nic Natanui of West Coast Eagles in that he had the same natural pace, leaping ability, courage and enthusiasm. And, like Natanui, he had physical characteristics that made him stand out. However, as someone brought up with Australian Rules he had a greater knowledge of the game than did Nic as a beginner.

His daughter, Britt Ditterich, has been in the public eye for country Victorians as a news reporter and reader for the WIN television channel.

Carl Ditterich played 203 games for the Saints for 156 goals and kicked 43 goals for the Demons in his 82 games with that club. He coached Melbourne from 1979 until 1981. Carl won the Best and Fairest award at both clubs. A volatile player he missed out on being in the Saints' 1966 premiership side as a result of suspension. In 2003 he was inducted into the Saints' Hall of Fame and he was named in the first ruck in the Saints' Team of the Century.

In the game against Lalbert, Carl's son, smaller than his dad but with a similar running gait, did quite well.

Dale Lewis

Wes, a brother of **Dale Lewis**, the Sydney Swans' star, was playing for Woorinen against Lalbert on that day and he had a reputation as an excellent Central Murray League player. Having a leadership role, he didn't let himself or the team down when I saw him play.

Swan Hill born Dale Lewis played for the Sydney Swans from 1990 until the end of 2001. During that period he played 182 games and kicked 186 goals. Since retiring he has had a successful career in the media and in 2012 was working for *Triple M* on their *Hot Breakfast* show.

Dale Lewis hit the headlines in 2002 when he stated that 75 per cent of AFL players use recreational drugs. Although he failed to provide evidence to back his statement and was widely ridiculed for it, there is no doubt that the AFL became more determined to ensure that drugs did not become an issue in footy. In March 2007 the AFL announced that "surprise drug tests will now be conducted on Saturday and Sunday mornings in an effort to catch recreational drug users". However clubs will only be notified if a player is in breach of the rule on three occasions. Many, including Magpie President, Eddie Maguire, and retired President of Hawthorn, Jeff Kennett, opposed this delay in telling the clubs as they believed that the clubs can best help the player with the problem. Kennett had a particular interest in this question as in 2010 Hawthorn player Travis Tuck was suspended for 12 weeks and fined $5000 for the illicit use of drugs.

Just as on-field issues such as player payments, violence and dangerous play, off-the-field player behaviour, player betting and bribery have required constant vigilance by football administrators throughout the history of the game, so today eliminating the taking of inappropriate or banned substances has become a major concern.

Tony Free

As noted in an earlier chapter, when I was playing cricket with Lalbert I was driven to the matches by a neighbouring farmer, Billy Free, whose two brothers David and Peter were also in the team. Peter's son, **Tony Free**, was an outstanding footballer for Lalbert before he went to Richmond in 1987 being promoted from the Under 19s to the seniors in that year. As a senior player at Richmond he proved to be a talented, determined, courageous mid-fielder who won the Club Best and Fairest award in 1989 and 1993. His outstanding leadership qualities were recognised by his appointment as captain in 1994. With Free in that role the team made the preliminary final in 1995. A serious knee problem caused him to retire at the beginning of 1997.

Like George Smeaton and Laurie Fowler, Tony Free was nominated for performing one of the Tigers' *Brave Acts of the Century*. As a nominee for this award, Tony Free is regarded as one of the *100 Tiger Treasures*.

The citation for Tony's nomination read as follows:

TONY FREE – August 14, 1994

The Richmond captain's reputation for bravery was further enhanced this particular day at the MCG against Sydney ... Free's jaw was broken in an off-the-ball incident with Dermott Brereton, after he'd put his body on the line to shepherd teammate Brendon Gale, prompting Tiger coach John Northey to urge his players to repay their skipper for his inspirational leadership.

Tony Free played 133 games for the Tigers and kicked 46 goals. He joined the Board of the Richmond Football Club in 2008.

It could be argued that apart from wheat, **Tony Free** is Lalbert's best known export.

Although he was making a rare re-appearance, and playing "on one leg" with Lalbert on the day of the Reunion, Free, only 32 at the time, was Lalbert's best player. His ability to be in the right place, his courage and his use of the ball made him outstanding.

Small World in Footy

Another ex-Lalbert player had success at Tigerland in a career which overlapped that of Tony Free. Playing 72 games with Richmond, Craig Smith came second in the Tiger Best and Fairest in his first season with the club. An aggressive half-back flanker, Smith had the highest compliment paid to him when he was given the guernsey with Jack Dyer's famous number 17 on its back. It was quite a thrill for folk from tiny Lalbert, even my Swans-supporting friend Frank Fogarty, to travel to the City to see two of their ex-players, running around the 'G in "yellow and black".

Lalbert was part of Richmond's recruiting zone in the 1960s and early 1970s. Francis Bourke told me (in an email) that he often went there during that period. He had another interest in Lalbert at that time in that his brother-in-law Chris Drum coached Lalbert in the mid-1970s. Francis wrote that "as a youngster, he (Chris Drum) played at Congupna and was mentored and coached there by that wonderful man, Jock (Jack)

O'Connor, who was a teacher and prominent citizen who played and coached at Lalbert, perhaps in your time there".

As we have seen, Jack was a star player at Lalbert when I was there. Chris Drum is Damian Drum's brother.

Snippet

Woorinen won the flag in the Central Murray League in 2002 but the most successful team in that League in the first decade of the new millennium was Balranald which played in the finals in every year from 2005 to 2009, winning flags in 2006 and 2009 and being runners-up in 2005 and 2007. In 2008 they lost to Swan Hill, the eventual premiers, in the first semi-final. A significant factor in their success was the fact that **Merv Neagle** coached them during that period.

Merv Neagle played 147 games for the Bombers before he was enticed by big money to transfer to the Swans in 1986. A member of the Essendon 1984 flag-winning team, Neagle was a tough and talented centre line player. Essendon supporters remember him for his epic one-on-one battles against such foes as Robert DiPierdomenico and David Rhys-Jones with both himself and his opponents "never giving an inch" in their contests.

Tragically Merv Neagle was killed in a trucking accident in August 2012.

Lalbert Football Club in the 2000s

The story of the Lalbert Football Club (now the Mallee Eagles Football Netball Club) over the past two decades is interesting and not atypical of rural clubs. Although Lalbert won premiership flags in 1992 and 1996, it was a credit to the club members that it had managed to survive as a single club and compete in a strong league.

Over the past couple of decades country leagues have been amalgamating as a result of declining numbers in the rural workforce, and clubs likewise have been either folding or joining forces with other clubs. The Mid-Murray League in which Lalbert had played for over a half a century has folded and the newly formed Central Murray League includes clubs from other leagues. For example, Kerang from the former Northern District League has joined the Central Murray League while nearby Quambatook has moved into a weaker neighbouring competition. Furthermore, the Nyahwest and Nyah clubs have merged in order to survive.

But it wasn't only the declining rural economy that hit Lalbert; it was the long drought at the turn of the century that really knocked the club. Not only were farmers less well off with less money to pay for club membership but a major source of the club's income disappeared. In good times it was usually able to obtain funds by share-farming a crop with voluntary labour. A farmer would make land available and volunteer workers would sow and harvest the crop. The football club would then receive a share of the returns. In a drought this couldn't happen. The desperate position of the club was told in the *Herald-Sun* in an article, headed *Drought puts bite on farmers*, by Jane Metlikovec on 18 October 2006. An excerpt from the article appears below:

> Also feeling the pinch are Mallee sports clubs.
>
> Lalbert Football Club, near Swan Hill, is desperately seeking funds after the club's crop failed. Its main source of income was lost a few weeks ago.
>
> Dedicated players had spent weeks tending to more than 80 hectares of donated barley and wheat seed worth $10,000 only to see it fall victim to the drought.
>
> But Lalbert Eagles president **Darren Scott** said the crop failure would not jeopardise the future of the Central Murray Football League side. "It is going to be tight over the next 12 months because we have had zero yield," he said. "But we are just going to have to work harder and think of other ways to raise the money. It is not uncommon for clubs in the area to share-crop with a

local farmer to raise money for their team", he said. "Lots of clubs around farming areas do this. Our crop hasn't been going great for a few years, but we will plant it again next year," he said. "You never know when it is going to come good and all the work will pay off."

Mr Scott said the club, with more than 80 registered players, was thanking its lucky stars it won the tender to stage this year's grand final. A grand final bid could cost a club up to $4000 but the returns were well worth it, he said.

The host club retains all profits aside from gate takings.

More than 5000 people descended on the tiny town, about 45 kilometres south of Swan Hill, for the match, won by NSW powerhouse Balranald.

"The grand final is our harvest this year," Mr Scott said. "We were really lucky we got the final, because with the crop as it is, if we didn't get it, we would have been stuffed."

The club survived the drought and it also improved its position on another front. As a club in a small community, declining in population, Lalbert had trouble recruiting junior players who would provide the backbone of the club in the future. The club changed this situation by merging with, not another senior club, but with St Mary's Junior Football Netball Club based in Swan Hill where most of the Lalbert children have traditionally travelled for their secondary education. The club now has a larger base from which to grow and there are signs of a successful future ahead of it. As it says on its Mallee Eagles (the current name of the club) website:

> While these were certainly hard years the club is now in an enviable position where, through a lot of dedication and hard work, it has an outstanding junior football program in place which is already producing some exciting young talent. This was demonstrated in some of the young players who were exposed to senior football in 2012. It is also in a strong position financially and is poised for success over the next few years.

Another factor which has contributed to the brighter future of the club has been the appointment of **Daniel Ward** as coach. Ward played 136 games for the Demons from 1998-2007. He was a back flanker who could run and deliver the ball well without being a known as a champion, although anyone who plays 136 games of AFL football must have what it takes. Tragically Ward had a gambling problem, well reported in the media, which almost ruined his life.

With financial assistance from the AFL Players' Association (AFLPA) he obtained professional help in Adelaide and returned a changed man.

Season 2011 saw him working in Swan Hill and coach of Lalbert.

The 2012 and 2013 seasons saw Lalbert continue as a competitive club on the football field, with their Reserves finishing runners-up to Swan Hill. However, what might be seen as a tragedy for the town happened in that year. The Lalbert pub closed. The following report in the *Herald and Weekly Times* in July 2012 tells the story:

"It's a sign of the times," hotel manager **Maurice "Lizard" Meehan** (photo at right of a young Maurice) said, before closing the door for the last time on Saturday.

First opened in more optimistic times in 1892, the Lalbert hotel has fallen victim to the depopulation of the region and a dry start to the season.

"The younger blokes who have taken over the farms don't drink as much as their fathers," Mr Meehan said.

The Lalbert pub may be the first of many hotels to close their doors in the next few years unless grain prices improve and the seasons stay kind. The dry start to the year also sapped confidence.

Maurice is the son of Phonse and Gladys Meehan with whom I boarded when I was working at my one-teacher school. Maurice was a

Prep pupil in my second year there. Seeing a former prep student, as a mature man, running the local pub certainly makes one feel old.

The closing of a school, pub or bank in a small town is a sad occasion. Each closure is another nail in the coffin of that town. No doubt the Lalbert pub houses many memories of stories told about good and poor harvests and footy and cricket matches won and lost. With dry seasons and poor grain prices the writing has been on the wall for Lalbert for some time. Instead of retiring from their farms to live in the Lalbert township, as farmers did when I was living in the district, the larger city of Swan Hill is now the retirement venue of their choice. David Meehan, tiring of the hot weather and the tough lifestyle chose, with his wife Kath, to live by the sea at Portland after they sold the family farm. Mallee towns are being depleted, as the article above indicates, and the Lalbert Pub won't be the last in the region to close.

Snippet

It was announced in *The Weekly Times* (23 October 2013) that the Lalbert school will close in 2014. During 2013 the school had only four pupils (the Meehan and Mullan sisters) who will catch the bus to Swan Hill in 2014. In excess of 1,000 children have attended the school since it opened over 120 years ago.

The paper reported that School Council President Peter Mullan said it was the story of rural Victoria. "Farms are getting bigger and there's not as many people around," he said.

Hall Of Fame Induction

Season 2012 wasn't a good one for Melbourne. Sadly they lost Jim Stynes, their President, before the season started and their form on the field was as poor as it had ever been. However there was some consolation for the club, mid-season, when **Big Bob Johnson** was one of six ex-champions who were inducted into the AFL Hall of Fame. The other inductees were Chris Grant (Western Bulldogs), Glen Archer (North Melbourne),

Robert Harvey (St Kilda), Shane Crawford (Hawthorn) and Graham Cornes (Glenelg). Barry Cable (Perth, North Melbourne and East Perth) was elevated to Legend status.

Big Bob was recognised particularly for the number of grand finals and premierships that he played in across two states – Victoria and Western Australia – as well as for his ability as a captain, coach and player, particularly as a ruckman/forward. Unfortunately Bob did not live to enjoy his award.

Tigers in Town

With our son Tim and his wife Marelyn living in Ballarat and starting a family there, Marj and I bought a weekender, "Shanagolden", at Learmonth a few kilometres north of Ballarat. The house would provide accommodation when we visited the young couple and their children. Learmonth at that time could be called a "dying town" as Lake Learmonth, which had been the town's life blood for most of the past hundred years, had been dry for five years. There were no more water-skiers, yachts or fishing boats to be seen on the lake. Two shops had recently closed in the town, with the only remaining open shop being the post office/general store. However the drought broke and in 2011 the Lake was back to its former glory. Unfortunately we had sold the property before this happened.

The first week of February, a year or so after we purchased the property, provided us with a special event. The Richmond Football Club, the famous Tigers, was running a training week in Ballarat and they were having their first intra-club practice match of the year at the Learmonth football ground. This was part of a new and very successful program where AFL teams move away from their home grounds and take the game to the people, usually to a regional centre or a country town.

Nothing like this had happened in the town for some years. Tiger officials visited the ground on six occasions (according to a local Tiger fan) to make sure that the surface of the ground was in good enough condition. The risk of a Tiger injury from an uneven surface could not be countenanced – too much money had been invested in the players. The rock hard cricket pitch in the centre of the oval was totally resurfaced with a rubber based super grass mat while the grass on the remainder of the surface was mown to perfection.

The big day came and the Tigers arrived.

Ballarat has a reputation for cold weather but it didn't turn out that way. In fact it was 33 degrees with a hot northerly blowing. But the weather did not diminish the enthusiasm of the players or the supporters. Some 2000 people attended the game which had a picnic-like atmosphere about it. All the stars were present: "Richo", two Bowdens, Kane Johnson, Andrew Krakouer and the ever popular David Rodan. A very eager **Daniel Jackson** was about the youngest player there. (He would win the Richmond Best and Fairest award in 2013).

The game was played in a good spirit with a local umpire officiating. Tiger-ware was on sale everywhere as were raffle tickets, drinks and lollies. After the game the players remained on the oval to chat with supporters and give autographs. All players had marker pens in readiness. Tim's son, William, actually "touched Joel Bowden" when getting his autograph.

Earlier in the day I arrived at the ground before Tim and his children and had trouble finding them in the crowd. A couple of weeks later when telling of the event to my son-in-law, Peter, I commented, "I didn't think I would ever have trouble finding someone in Learmonth."

To which Pete replied, "I've always thought you would have trouble finding *anyone* in Learmonth."

That might have been the case on the next day, but when the Tigers were in town, Learmonth really came alive.

21
Back to Costerfield and the MUGARS

Melbourne University Girls' Aussie Rules Squad (MUGARS), Flag-winning teams, In the club rooms, Indigenous stars, Tiwi Islands, Goldfields' heritage; Geelong FC, Port Adelaide FC, Hawthorn FC, Collingwood FC, Carlton FC, Costerfield FC; Reg Hickey, "Buddy" Franklin, Cyril Rioli, David Rodan, the Abletts, Adam Goodes, Tom Hawkins, Jess Egan and Michelle Dench.

In 2005 our youngest child, Natalie, and her husband Gavin, both keen on footy, journeyed to Canada. They lived in London, Ontario, a city not far from Toronto, for six months.

When the couple arrived in London they found that there was an Aussie Rules football competition based in Toronto and that London had a team in the competition. Gavin was keen to play while in Canada.

The absence of a coach at the time gave Gavin and Natalie a chance to play leadership roles in the club; Gavin on the field and Nat off the field. As the club was sometimes short of players, Nat, an experienced basketballer, occasionally took to the field and ran around in a forward or back pocket. Both of them enjoyed the experience.

On returning to Melbourne, Nat decided she would continue to play football and, as close friend, **Jess Egan**, was a top player for the Melbourne University Girls Aussie Rules Squad (MUGARS), she joined that club. In some email correspondence with me in 2012 about the MUGARS, Jess told me the following about the club:

The MUGARS (Melbourne University Girls Australian Rules squad, now more often called Melbourne University Women's FC), first competed in the VWFL in 1997. I joined the following year and have played most seasons since.

The club has won three Division One premierships (2002, 2003, 2005). I was a playing member of all three premiership teams. The club's second division team has also won 2 premierships (2003, 2005). The club played in eight consecutive division one grand finals from 2001 to 2008.

The club has changed its team makeup a number of times over the past 15 years. Starting with one team in season 1997, we expanded to also include a Division Two team in 2000. A Division Three team was created in 2003 but was removed prior to season 2009. Our Youth Girls (junior girls) side was created in 2005, expanding to two teams for seasons 2007-08. We currently have one Division One (Premier Division); one Division Two (Premier Reserves) and one Youth Girls team.

Jess had an outstanding career as a player with the MUGARS. She won the Medal for Best on Ground in the 2003 Grand Final and won the Best and Fairest award for Division One in 2004 and was also a member of the Victorian State teams at the National carnivals in 2006 and 2007. She was elected to either vice-captain or deputy vice-captain positions at her club each year between 2006 and 2009, but stood aside from on-field leadership roles prior to season 2010.

During her career, Jess twice required surgery to correct knee injuries. The hard working Jess has also been active in off-field roles with the club. She was on the club executive for six years (2006-07: Sponsorship and Merchandise Officer; 2008-10: Secretary; 2011: President) and also had a stint coaching one of the junior teams in 2008. She recently joined the umpiring ranks and currently umpires the Youth Girls' games on a Saturday morning.

Snippet

The Victorian Women's Football League was formed in 1981 with four teams competing. By 2007 there were five playing divisions: Premier (seniors and reserves) North West, South East and Country. Twenty-two clubs with 30 teams and over 1000 players were competing in the various divisions. An Under 17 Youth Girls Competition was established in 2004 to provide a pathway for young players to the WVFL. As the competition obtains a higher profile, with better media coverage, both participation rates and attendance numbers at the games are increasing, in Victoria and across the nation.

A report in the *Herald Sun* in 2012 noted that "AFL figures show females are flocking to play, and Victorian participation is expected to soon be three times that of 10 years ago" and that "Australia-wide last year there was a 43 per cent surge in females playing a footy season of six weeks or more – 136,000 girls compared with about 94,000 the year before."

Michelle Dench

Our daughter Natalie had a couple of satisfying seasons with the MUGARS, graduating from the thirds to the reserves during that period. Being a tall girl, with overhead skills from basketball, she was a very handy key position defender. Marj and I often went to see Natalie play and enjoyed seeing the girls in action. During Nat's playing years at the MUGARS, Michelle Dench was captain of the senior team. Jess Egan has the following to say about Michelle:

> According to many people at my club and in the league, Michelle is one of the best female footballers ever to play the game ... in 2002 after switching from basketball ... she started as a half forward flanker but moved into the midfield half-way through her career ... She was a triple premiership player, played 111 games for the club, was four times Best and Fairest ... was an outstanding finals

performer winning the club's player of the finals award four times. She was no stranger to representative football either, playing for Victoria on four occasions (including as Victorian Co-Captain in 2006). Her work commitments prevented her from being available for state selection during the years she didn't play for the Big V. She was selected to the All-Australian team on three occasions and also represented Australia in Ireland in an International Rules tournament ... she was a prolific goal scorer.

Michelle was also on the club executive for a couple of years and was captain for three years (after holding the vice-captaincy role). Denchy was not overly tall (but taller than average) ... she definitely played tall. She was very competitive in the air and had very safe hands. Probably the things that stood out to me most were her silky skills and agile movements. She would collect the ball at pace and sidestep out of the defender's way, then accelerate with much pace. She loved running the ball and having a bounce, but was very fair too and brought her team mates into the game. She was a much loved leader ... She was also a hard worker, using her many talents to full potential with a great attitude to training and fitness.

Michelle's dad, David Dench, was also a very good player. A dual premiership full back for North Melbourne, Dench was tipped by many to be named as full back in the AFL/VFL Team of the Century. David Dench was both reliable and dashing. Michelle proudly wore her dad's number 23.

Michelle Dench and Jesse Egan played in the MUGARS premiership team in 2005.

MUGARS Division 1 Premiership Team, 2005

Back L-R: Karen Reece, Stephanie Kierce, Jess Smyth, Adam Rieusset (Coach), Clare Woodhouse, John Stewart (Runner), Belinda Blay, Bronwyn McGorlick, Rebecca Jennings, Kylie Lush (hidden), Emma Phillips.

Middle L-R: Elizabeth Skinner, Lucy Puls (Vice Captain), Chyloe Kurdas (Captain, holding Premiership Cup), Michelle Dench (Deputy Vice Captain), Lucy Shiels (partially obscured), Jess Egan, Rebecca Ball, Kirsty Suffield, Kristen Douglas

Front L-R: Amma Bridgeman (sitting), Erini Gianakopoulos, Sarah James, Janine Milne.

(Photograph by Nick Featherston)

The Grand Final was played at the Whitten Oval in Footscray against Darebin. **Scores:** Melb Uni 11.12.78 defeated Darebin 4.3.27. **Goals:** Rebecca Ball 2, Belinda Blay 2, Kristen Douglas 2, Amma Bridgeman, Erini Gianakopoulos, Sarah James, Rebecca Jennings, Chyloe Kurdas. **Best:** Chyloe Kurdas, Michelle Dench, Jess Egan, Liz Skinner, Lucy Puls, Karen Reece.

In the Rooms at an AFL Game

In 2004, Brendan took up a teaching position in the Geelong area. Living two doors away from them in Grovedale were Chris and Keith Primus, the parents of well-known football identity Matt Primus who had a successful AFL career with Fitzroy and Port Adelaide. He won the latter club's Best and Fairest in 2002, being in the All Australian team in 2001 and 2002 and playing in the International team against Ireland twice. He captained the team for five years and on retirement through injury was assistant coach to Mark Williams, taking over the coaching position from him in 2010.

Matt Primus had the right pedigree to be an AFL footballer as his mother Chris is the daughter of Reg Hickey, one of the most famous footballers that Geelong has produced. With pace, strength, courage, high marking skill and the ability to kick with either foot, Hickey was a great part of Geelong's successes over three-and-a-half decades, captaining the Cats to the 1932 flag, being captain and coach of their 1937 premiership team and non-playing coach of their back-to-back flags in 1951 and 1952. He was named captain and coach of the Geelong Team of the Century and was also named in the AFL Team of the Century. The Reg Hickey Stand at Kardinia Park is named after him.

Brendan Reed, like his dad, is a Richmond supporter with a soft spot for the Cats. Bren's son, Patrick, is an avid football fan. His idol is Gary Ablett Jnr.

Knowing of their love for the game, Keith and Chris Primus invited Bren and Pat to go the 'G with them to watch Port Adelaide play Hawthorn in 2011. "Pat can come into the rooms after the game," promised Chris.

Sure enough, Bren and Pat joined Chris and Keith for the Port Adelaide match against Hawthorn in Round 21 of the season. The Reeds were thrilled to do so, but there was a dampener on the game as Port was well beaten, with the Hawks scoring 31.11.197 to Port's 5.2.32.

It was a pity that the game was so one-sided Hawthorn's way, but young Pat had the consolation of seeing **Buddy Franklin** kicking eight goals and **Cyril Rioli** kicking six. One needs little imagination to understand that the atmosphere in the rooms of a team that had just been beaten by 165 points was somewhat heavy but young Patrick had a smile on his face as he saw a lot of AFL footballers close up. Star Port rover, **David Rodan** was kind enough to have a chat to him. All in all it was a great day for Bren and Pat, thanks to the generosity of the Primus family.

Snippet

David Rodan is the first Fijian-born footballer to play 100 games of AFL football. David grew up in Lami near Suva and, on coming to Australia, he played Aussie Rules. Initially signed by the Tigers, he played 66 games there before transferring to Port Adelaide at the end of 2006. A very fast on-baller, willing to take on an opponent, he is exciting to watch and very popular with fans. To the end of the 2011 season he had played 105 games for Port Power. He is dangerous around goals. In 2013 he finished his career with the Demons.

Grand Final Day – 2011

Marj and I often watch the Grand Final on the telly at home but in 2011 we were invited to watch the match at the home of my cousin Maurice Reed and his very hospitable wife, Merle, long-time Geelong residents and Cats' supporters. It is well known that the 2011 Grand Final was "a ripper" with an even first quarter and the Magpies having a slender lead at half time. In the 3rd quarter, **Tom Hawkins**, who had been marking brilliantly, kicked three goals to give the Cats a seven point lead at the final break. In the last term the Cats consolidated their victory by kicking four goals while the Magpies failed to goal. It was a great afternoon, particularly for our Cats-loving hosts.

The Ablett Family

Gary Ablett was an integral part of the Cats' 2007 and 2011 premierships. He and his father were not the only members of the Ablett family to play VFL/AFL football.

As far back as 1939 an Ablett was playing VFL football. Len Ablett, a cousin of Gary Snr's dad played for the Tigers. He had 70 games during his five year stint with the club and was 19th man in Richmond's winning 1943 Grand Final side. The following article, by Scott Palmer in the *Herald Sun* on 19 May 2012, details later Ablett involvement in the game:

> The Ablett clan will chalk up 900 league games tonight when Gary Jnr plays for Gold Coast against Western Bulldogs.
>
> Six members have played at top level starting with Geoff, the first of three brothers to turn out with Hawthorn.
>
> Geoff played 229 games for the Hawks, Richmond and St Kilda and was joined by Kevin (38 games with Hawthorn, Richmond and Geelong) and Gary Snr (248 games with Hawthorn and Geelong).
>
> Kevin's son Luke appeared in 133 games for Sydney, while Gary Jnr has played 217 games for Geelong and Gold Coast, and his brother Nathan 34 for the Cats and Suns. The tally would be greater if you count the games played by the sons of Ablett's sister Faye.
>
> Shane (147 games with Richmond) and Travis Tuck (20 with Hawthorn) are still playing while their father Michael (Tuck) is the AFL games record holder with 426.

Our grandson Pat's admiration for Gary Ablett Jn was so great that he decided to follow the Gold Coast Suns in 2011 and was often the only budding AFL champion bravely wearing a Suns' outfit among a sea of hooped footy jumpers at the Auskick program, held at Kardinia Park.

Snippet

Bren Reed worked as the specialist physical education and music/drama teacher at a Geelong school. One day, he was in a chemist shop and **Gary Ablett Snr** walked in and stood beside him at the counter.

Noting that Bren was purchasing medicines Gary asked,

"Got a sick kid at home, mate?"

"Yes, in fact we have three kids sick, all under four."

"That's hard work."

"Yes. You had your kids close didn't you?"

"Yep we had four under six at one stage."

Just then a couple came into the shop with a young lad about eight years old.

"Look over there dad. See who's there. Can I go and say 'Hello' to him?" exclaimed the boy.

"OK, but remember your manners."

With that the boy rushed across to Gary and Bren and called out, "Hello Mr Reed."!!!

The lad was a pupil at Bren's school and Bren took him for PE. The boy and his parents were from India and probably hadn't heard of Gary Ablett Snr.

It doesn't often happen that Gary Ablett is upstaged.

Flag-Winning Teams

Brisbane, with Leigh Matthews as coach, Michael Voss as captain and ex-Warrnambool youngster Jonathan Brown as centre half-forward, won the first of its three consecutive premierships in 2001. They were runners-up to Port Adelaide in 2004. When teams have a run of success they are usually quite innovative and it takes time for other teams to catch up.

Information obtained from *The Enclclopedia of AFL Footballers* reveals some features of the 2001 Premiership side, Brisbane, that are worth noting. Eleven of the 22 team members had played over 100 games of AFL football. Seven of the team weighed at least 90 kilograms with two of the remaining players weighing 88 kilograms or more. Even more importantly, there were 11 players in the team who had kicked over 100 goals in their careers at the time of the Grand Final. And those players did not include youngsters Jonathan Brown and Luke Power who had 43 and 88 goals respectively with both averaging more than a goal per game.

The Brisbane Premiership Team, 2001

Backs: C. Johnson, J. Leppitsch, D. White
Half-backs: N. Lappin, C. Scott, M. Ashcroft
Centres: J. Akermanis, M. Voss, R. Copeland
Half-forwards: S.Hart, J. Brown, L. Power
Forwards: D. Bradshaw, A. Lynch, M. Pike
Rucks: C. Keating S. Black, B. Scott
Int: B. McDonald, C. McRae, T. Notting, M. Michael

The group comprised mature big-bodied, experienced players. They were not easily brushed aside in going for the ball and used their tough bodies to tackle hard when the opposition had the ball. Furthermore they had lots of players who could kick goals.

Premiership teams of the next decade were of a similar ilk, with the Geelong team under Mark Thompson and Chris Scott being the best of that type over that period. Grand Finalists for five of the seven years from 2006 to 2012, they too had experienced hard-bodied footballers who tackled fiercely, with many players, from all over the ground having the ability to kick goals.

Magpie star Scott Pendlebury summed the value of hard-bodied players after his team's loss to Geelong in the 2011 Grand Final. He said in the *Herald Sun* during the following week:

> Geelong's bigger bodies got us. When the heat was on in the last term on Saturday, the Cats' physicality and strength was a decisive factor.
>
> When their mature bodied players come at you with the ball it's as if they think: "I'm going to nail this guy".
>
> It's as if they want you to try to tackle them because they just want to break straight through you.
>
> Eventually it just wore us down.
>
> … On top of our "to do" list over summer is to get bigger and stronger. The entire list will face a tough pre-season adding size. We need to make tackles stick. The ones the Cats busted through on Saturday (*Herald Sun,* 3 October 2011).

That wasn't to be. Neither side reached the Grand Final in 2012.

The Hawks and the Swans did make it, with both teams having big-bodied men in their side. The Swans' victory also showed the importance of Grand Final sides having a large number of potential goal kickers. They had nine goal kickers to the Hawks six in the Grand Final.

In 2013 the experienced Hawks went into the ultimate game with 10 players who had kicked 15 goals or more for the season and over 50 in their careers. All of their Grand Final goal kickers came from this group. Fremantle had only five in that category with three of these players kicking six of the team's eight goals. Big bodied sides with many players accustomed to kicking goals seem to be the most important ingredients for success to date in the 21st century.

The 2011, 2012 and 2013 flag-winning teams also had an extra ingredient – indigenous players.

Indigenous players

We have seen that there has been a sprinkling of indigenous players, mostly highly talented, throughout the 20th century. Sir Douglas Nicholls, Norm McDonald, Eddie Jackson, Polly Farmer and Barry Cable readily come to mind. Syd Jackson was among Carlton's best in the 1970 Grand Final. Sydney Swans stars, Michael O'Loughlin and Adam Goodes were beginning to make their names at the end of the 1990s, while Darryl White was perhaps the most exciting player in the Brisbane team in their run of premierships at the beginning of the new century. However Geelong took the trend a step further with three indigenous players (Matthew Stokes, Travis Varcoe and Allen Christensen) on the field in their flag-winning line-up in 2011. The Swans had Adam Goodes and Lewis Jetta in their 2012 team while the runners-up, Hawthorn, had Lance Franklin, Cyril Rioli and Shaun Burgoyne.

Indigenous players are certainly a spectacular feature of the Aussie game today. Perhaps the best over the long haul is **Adam Goodes** who has won two Brownlow Medals and has been a member of two premiership teams, playing in the centre in the 2005 Grand Final and at full forward in 2012.

Named at centre half-back in the Indigenous team of the Century, Goodes has also played in the Indigenous All Stars team which plays a pre-season match against an AFL team every second year. He was selected as captain of that team in 2011 (but the game was washed out) and he won the Polly Farmer Medal for the best All Stars player in 2003. On top of this he had played a club record of 321 games for the Swans to the end of 2012, 204 of these being consecutive. Furthermore, he has won the Bob Skilton Medal for the Swans' Best and Fairest on three occasions.

Goodes' ability to play well in any position on the ground and in "big" games makes him an outstanding footballer. His effort in the 2012 Grand Final is a case in point. Seriously injuring his knee in the second quarter, Goodes played on despite the pain and kicked a telling goal in the last quarter to seal the game.

"To have a knee that was essentially gone and hang in like he did was a sensational effort," coach John Longmire said of Goodes' performance. While the *Sunday Herald Sun* commented on the following day that the "courageous performance of the dual Brownlow Medalist elevated him to similar status in Swans' folklore as past great Bob Skilton, who presented the Premiership Cup to coach John Longmire at the MCG yesterday."

As more and more indigenous players are proving to be outstanding exponents of our game, it can be safely said that Adam Goodes won't be the last such footballer to be seen as one of the best in a particular era.

Snippet

Brother John Pye, a missionary, was responsible for taking Aussie Rules to the Tiwi Islands in 1941. He believed that the natural physical attributes of the people there lent themselves to that game rather than to rugby, the other game with which Brother Pye was familiar – and he was proven to be correct.

With a local competition on the islands and one in Darwin, where many Tiwis played with the St Mary's team, players from the Tiwi Islands became sought after in the Southern states. David Kantilla went to South Adelaide in 1961 and Sebastian Rioli, Maurice's brother, played with South Fremantle from 1972 until 1976. Both were highly successful. Ronnie Burns and Dean Rioli, Sebastian's son, are others from the Tiwi Islands who have had great success with Victorian teams.

In 2012 there were eight teams in the Tiwi Islands Football League (TIFL). Each year the Grand Final in the TIFL is a great tourist attraction with around 3,000 people attending the game. The Islands field a team, the Tiwi Bombers, in the eight team Northern Territory Football League (NTFL) winning the flag in the 2012 season. The Northern Territory has also fielded a side in the AFL Queensland League since 2009.

What's so Good about Footy?

Sure it can be argued that football is good for boys and girls to play because it keeps them fit. It also gives them the experience of playing in a team game where they may have to make sacrifices for the benefit of the side. Hopefully they learn to be gracious in defeat and humble in victory. And, of course, the game itself is fun to play and gives a great adrenalin rush.

But from my perspective, another plus from my family's interest in football is that it has provided a source of communication between members of families and people in the community at large. To see a a couple and two or three children decked out in their team's colours obviously going to an AFL game, sitting in a train and chatting eagerly to each other, and sometimes to other passengers, about the day ahead, warms my heart.

In my own experience, going to an AFL game with grandchildren and their parents is great fun. I was at the 'G with Tim and his son William, both Richmond supporters, when the Tigers beat the Doggies and **"Richo"** kicked 10 goals. William put as much energy and gusto into singing "We Come From Tigerland" after the final siren, as Richo did in kicking the goals, and enjoyed it just as much. It couldn't come any better than that for Willam (or his dad and grandfather). We had plenty to talk about on the way home.

Return to Costerfield

In November 2009 a "Back to Costerfield" was held to launch Anne Bradley's book *Pioneers of Costerfield*. Marj and I, as well as 22 other descendants of George and Annie Reed, were among the large crowd at the function.

The town then comprised the hall and only a few nearby houses. The old school was being used as a home and the tennis court had trees growing through the bitumen surface. However the hall itself, colourfully decorated with streamers in the Costerfield colours of red, white and blue, was a great surprise. The locals had been able to continually raise funds or obtain grants to keep it in very good repair. The floor was highly polished hardwood and the walls and ceiling were tongue and groove Baltic pine.

I was thrilled to see artifacts and photos around the wall. These included photos of Costerfield Football Teams and the bronze War Memorial to Ex-Costerfield Primary School students who served in the First World War.

In pride of place over the entrance doorway was a large photo of the 1919 Premiership team with Mick Reed seated in front of a standing George Hird, while the names of Jack and Ted Reed were included on the bronze War Memorial and Ted Reed was also in a photo of the 1924 Costerfield Rovers premiership team.

I was surprised to see at the Back To a tall gentleman with the name tag "Raymond Hird" on his lapel. He told me that he was the son of George Hird and the brother of Allan Hird Snr. I asked him if he had played footy. "No, not me and that's why I'm so fit in my nineties." was his reply.

The Le Deux family

Also present at the "Back to Costerfield" was **Fred Le Deux III**. Fred was a descendant of **Frederick Le Deux I** who came from France to Australia in September 1858 with his son Claude to work as a blacksmith. Eventually he worked on the goldfields not far from Costerfield. Although **Frederick I** later left Australia, his son Jean Claude remained and some of his descendants, of whom **Fred III** is one, settled on a farm between Costerfield and Nagambie. As we have seen, Fred's father, **Fred Le Deux II**, played footy alongside **George Hird** and **Mick Reed** for Mooroombool West in 1918.

Fred III grew up living near my cousin Ted Oliver (a grandson of George and Annie Reed) and both Fred and Ted went to Assumption College Kilmore where Fred was an outstanding schoolboy athlete and footballer.

On leaving school **Fred III** played 18 games with Geelong, from 1956 to 1958. He then transferred to Mordialloc in the VFA. After three enjoyable seasons at Mordialloc, Fred Le Deux moved on to play with nearby Chelsea, retiring from football in 1962.

Fred Le Deux III married and settled in Geelong to raise his family. It was there that his daughter **Jenny Le Deux** met and married a prominent Geelong footballer **"Jumping Jack" Hawkins**. Recruited from Finley in New South Wales, Jumping Jack, as his nickname suggests, was a brilliant high mark who played mainly in defence. He played 182 games with the Cats and represented Victoria in an interstate match against Tasmania in 1979. Returning to live at Finley, Jenny and Jack had four children including a son, **Tom Hawkins** (photo below with Pat Reed, Bren's son), who grew up on the family farm and went to school

(With permission from Andrea Woodhead)

at Melbourne Grammar, as did his father before him. There Tom was a champion footballer and athlete like his dad had been at that school, and his grandfather **Fred Le Deux** at Assumption College, Kilmore.

Tom was drafted to Geelong under the father-son rule, and was a member of the Geelong 2009 and 2011 premiership teams, kicking two goals in the 2009 Grand Final and starring in 2011. In 2012 Tom had a very consistent season coming second in the Coleman Medal with 62 goals, many of which came from contested marks. He was chosen as the All Australian full forward and won the "Carjie" Greeves Medal for Geelong's Best and Fairest.

From the Goldfields to the 'G

Like Matthew Francis, George Reed's great-great-grandson, and James Hird, George Hird's great-grandson, **Tom Hawkins,** had family roots in the mining district of Costerfield. And like James, Tom had a father and a grandfather who played VFL football. Matthew, James and Tom are examples of footballers who, in their family trees, can trace a journey "from the goldfields to the 'G".

And there may be many more, including, as we have seen, Aussie Rules greats – Jack Worrall and Ron Barassi.

Just how many more is an interesting question. If that number is still a very large proportion of AFL footballers in 2013, then perhaps there is the implication that Aussie Rules has failed to capture the imagination and love of many of the massive migrant intake since WWII.

In 1947, all of the Richmond first semi-final team had Anglo/Celtic surnames, and if Bob Katter Jnr MHR is correct about the composition of the Australian population at that time, the vast majority of these could have traced at least one line in their family tree back to the goldfields. Over 50 years later, the 2001 Brisbane premiership side contained only four players (Voss, Lappin, Akermanis and Leppitsch) who did not have names with Anglo/Celtic backgrounds. The flag-winning Hawthorn side of 2013 had only five players whose names were from non-Anglo/Celtic origin (Guerra, Burgoyne, Breust, Rioli, Puopolo).

If the above situation means that the continuing very large numbers of new arrivals since WWII have not had a huge impact on the composition of VFL/AFL sides, then AFL administrators ought to have some worries about the long-term future. The changing nature of our population and its effect on our game is an issue that needs continual research. I wonder if such research is being undertaken. Have the families of the bulk of our Aussie Rules footballers (and supporters) still travelled, in their familes' stories, the journey from the Goldfields to the 'G? What would the faces in the crowd at an AFL final suggest? Do they have the same multi-national composition as would be found among the crowd at any major suburban shopping complex? Or do the bulk of them appear to have come from Anglo-Celtic backgrounds?

Epilogue

In our one-eyed look at Aussie Rules a number of themes have, in turn, become the focus of the story.

An obvious one is that the Australian sport grew from a game being played amongst groups of men in the major cities and rural areas, initially in a very informal manner, until it became a truly national sport. Matches are now played in the AFL competition in every state and territory of the Commonwealth. Furthermore, women have moved from being spectators to players.

It has been noted that the game is a family affair in that family members, often across generations, play, work for and support Aussie Rules at local and regional levels and also loyally follow their teams at the higher levels of the game. We have seen examples of Meehans and O'Sheas at the local levels and Hirds, Bourkes and O'Connells at top levels. This involvement is good for footy and is also good for the families themselves as it gives family members a common interest.

The evolving nature of the game is also apparent. Although the game today would be clearly recognisable as the same game that was played over 100 years ago, significant changes have often been made to the rules. Examples of such are the number of players allowed as reserves and the introduction of a penalty for kicking the ball out of bounds on the full. Players' skills have improved and new skills are being constantly fostered. In the 21st century the skill of using handball has become more highly developed while the technique of dribbling the ball through for angled goals is a relatively new skill.

Australian Football is highly competitive as there is "no prize for second" so there is an on-going challenge for administrators to ensure that the game is played fairly and that infringements of the rules, both on and off the field, are consistently and appropriately punished. The monitoring of player involvement in activities such as dangerous tackling, betting on results of games, and taking performances drugs is an ongoing necessity of our game.

Another key concern for administrators is to ensure that it isn't only the wealthier clubs that have success. Outstanding players are in great demand, and the more financial clubs can pay top money for the better players. Measures such as the Coulter Law, salary caps and the draft have been part of on-going attempts to ensure a level playing field when it comes to player recruitment by clubs.

A number of wars have been fought over the years that our game has been played. Aussie Rules footballers, such as Ron Barassi Snr and Bluey Truscott, and others from different echelons of the sport, have served and continue to serve our nation with great honour in these encounters – many of them paying a heavy price in so doing.

Footballers, such as Jim Stynes and Brendan Keilar, have also shown themselves to be heroes in peace time too.

Although Doug Nicholls was an early VFL champion, very few of our indigenous community were prominent in much of the story of Aussie Rules. However, in recent times, not only are they playing in larger numbers at all levels, they are also displaying a unique brand of skill that is a feature of the game, particularly at the AFL level. And indigenous champions such Michael Long and Adam Goodes bring spectators through the gates.

Economic and demographic changes have seen teams and competitions fold or amalgamate, again at all levels of the sport. The changing face of the Oakleigh population with post-WWII migration caused the demise of the Oakleigh Football Club and forced clubs in the Oakleigh area to lose a historically Aussie Rules venue (the Rec) to soccer. This raises some questions, along the following lines, the answers to which will affect the future of our game.

Which group (or groups) now encompasses the bulk of our game's followers in terms of players and supporters?

Is it still largely the descendants of people who came here in the gold rushes and later produced the post-WWII baby boomers who, in turn, were the core group of Aussie Rules supporters in the game's halcyon days of the 1960s, '70s and early '80s?

With about one quarter of our population being born overseas, to what extent are our new citizens, particularly those from Asia and Africa, developing a love of Australian Rules? (Brendan Reed's pupil from an Indian family didn't recognise Gary Ablett Snr in the chemist's shop.)

Are our newcomers, in general, simply continuing their attachments to interests and sports which they brought with them, and which are nowadays well set up for new citizens when they arrive? Is there any need for them to become interested in Aussie Rules in order for them to fit into their new community?

Of course, it is not only demographic change that is affecting the leisure-time activities of our population. Technology, including television, is also bringing about change.

Australians used to be seen, and in many cases saw ourselves, as lovers of sport, and in the southern states particularly, as lovers of Australian Rules. With multicultural influences and the continuing introduction of new technology are we becoming a nation of computer whizzes, food connoisseurs, dancers, musicians, entertainment buffs as well as lovers of other sports, all of whom take a decreasing interest in Aussie Rules?

Demographic changes in Oakleigh, with consequent changes in recreational habits, forced Aussie Rules to share centre stage with soccer as the suburb's major football interest. Is it likely that, in the not too distant future, with the changing face of the Australian population and its variety of cultural backgrounds and interests, our game will be forced to take a position further back on the stage? If so, is this a good or bad thing for the nation as a whole?

People will have differing answers to that question, but I am pleased that our Australian game has been a continuing part of the life of my family across the generations.

Classic Photo of a Premiership Team
(Costerfield's second premiership – 1908)

Photo features:

- The remnants of the forest cleared for the footy oval.
- Two types of jumpers used (vertical and horizontal stripes).
- Silverware trophy, with officials' arms arched above it.
- Photo details written on a chalkboard (borrowed from the school?).
- Fewer players than "extras" (some may have played during the year).
- Player George "Kelly" Reed – second row, extreme left.

Costerfield's last season was 1947. George and Annie Reed's grandson, Jack Oliver, was in the team.

The forest has since reclaimed the land where the footy oval used to be.

References

Books

Ashford, M., *Pride and Premierships – A History of De La Salle Old Collegians Amateur Football Club 1955-1980* Melbourne: De La Salle Amateur Football Club, 1981.

Barassi, R., *Australian Football Stories*, Melbourne: Methuen, 1981.

Bartlett, K. and Phillips, S, *Kevin Bartlett's Footy Trivia*, Melbourne: Herald and Weekly Times (Undated).

Bartlett, Rhett, *Richmond F.C. "The Tigers" A Century of League Football*, Victoria: Geoff Slattery Publishing Pty Ltd, 2007.

Billings, C. M. (Editor), Stonnington, *1969*, Toorak: Student's Representative Council of Toorak Teachers' College, 1969.

Black, H., with Lisa Holland-McNair, *Black*, Melbourne: Agenda Publishing, 2012.

Blainey, Geoffrey, *A Game of Our Own – The Origins of Australian Football*, Victoria: Black Inc, 2003.

Bradley, Anne, *Pioneers of Costerfield*: Bendigo, Victoria: Anne Bradley, 2009.

Cartledge, E., *Footy's Glory Days – The Greatest Era of the Greatest Game*, Melbourne: Hardie Grant Books, 2013.

Cole, R., Keilar, H., McCorkell, R., and Wright, I., *Birth of the Blues: Warrnambool Football Netball Club 1861-2008*, Warrnambool: Warrnambool Football Club.

Collins, B., *The Red Fox – The Biography of Norm Smith, Legendary Melbourne Coach*, Melbourne: The Slattery Media Group, 2008.

Education Department, Victoria, *Vision and Realisation, Volume 2*, Melbourne: Government Printer, 1973.

Fiddian, M., *Devils at Play, A History of the Oakleigh Football Club*, Pakenham: Pakenham Gazette, 1982.

Fitzgerald, B. and Wooderson, K., *Through Football Better Citizens: A Pictorial History of the Oakleigh Youth Club Football Club*, Oakleigh: Oakleigh Youth Club Football Club, 2005.

Flanagan, M., *The Game in Time of War*, Sydney: Picador, 2003.

Gilchrist, James, *Collingwood Tragic*, Ballarat: Connor Court, 2011.

──────── *Wednesday Warriors*, Ballarat: Connor Court, 2010.

Hirst, J. B., *The World of Albert Facey*, North Sydney: Allen and Unwin Pty Ltd, 1992.

Holmesby, R. and Main, Jim, *The Encyclopedia of AFL Footballers*, Melbourne: Crown Content, 2002.

Hutchinson, G., *Great Australian Football Stories*, Ringwood: Penguin Books Ltd, 1983.

Katter, B., *An Incredible Race of People – A Passionate History of Australia*, Millers Point: Pier 9, 2012.

Madigan, A. and M., *Bush Legends – South Australian Country Footy Stories*, Adelaide: Elvis Press, 2003.

MacDowell, R., *Inside Story: 20 Famous Australians Tell Their Story*, Brighton: Hobson Dell Publishing, 2001.

Macklin, Robert, *Jacka VC Australian Hero*, Crows Nest, N.S.W.: Allen and Unwin, 2006.

Main, J., *Plugger and the Mighty Swans*, Melbourne: Wilkinson Books, 1996.

Main, J., *When It Matters Most – The Norm Smith Medallist and Best on Ground in Every Grand Final*, Melbourne: Bas Publishing, 2006.

Oakleigh Football Club, 1929 – Year Book – 1950, Oakleigh: Oakleigh Football Club, 1950.

O'Neill, T., *Barassi*, Strawberry Hills, N.S.W.: Currency Press Ltd, 2012.

Piesse, K., *Football Legends of the Bush – Local Heroes and Big Leaguers*, Ringwood: Viking-Penguin Books Australia Ltd, 2011.

Pook, Andrew, *Life, Work and Travels*, Melbourne: Maurice Reed, 2007.

Prior, Tom, *A Knockabout Priest – The Story of Father John Brosnan*, North Melbourne: Hargreen Publishing Company, 1986.

Reed, K., *Good Paddock Footballers – The Reeds of Costerfield*, Melbourne: K. Reed, 2010.

Rodgers, S. and Browne, A., *Every Game Ever Played – VFL/AFL Results 1897 -1995*, Ringwood: Viking-Penguin Books Australia Ltd, 1996.

Sheedy, K., *Stand Your Ground Life and Football*, Sydney: Pan MacMillan Australia Pty Limited, 2008.

Slattery, G. (Introduction), *Grand Finals Vol II – The Stories behind the Premier Teams of the Victorian Footbal League*, Richmond: The Slattery Media Group, 2012.

Smart, R., (Ed), *The Penguin Book of Australian Anecdotes*, Ringwood: Penguin Books Australia, 1996. (A number of humorous statements from persons associated with football came from this book.)

Stynes, J., *Whatever It Takes*, Melbourne: Celebrity Publishing, 1995.

Wilson, P., *Broadway and Beyond – The Story of Sacred Heart Parish, Oakleigh 1888 – 1988*. Oakleigh, Victoria: Sacred Heart Parish, 1988.

Magazines and Journals:

Flaherty, Peter, *Our Land Our Century*, Melbourne: The Herald and Weekly Times Ltd, 1999.

Relevant Editions of VFL/AFL publication *Football Record*, and *Finals Souvenirs*.

Peters, T. and Diggerson, K (editors), Premiers 2011, *The Cats Insider Annual Report 2011*, Geelong: Geelong Football Club, 2011.

Murray Sports Nostalgia Series, *Australian Rules 100 Greatest Players* (Undated).

Greenwood, G. *Grand Finals* Publisher: Unknown, (Undated).

Various Herald-Sun Publications including *The Top 240* (1982), *Football 1963*, *Superfooty 2011*.

Allan, David (Editor), *Footy Fan Magazine* West Melbourne: Tennyson Publishing Company, (Undated)

Argus Publishing: *Footy and the Clubs That It*, (1953).

Relevant Editions of *Blue and Gold* (The De La Salle College Annual Magazine), Melbourne: De La Sale College.

Relevant Editions of *The Emmanuel College Connection*, Warrnambool: Emmanuel College.

Emmanuel College Warrnambool, *Celebrating 140 Years of Catholic Secondary Education in Warrnambool*, Warrnambool: Emmanuel College, 2012.

Chapple, M., Coppock, M., Fitzgerald, *80 – 50 – 20 Anniversary, A Celebration of Oakleigh Football,* Oakleigh: Oakleigh Amateur Football Club, 2012.

Warrnambool Institute of Advanced Education, Football Club, Shark *Power – Almanac (1976-1990),* Warrnambool: Warrnambool Institute of Advanced Education, 1990.

Catholic Education Office, *Catholic Education Today,* Melbourne: Catholic Education Office, August 2012.

Newspapers

Relevant editions of *McIvor Times, Shepparton News, Traralgon Journal, The Sun, The Herald Sun, The Swan Hill Guardian, The Quambatook Times, The Charlton Tribune, Inside Football, Waverley Leader, The Warrnambool Standard.*

Internet

McDonald, Peter, *Demography, eMelbourne, the City past and Present – The Encyclopedia of Melbourne.*

Relevant articles on *Wikipedia, fullpointsfooty.net, Fox Sports Pulse, Australian Football.com, Boyles Footy Photos* as well as Aussie Rules Football Clubs' websites including VFA, VFL, AFL clubs.

Nadel, Dave, *Melbourne the City Past and Present.*

The Australian Dictionary of Biography Online.

Source for information on Pastor Doug Nicholls: *http://www.teachers.ash.org.au*

Genealogy Centres

Databases and CR-Roms at Genealogy Centres at various libraries.

Acknowledgements

It would not have been possible for me to produce this book without the assistance of many people; the first of whom I must thank is my wife Marj for her support, patience, encouragement and proof-reading. She had to endure many lonely hours whilst I typed in our study. Dr Reg Chapple also gave much of his time in proof-reading the whole book, and making helpful suggestions, for which I am extremely grateful.

Other members of my family were helpful too; Elizabeth, with her proof-reading, and her siblings; Michael, Tim, Jane, Brendan and Natalie who gave their time to talk about material which might be relevant to my writing. In particular Brendan and Pat Reed as well as Natalie's husband, Gavin Pocock, were generous in lending me books from their libraries. These proved to be very useful source materials. My siblings, Maureen Kelly and Ramon Reed (with his wife Margaret) were always on hand if I had to check on information.

I have been lucky to have a group of "football friends" with whom I have talked about footy over many years. I am grateful for their contributions to my book, even though they may not have known that they were doing so at the time. Included in this group are the following friends from teachers' college days who were also team-mates at Oakleigh YCW: Jim McKenna, Ray Clarke, Kevin Jenkins and the late Paddy Rohan. Bill O'Shea, Peter Quinn and the late Barry Carr, other former team-mates with Oakleigh YCW, must also be included in this category.

Perhaps the most exciting part of writing this book has been making contact with people whom I thought would be able to help me with useful information and/or the reading of early drafts. Many of these were associated with a football club (FC). Included in this group are the following:

Francis Bourke and Graham Burgin from Richmond FC, John Bolt, Simon Humphries, John Murphy, Barry Lyons and Colin Glover from De La Salle Old Collegians FC; Paul Nikakis, Barry Alexander and Mark Chapple from Oakleigh Amateurs FC; Jess Egan from Melbourne University Women's Football Club; Brian Brown and Leigh McCluskey from South Warrnambool FC; Alan Aulsebrook, Luke Jackson, Dr John Sherwood and Dr John Warhurst from Deakin University/WIAE FC; John Callanan, Greg Cahill, Dr Paul Callery and Frank Davis from Oakleigh YCW FC; Greg Kiellerup, Phil Wilson and others from Oakleigh Districts FC; Dr Peter Hay, ex-Wynyard FC; Fred Le Deux, ex-Geelong FC; David Meehan, Tony Free, Frank Fogarty and Margaret Shepherd from Lalbert FC/Mallee Eagles Football Netball Club; Ian Slockwitch, ex-Richmond FC; Brian Carroll ex-Watchem-Corack and ex-Fitzroy FCs; John O'Connell ex-Geelong and ex-Claremont FCs; Bill McMaster ex-Geelong FC; Paul Gadsen from Lake Boga FC; John Kennedy and John O'Mahony from Hawthorn FC.

Harry, Moya and Alice Keilar were very generous in their giving of time to the project. Their help was much appreciated.

My sincere thanks go to Dr Paul Callery for writing the Introduction to the book. His thought-provoking comments are an excellent starting-point for readers.

Michael Gilchrist has been extremely skilful, thorough and very patient in getting the text with the accompanying photographs into a publishing format. I am deeply grateful to him for his work.

Special thanks are extended to archivists, Jenny Larsen from Emmanuel College, Warrnambool, Louisa Moscato from De La Salle College Malvern, Angela Forgan from the Catholic Education Office, Melbourne, and also to Kevin Parker for the use of his videos.

I must also mention that I was able to make use of invaluable material that had been collected by my late dad, Mick Reed. Some very old magazines were particularly relevant.

Other helpers to whom I am grateful include Marcia Howard and other members of the Howard family.

Lastly I must apologise to anyone who has helped me with my efforts and may have been unintentionally overlooked in these acknowledgements.

Without the help of those mentioned above (and those overlooked), this work would not have seen the light of day.

Photographs

In addition to those photographs acknowledged in the text, I wish to thank the following groups and individuals for particular photographs used in the book:

John O'Mahony (p. 87)

John O'Connell (p. 116)

Mick Reed (dec) (p. 131)

Gladys Meehan (dec) (p. 296, p. 157)

Graham Burgin (p. 215)

The Bourke family (p. 217)

The Keilar family (p. 234)

Emmanuel College Warrnambool (p. 240)

South Warrnambool Football Club (p. 245)

Dr John Sherwood (p. 261)

Gary Francis and Deakin University Football Netball Club (p. 258, p. 264)

Oakleigh Amateur Football Club (p. 276)

The Geelong Football Club (p. 315)

With regard to the photograph of Jeffrey Rosenfeld (p.180), it is uncertain as to who holds the copyright on this photo. If it is the

Ministry of Education and Early Child Development, then the photo is out of copyright. If it is the photographer, we have no knowledge of who he/she is and would be pleased if he/she made contact with the publisher.

With regard to the photograph of Graham Robbins (p. 223), it is thought that either Mark Plummer or Ross Beale (ex-students at Toorak Teachers' College) took this photo in 1969. Attempts to contact these people have been unsuccessful. We would be pleased if any person who believes who he/she owns the copyright to this photograph made contact with the publisher.

With regard to the photograph of Frank, David and Francis Bourke (p. 217), this was given to the author by the late Frank Bourke. The owner of the copyright to the photograph is unknown. The Bourke family has given permission for it to be used in the book. If anyone believes that he/she holds the copyright to this photograph, we would be pleased if he/she made contact with the publisher.

With regard to the photograph of South Warrnambool Under 18 Premiership Team, 1984 on page 245 of the book, permission has been given by South Warrnambool Football Club to use this photograph in the book, although it is uncertain as to who owns the copyright to the photograph. The question is still being pursued. If anyone believes that he/she holds the copyright to the photograph, we would be pleased if he/she made contact with the publisher.

Key Player Index

Ablett Family 307
Ablett, Gary Snr 155, 255, 268-270, 285, 287, 288, 308, 320
Ablett, Gary Jnr 269, 305
Allan Family 212
Anderson, Frank 175
Anderson, Graeme 174-175

Baker, Des 271, 275-277
Barassi, Ron Jnr 78, 165-166
Barassi, Ron Snr 14, 78, 319
Bence, "Tiger" 230, 247
Black, Heath 196, 210
Bourke, David 216
Bourke, Francis 104, 216, 218, 292
Bourke, Frank 217
Bow, Glen 150, 155, 158, 163, 178, 228, 233
Bradmore, Phil 251, 257
Brereton, Dermot 207, 255, 267
Brown, Brian 202, 249, 250-252
Brown, Jonathan 234, 259, 251, 308, 309
Brownlow, Charles 1, 15
Burgin, Graham 212, 215, 216

Callanan Family 274

Callanan, Jack Snr 274
Callanan Jack Jnr 223, 270, 274
Callery, Paul 133, 196, 205, 208, 265
Capper, Warwick 94, 101
Carroll, Brian 165, 175, 281, 282
Carroll, Damian 203, 281, 282
Carroll, John 281
Casey, Richard 1, 5
Cazaly, Roy 230, 245-247, 281
Coulthard, George 1, 17
Challis, George 37, 40, 41
Chitty, Bob 172
Chitty, Peter 172
Clark, Norman 19, 26
Cleary, Phil 196, 261, 282
Cloke, Aaron 275
Cloke, David 104, 275
Closter, Wayne 212, 219, 225
Coleman, John 70, 73, 84, 136, 288
Collier, "Leeter" 58, 59
Collier, Harry 58, 59
Cook, "Peter" 230, 232, 233
Cook, Fred 196, 197
Cooper, Geoff 150, 158
Cordner Family 31
Cornes, Graeme 134, 145, 146, 212, 220, 249

Couch, Paul 230, 248
Coughlan, John 171, 189, 191-196
Coventry, Gordon 59, 60
Coventry, Syd 60, 61
Cox Family 274
Cumberland, Vic 28, 33, 34

Dench, Michelle 300, 302-304
Devine, John 180, 194, 195, 214
DiPierdomenico, "Dipper" 255, 267, 293
Ditterich, Carl 285, 289, 290
Douglas, Jack 86, 87
Dunstall, Jason 255, 267, 269
Dyer, Jack 65, 70, 73, 88, 104, 105, 109, 136, 229, 292

Egan, Jess 300, 302, 304, 331

Fanning, Fred 94, 96, 217
Faul, Bill 69, 180, 187
Finn, Ray 140, 141
Finn, Stan 140, 141
Flanagan, Fred 150, 155, 159
Ford, Brian 212, 225, 226
"The Foreign Legion" 58, 68, 70, 187
Fowler, Laurie 94, 101, 103, 104, 128, 281, 191

Fox, Rob 165, 172
Francis, Matthew 285-287, 316
Franklin, "Buddy" 300, 306, 311
Franks, Albert 1, 5, 23
Fraser, "Mopsy" 89
Free, Tony 285, 289, 291, 292

Gent, William 1, 5, 23
Gleeson, Adrian 230, 238
Goodes, Adam 91, 300, 311-312, 319

Hafey, Tom 103, 212, 214, 231
Hardiman, "Splinter" 136
Hardiman, Peter 136
Hawkins Family 315
Hawkins, Jim 189, 181, 182
Hawkins, Tom 300, 305, 316
Herbert, Barney 45, 51, 53
Hickey, Reg 68, 134, 136, 158, 300, 305
Higginbotham, David 10, 11
Hird, Allan Snr 73, 90, 92, 148, 314
Hird, Allan Jnr 92
Hird, George 37, 41, 42, 45, 92, 148 287, 314, 316
Hird, James 92, 285-287, 296, 316
Howard Family 239
Howard, Leo 239
Howell, "Chooka" 120, 132

Howell Family 132

Jackson, Eddie 311, 165, 172, 173
James, Glen 212, 221, 222
Johnson, Bob Snr 114, 115, 255
Johnson, Bob Jnr 99, 106, 109, 114-117, 120, 165, 176, 177, 196, 201, 225, 226, 255, 268, 278, 297

Keilar, Brendan 230, 234-237, 319
Kelly, Dan 134, 143
Kelly, Greg 134, 143, 144
Kennedy Family 112
Kennedy, John Snr 87, 105, 110, 111, 113, 188, 207
Kennedy, John Jnr 111, 113
Kernahan, Stephen 285, 288

Le Deux Family 314
LeDeux, Fred III 314, 315
Le Lievre, Stan 94-97
Lee, "Dick" 22, 28, 34, 51, 53
Lewis, Dale 285 289, 290
Long, Michael 285, 288, 316, 319

Maguire, "Goose" 230, 249
Maguire, Matthew 234, 249
Maher, Frank 45, 55, 125
Marshall, Theophilus 1, 8, 9

Matthews, Leigh 207, 229, 255, 267, 269, 303, 308
Maylin, Phil 271, 281
McAlister, Jack 120, 121, 126, 127
McCorkell Family 257
McCorkell, Leigh 256
McDonald, Norm 91, 311
McMahon, Noel 150, 164, 165, 167
McMaster, Bill 150, 153-155,
McNamara, Dave 19, 22, 23
Metherall, Jack 134, 137
Metherall, Len 134, 137
Miller, "Frosty" 196
Minogue, Dan 45, 52
Moran, Jeff 196, 207
Morris, Bill 89
Murphy, John 188
Murphy, Maurice 181, 187, 188
Murphy, Robert 188, 189

Nicholls, Sir Douglas 91, 120, 125, 319

O'Connell, John 115, 116, 118, 119
O'Connor, Jack 150, 156, 162, 164, 170, 171, 289, 292-293
O'Mahony, John 87, 111, 266
O'Meara Family 212
Oppy, Max 89

O'Shea Family 278

Paez, Ron 150, 160, 228
Pannam Alby 90, 92, 189
Pannam Family 92, 93
Park, Roy 28, 32
Pearce, "Joe" 19, 22, 41
Poulter, Ray 85, 86, 164
Power Family 212
Power, Luke 271, 284, 309
Pratt, Bob 58, 69-71, 101, 207

Rankin, Cliff 56
Rankin Family 56
Reed, George 1, 2, 4, 6, 12-14, 17, 24, 25, 34, 38, 203, 285, 316
Reed, Mick 43, 44, 53, 54, 62, 64, 65, 85, 88, 146, 147, 196, 206, 229, 314, 355
Rice, Colin 150, 159
Richardson, Mal 170, 178, 213, 228
Rioli, David 221
Robbins, Graham 212, 222, 223, 225-228
Rodan, David 299, 300, 306
Rose, Bob 152
Rose Family 153
Rowe, Des 230, 231
Rudolph, George 120, 125
Russo Family 112

Russo, Felix 112, 113
Ruthven, Alan 73, 75
Ryan, Bill 150, 158, 159
Ryan, Shaun 230, 242

Salmon, Paul 285, 288
Schwass, Wayne 230, 243, 248
Sheedy, Kevin 285, 286
Shelton, "Bluey" 165, 167-169, 173, 176
Shelton, "Mulga" 165, 167-169
Sherwood, John 255, 260, 261-263
Skilton, Bob 120, 123, 311, 312
Slockwitch, Ian 231
Sloss, Bruce 37, 39, 40, 53, 224
Smeaton, George 120, 128, 129, 225, 291
Smith, Norm 58, 96, 103, 165, 166, 177, 202, 216, 221, 268, 288
Smith, Ross 196, 208
Symons, Jack 67, 73-75

Taylor, Kain 271, 281
Thorpe, Vic 45, 51-53
Todd, Ron 77, 97, 130, 136, 177, 180, 190
Truscott, "Bluey" 73, 78, 319

Vallence, "Soapy" 94, 97

Wanganeen, Gavin 285, 288
Warburton, Keith 150, 160, 228